Oxford

NEW ENJOYING
MATHEMATICS

Class 5

Aashalata Badami

Series Editor
Jose Paul

OXFORD
UNIVERSITY PRESS

OXFORD
UNIVERSITY PRESS

Oxford University Press is a department of the University of Oxford.
It furthers the University's objective of excellence in research, scholarship,
and education by publishing worldwide. Oxford is a registered trademark of
Oxford University Press in the UK and in certain other countries.

Published in India by
Oxford University Press
YMCA Library Building, 1 Jai Singh Road, New Delhi 110001, India

First Edition published in 2006
Second Revised Edition published in 2009
Third Revised Edition published in 2014
Second impression 2014

ISBN-13: 978-0-19-809439-5
ISBN-10: 0-19-809439-6

Typeset in Times New Roman
by Mukesh Technologies Pvt. Ltd., Puducherry 605005
Printed in India by Repro India Ltd., Navi Mumbai

Illustrations by Pankajakshan K, Amit John, Santosh Gupta,
Pradeep Nayak, Nilabho Dhar Chowdhury and Mammoth Designz

Preface

Children can be taught mathematics in two ways, either as abstract numbers on a page, or through the lines that rule the page, the angles of their desks, and the shadows of trees outside their classrooms. While drawing strength from the previous edition, the *New Enjoying Mathematics* **revised edition** series promotes the latter approach. It places emphasis on developing thinking and reasoning skills among students, by connecting the mathematics curriculum with real-life situations.

New Enjoying Mathematics **revised edition** is a series of ten books that conforms to the vision of the National Curriculum Framework (2005). It is designed to help teachers understand and effectively use the Continuous and Comprehensive Evaluation.

Keeping CCE requirements in mind we have incorporated suggestions for formative and summative assessments. These are for the teachers and we are aware that they will be able to pick out many more ideas from the text for the same. Similar suggestions have been made in the teacher's manuals that accompany the books.

Key Features

- *Looking Back* for refreshing the concepts learnt earlier
- *Chapter Check-Up* at the end of each chapter for easy recapitulation
- *Worksheet* to provide an interactive and motivating form of practice
- *Challenge* questions to build thinking skills
- *Enrichment Time* and *Activity Bag* to explore the subject and think creatively
- *Maths Lab Activity* to help build concepts through different activities
- *Project* to help students connect the topics with everyday life
- *Keeping in Touch* to enable children to revisit the concepts previously learnt
- *Test Your Skills* after every three chapters to revise the previously learnt concepts

New features of the revised edition

- *Mental Maths* worksheets focusing on special strategies followed by exercises for fast calculation
- The symbols **F A** and **S A** have been provided to highlight the features which can be used for *Formative* and *Summative Assessments*
- *Journal* to help the child express in her own words what she has learnt in class
- *Value Based Questions* **VB** a requirement and a necessity in today's world
- A new technique to problem solving where quantities are visually represented and approached

Revising a successful and well-accepted mathematics course would have been a daunting task, were it not for the feedback and support of all those exceptional teachers who took the time to make sure we received, and incorporated their feedback. I hope that this book can match up to their expectations.

My sincerest thanks to the dedicated, creative and hardworking editorial, design and production teams at Oxford University Press for their motivated and inspired inputs. I would also like to thank the dynamic sales and marketing team through whose untiring efforts this book has reached thousands of students and teachers across the country. A big thank you to my family for their never ending support and patience – I take it for granted now. As to the cosmic force that keeps me working happily – thank you is not enough.

Aashalata Badami

An overview of CCE and its implementation in

New Enjoying Mathematics Revised Edition

Continuous and Comprehensive Evaluation (CCE) assesses students continuously and comprehensively through various tools and techniques. Its purpose is diagnosis, feedback, remediation, and effectiveness.

Continuous

This refers to the regularity in assessment, i.e., assessment integrated while teaching. Assessment should be done both in formal setting (inside the classroom) and informal setting (outside the classroom, such as playground, outdoor activities, etc.)

Comprehensive

This refers to the application of a variety of tools and techniques (both testing and non-testing) and aims at assessing a learner's development in areas of learning such as

- Knowledge
- Understanding
- Applying
- Analysing
- Evaluating
- Creating

Evaluation

FORMATIVE ASSESSMENT

This continuously assesses students in everyday learning situations during teaching. It helps the teachers diagnose learning gaps and acts as feedback to the teacher to take remedial action immediately.

SUMMATIVE ASSESSMENT

This sums up how much the student has learned at the end of teaching.

- Objective type
- Very short answer type
- Short answer type
- Long answer type

TOOLS

- Questions
- Observation
- Interview schedule
- Anecdotal records
- Document analysis
- Tests and inventories

TECHNIQUES

- Examination
- Assignments
- Quizzes
- Competition
- Projects
- Debates
- Elocution
- Group discussion
- Club activities
- Experiments
- Research

The tools and techniques of evaluation are important components of CCE. A review of the features in *New Enjoying Mathematics* **revised edition** to support tools and techniques suggested by the CBSE for assessment under CCE is shown overleaf.

CCE implementation in
New Enjoying Mathematics Revised Edition

Journal

What it does: Helps the learner articulate her mathematical thinking in words, which in turn helps in diagnostics
Skills assessed: Understanding
Tools: Observation
Techniques: Examination

Worksheet

What it does: Assesses a learner's ability to tackle questions based on mixed chapters
Skills assessed: Remembering and understanding
Tools: MCQs, Objective type, very short answer type, short answer type
Technique: Assignment, examination

Mental Maths

What it does: Provides questions to develop mathematical thinking skills
Skills assessed: Knowledge of mathematical calculations
Tools: Objective type, Fill in the blanks
Techniques: Examination, Quizzes

Test Your Skills

What it does: Assesses a learner's knowledge based on mixed chapters
Skills assessed: Remembering and Understanding
Tools: Very short answer type, Short answer type, Long answer type
Techniques: Assignment, Examination

Project

What it does: Helps the learner find usefulness of mathematics in everyday life
Skills assessed: Creating and Analysing
Tools: Tests and inventories, Observation
Techniques: Research, Group discussion, Experiments, Project

FOR TEACHERS

Oxford Educate

Oxford Educate is an exciting digital teaching aid that integrates in a single resource an e-book with interactive teaching tools and learning materials.

- Animations, video clips and QTime for relevant topics are included.
- Interactive tools such as zoom in or out, sticky notes, hide text, spotlight, a pencil, an eraser, and a highlighting pen are also inbuilt.
- Geometool, an interactive tool that comes with each Oxford Educate has been designed to help teachers visualise, construct and manipulate geometrical shapes.

A comprehensive and easy-to-use **Test Generator** is an effective assessment tool designed to benefit teachers by enabling them to create a variety of test papers as well as worksheets.

- The teacher can choose from a variety of types such as solve, simplify, true or false, fill in the blanks, short answer and long answer questions.
- The Test Generator can be used to create test papers for one or more chapters. Answers are provided for efficient and effective evaluation.
- Teachers can decide to choose questions from a pool of questions from the book or outside the book or both.
- It can also be used to generate worksheets.

Maths Lab Activity

What it does: Aids learning by doing through hands-on activities based on concepts studied in the chapter.
Skills assessed: Analysing, Understanding and Evaluating
Tools: Observation
Techniques: Project, Group discussion, Experiments

Challenge

What it does: Provides higher level questions for learners
Skills assessed: Higher order thinking skills
Tools: Questions
Techniques: Group discussion, Examination

Contents

Place Value

Looking Back

Read this sentence.

India has 65,590 km of National Highways and 1,31,899 km of State Highways.

L	TTh	Th	H	T	O
1	3	1	8	9	9

— 9
— 90
— 800
— 1,000
— 30,000
— 1,00,000

> 65,590
> These digits tell us how many thousands.

> 1,31,899
> This digit tells us how many lakhs.

In words: One lakh, thirty-one thousand, eight hundred ninety-nine
Expanded notation: 1,00,000 + 30,000 + 1,000 + 800 + 90 + 9

1. Use the digits 5, 6, 3, 8, 9, 1 to:
   (a) build the greatest number possible.
   (b) build the smallest number possible.
   (c) give the expanded notation and number name for both.

2. Fill in the blanks.
   (a) 75 rounded to the nearest 10 is __80__ .
   (b) 774 rounded to the nearest 10 is __70__ .
   (c) 476 rounded to the nearest 100 is __500__ .

3. Give the Roman numeral for
   (a) 12: __VII__   (b) 24: __WIV__   (c) 39: __VVV__

Lakhs and Crores

7-Digit Numbers

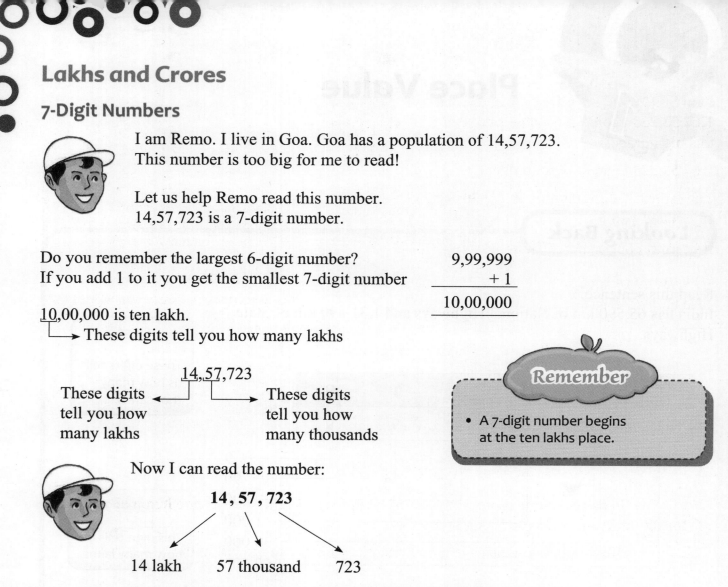

I am Remo. I live in Goa. Goa has a population of 14,57,723. This number is too big for me to read!

Let us help Remo read this number.
14,57,723 is a 7-digit number.

Do you remember the largest 6-digit number?
If you add 1 to it you get the smallest 7-digit number

$$\begin{array}{r} 9,99,999 \\ +\ 1 \\ \hline 10,00,000 \end{array}$$

10,00,000 is ten lakh.
└──→ These digits tell you how many lakhs

14,57,723

These digits tell you how many lakhs ←→ These digits tell you how many thousands

Remember
- A 7-digit number begins at the ten lakhs place.

Now I can read the number:

14 , 57 , 723

14 lakh   57 thousand   723

Fourteen lakh, fifty-seven thousand, seven hundred twenty-three

Take the number 27,68,435.

Lakhs		Thousands		Ones		
TL	L	TTh	Th	H	T	O
2	7	6	8	4	3	5

← Period
← Place

TL stands for ten lakh.

In words: Twenty-seven lakh, sixty-eight thousand, four hundred thirty-five

Expanded notation:

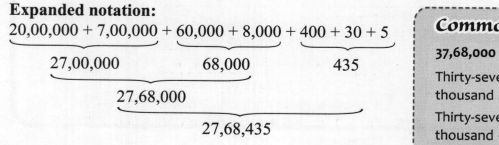

20,00,000 + 7,00,000 + 60,000 + 8,000 + 400 + 30 + 5

27,00,000   68,000   435

27,68,000

27,68,435

Common Mistake

37,68,000

Thirty-seven lakhs sixty-eight thousand ✗

Thirty-seven lakh, sixty-eight thousand ✓

8-Digit Numbers

I am Surjeet. I live in Delhi. My city has 1,67,53,235 people. I need help to read this big number!

1,67,53,235 is an 8-digit number.

The largest 7-digit number is	99,99,999
If you add 1 to it	+ 1
It becomes one hundred lakh	100,00,000

One hundred lakh is also called one crore.

1,00,00,000

→ This digit tells you how many crores

1, 67, 53, 235

This digit tells you how many crores

These digits tell you how many lakhs

These digits tell you how many thousands

So there are one crore, sixty-seven lakh, fifty-three thousand, two hundred thirty-five people living in my city.

8-digit number means we move one place further to the left in the place value chart.

Take the number 9,27,68,435.

Crores	Lakhs		Thousands		Ones		
C	TL	L	TTh	Th	H	T	O
9	2	7	6	8	4	3	5

9   27   68   435

It is easy to read a number with three commas. The first comma says crore, the second says lakh, the third comma says thousand.

9 crores	27 lakhs	68 thousands	4 hundreds 3 tens 5 ones
9,00,00,000	20,00,000 + 7,00,000	60,000 + 8,000	400 + 30 + 5

In words: Nine crore, twenty-seven lakh, sixty-eight thousand, four hundred thirty-five
Expanded notation: 9,00,00,000 + 20,00,000 + 7,00,000 + 60,000 + 8,000 + 400 + 30 + 5

Understanding Numbers Better

How do I write the number four crore, fifty-three thousand, one?

Write the place value chart and fill in the numbers according to the periods and places.

C	TL	L	TTh	Th	H	T	O
4			5	3			1

Then fill in all the vacant places with zeros.

C	TL	L	TTh	Th	H	T	O
4	0	0	5	3	0	0	1

Answer: 4,00,53,001

How do I find the number before and after a large number?

You can think of the number after as '+1' and the number before as '−1'.

The number **after** 56,79,999 is 56,80,000.
The number **before** 6,78,800 is 6,78,799.

Let us compare numbers now

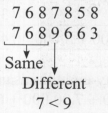

My number is
5,67,890

My number is
11,98,087

The number with more digits is the bigger number.

5,67,890 < 11,98,087

Now I pick
76,87,858

I pick
76,89,663

• Both numbers have the same number of digits. Start from the left and compare the digits until you find two digits that are different.

7 6 8 7 8 5 8
7 6 8 9 6 6 3

Hence, 76,87,858 < 76,89,663

Same
Different
7 < 9

What comes next?

23,45,678	40,46,300
23,46,678	40,56,300
23,47,678	40,66,300
?	?

Answer: 23,48,678   *Answer:* 40,76,300

How many numbers have 4 digits?
Let us start by finding out how many numbers have 1, 2 and 3 digits.
We may find a pattern!

(a) The smallest one-digit number is 1.
The greatest one-digit number is 9.
$9 - 1 = 8$
$8 + 1 = 9$
There are 9 one-digit numbers.

Put back the extra number that was taken away.

(b) Smallest 2-digit number is 10.
Greatest 2-digit number is 99.
$99 - 10 = 89$
$89 + 1 = 90$
There are 90 two-digit numbers.

(c) Smallest 3-digit number is 100.
Greatest 3-digit number is 999.
$999 - 100 = 899$
$899 + 1 = 900$
There are 900 three-digit numbers.

I can see the pattern!
1-digit numbers – 9
2-digit numbers – 90
3-digit numbers – 900

There must be 9000 4-digit numbers!

Try This

There are:
_____ 5-digit numbers
_____ 6-digit numbers
_____ 7-digit numbers
_____ 8-digit numbers

Project

Make a "FACT BOOK".
Research facts in encyclopedias or on the internet to fit in these groups of your FACT BOOK. Use at least one page per group. Find as many interesting facts as you can. One example is done for you. You can illustrate the facts if you wish to.

1–99
100–999
1000–9999
10000–99999
100000–999999
1000000–9999999
10000000–99999999 ⟶
More than–99999999

Mercury is about 5,79,37,000 km away from the sun.

Exercise 1.1

1.

1			2 6 2		3		4 9	5 9

(Crossword number grid with handwritten entries)

Row 2: 6 **3 3 3 8 4 0 1**
Grid cells down from 2: 3, 4, 5, 1, 2
Row 8: **1**

Clues across	**Clues down**
(1) The value of a digit is divided by this number as it moves to the right in the place value chart.	(1) Give the difference between the face value and the place value of the digit 2 in the number 5,27,87,890.
(6) What is 10,000 more than 23,38,901?	(2) What is 1,00,000 less than 64,45,121?
(4) The largest two-digit number.	(3) Give the next number in the pattern. 38,33,659 38,43,659 38,53,659
(7) Rearrange the digits 3, 7, 5, 2, 5, 9, 0, 0, 6 to form the biggest number possible.	(4) How many six digit numbers are there in all?
(8) Give the next number in the pattern. 80,11,497 81,11,497 82,11,497	(5) Give the standard form of ninety-one lakh twenty thousand four hundred twelve.

2. If you are 10 years old, you would have lived 52,56,000 minutes. Compare the numbers given below and match the age to the minutes lived. Do not calculate. Match by putting the numbers in ascending order. One has been done for you.

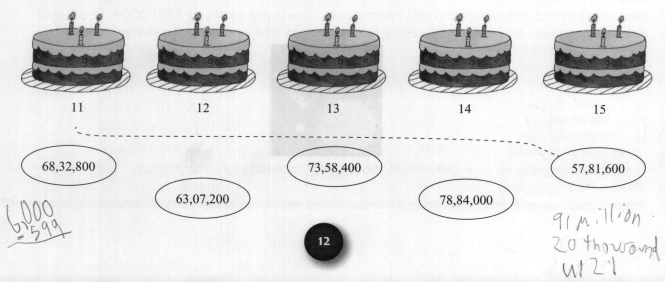

11   12   13   14   15

68,32,800   73,58,400   57,81,600

63,07,200   78,84,000

12

3. Give the word form and the expanded notation for these numbers.

   (a) 67,09,654   (b) 9,83,10,809   (c) 2,10,23,008   (d) 45,00,091

4. Write in figures (with commas).

   (a) Eight lakh thirty-nine thousand twenty-three
   (b) Twenty lakh nine hundred five
   (c) Thirty-five thousand eight hundred fifty-seven
   (d) Four crore thirty-seven lakh nineteen thousand

5. Give the place value of the coloured digit.

   (a) 89,00,345   (b) 30,34,112   (c) 87,93,389   (d) 2,67,23,592   (e) 7,08,19,004

6. Compare using <, >, or =.

   (a) 5,87,90,456 ◯ 5,78,23,567   (b) 90,40,908 ◯ 9,04,908

   (c) 8,20,45,899 ◯ 8,20,54,899   (d) 1,40,10,178 ◯ 1,40,10,720

7. Make the smallest possible 7-digit number by repeating the digits.

   (a) 5, 8, 2, 9, 1   (b) 4, 7, 1, 9, 0

8. Make the smallest and the greatest possible 8-digit numbers by repeating the digits.

   (a) 3, 6, 1, 7, 8, 9, 2   (b) 4, 7, 1, 0, 3, 5

9. Give the number before:

   (a) 45,69,500   (b) 87,16,000   (c) 5,10,000   (d) 20,00,000

10. Give the number after:

   (a) 9,29,499
   (b) 79,98,999
   (c) 99,99,999
   (d) 1,98,97,950

You may keep a separate notebook as your maths journal. You can use it to express thoughts, ideas and experiences about the different things you have learnt in the maths class.

Journal

We use numbers to **count** (there are 28 people in the room) to **identify** (my house number is 738) or to tell the **order of things** (Sabina picked the 9th book on the shelf.)

Can you find two more examples of each of the different ways we use numbers?
Can you think of any other way we use numbers too?

International System

Two lakh, thirty-four thousand, one hundred ninety-six people visit the book fair.

Two hundred thirty four thousand, one hundred ninety-six people visit the book fair.

234196 people visit the Book Fair

5-digit numbers are read the same way in India and the rest of the world.

234196 is a 6-digit number. **6-digit and greater numbers are read differently in the Indian and international systems**.

INDIAN		INTERNATIONAL
10,000 Ten thousand	←—— 5 digits ——→ 10000	10,000 Ten thousand
1,00,000 One lakh	←—— 6 digits ——→ 100000	100,000 One hundred thousand
10,00,000 Ten lakh	←—— 7 digits ——→ 1000000	1,000,000 One million

INTERNATIONAL SYSTEM

The international system has 3 places in each period.

The periods are separated by commas. The commas help us read the number.

M	HTh	TTh	Th	H	T	O	
	1	0	0	0	0	0	One hundred thousand
1	0	0	0	0	0	0	One million

Comparing the Indian and International Systems

	10 lakh	1 lakh	TTh	Th	H	T	O
Indian System	10 lakh	1 lakh	TTh	Th	H	T	O
International System	1 million	100 thousand	TTh	Th	H	T	O

Different   **Same**

Let us read the number 5237819 in both international and Indian systems.

INTERNATIONAL SYSTEM

M	HTh	TTh	Th	H	T	O
5	2	3	7	8	1	9

5 million   237 thousand   819

Five million, two hundred thirty-seven thousand, eight hundred nineteen

INDIAN SYSTEM

TL	L	TTh	Th	H	T	O
5	2	3	7	8	1	9

52 lakh   37 thousand   819

Fifty-two lakh, thirty-seven thousand, eight hundred nineteen

M	I	L	L	I	O	N
1	0	0	0	0	0	0

I remember that a million has 6 zeros with the help of this grid.

Read these figures in international system.

(a) 439,168—Four hundred thirty-nine thousand, one hundred sixty-eight

(b) 705,001—Seven hundred five thousand, one

(c) 1,201,590—One million, two hundred one thousand, five hundred ninety

(d) 5,500,109—Five million, five hundred thousand, one hundred nine

Exercise 1.2

1. Read these out.
   (a) There are more than 400,000 species of plants in the plant kingdom.
   (b) There are about 250,000 flowering plants.
   (c) Mr Acharya's new house costs ₹ 5,703,800.
   (d) Himachal Pradesh has a population of 6,856,509.

2. Rewrite using figures.
   (a) Ten people have about one million hairs.
   (b) The moon is about three hundred fifty-six thousand, four hundred kilometres from the earth.
   (c) There are one million, thirteen thousand, nine hundred thirteen words in the English language.

3. Insert commas and rewrite in words according to the international system.

   (a) 712801 = _712,801_, _____
   (b) 602590 = _____, _____
   (c) 1016800 = _____, _____
   (d) 5397284 = _____, _____

4. Give the value of the coloured digit using the international system.
   (a) 234198   (b) 6042381   (c) 191291   (d) 7184089

5. Write the following numbers in the Indian and international systems, using both figures and words.
   (a) 850009   (b) 1670112   (c) 4290281   (d) 530563

Rounding

The figure shown below is not an exact figure. It only gives an idea of **about** how many birds came to the sanctuary. It is a rounded figure.

5,000 birds arrive at the Bharatpur Bird Sanctuary.

Rules of Rounding

Revise the rules of rounding.
- When we round a number to the nearest 10, we use the **nearest multiple of 10.**
- When we round a number to the nearest 100, we use the **nearest multiple of 100.**
- When we round a number to the nearest 1000, we use the **nearest multiple of 1000.**

(a) Round 1,135 to the nearest 10.

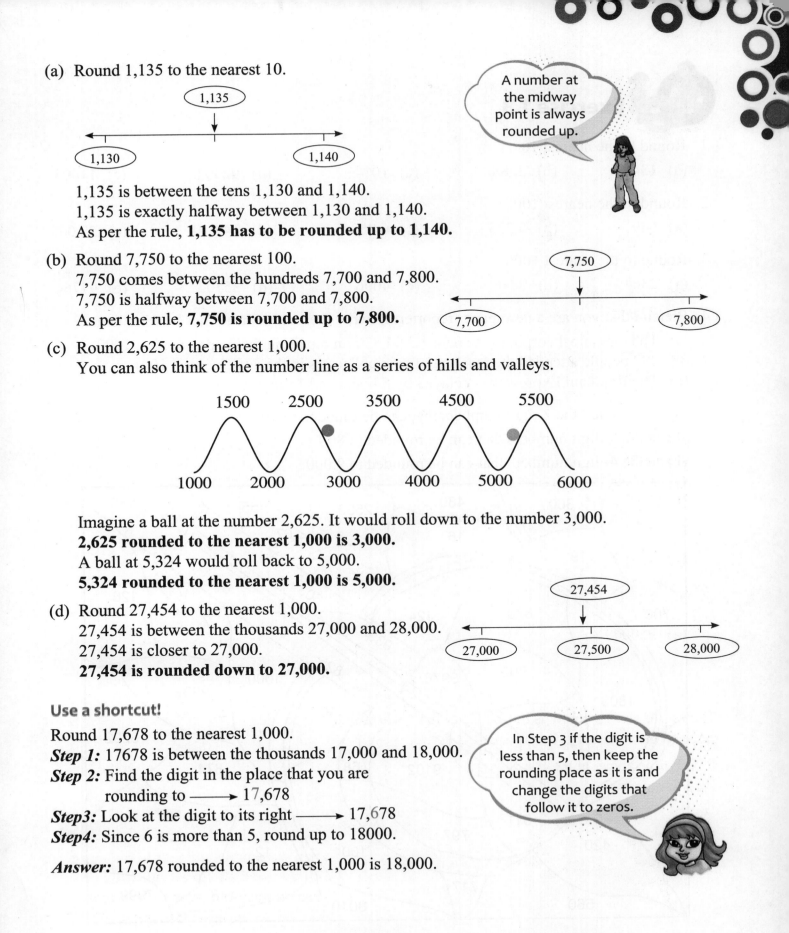

1,135 is between the tens 1,130 and 1,140.
1,135 is exactly halfway between 1,130 and 1,140.
As per the rule, **1,135 has to be rounded up to 1,140.**

> A number at the midway point is always rounded up.

(b) Round 7,750 to the nearest 100.
7,750 comes between the hundreds 7,700 and 7,800.
7,750 is halfway between 7,700 and 7,800.
As per the rule, **7,750 is rounded up to 7,800.**

(c) Round 2,625 to the nearest 1,000.
You can also think of the number line as a series of hills and valleys.

Imagine a ball at the number 2,625. It would roll down to the number 3,000.
2,625 rounded to the nearest 1,000 is 3,000.
A ball at 5,324 would roll back to 5,000.
5,324 rounded to the nearest 1,000 is 5,000.

(d) Round 27,454 to the nearest 1,000.
27,454 is between the thousands 27,000 and 28,000.
27,454 is closer to 27,000.
27,454 is rounded down to 27,000.

Use a shortcut!

Round 17,678 to the nearest 1,000.
Step 1: 17678 is between the thousands 17,000 and 18,000.
Step 2: Find the digit in the place that you are
rounding to ⟶ 17,678
Step3: Look at the digit to its right ⟶ 17,678
Step4: Since 6 is more than 5, round up to 18000.

Answer: 17,678 rounded to the nearest 1,000 is 18,000.

> In Step 3 if the digit is less than 5, then keep the rounding place as it is and change the digits that follow it to zeros.

Exercise 1.3

1. Round to the nearest 10.
   (a) 1346   (b) 2388   (c) 1014   (d) 92407   (e) 11003

2. Round to the nearest 100.
   (a) 649   (b) 5,325   (c) 6,850   (d) 14,910   (e) 58,009

3. Round to the nearest 1000.
   (a) 2364   (b) 9846   (c) 4096   (d) 35502   (e) 97764

4. Pretend that you are a newspaper reporter. Rewrite these news headlines by rounding.
   (a) The municipal corporation spent ₹ 5,94,830 on repairing the roads. (nearest 1000)
   (b) 389 people attended the meeting of coin collectors in the city. (nearest 100)
   (c) The Rajdhani Express was delayed by 5 hours and 15 minutes. (nearest hour)

5. Shade in pencil the 2-digit numbers that can be rounded to 70.
   Shade the 3-digit numbers that can be rounded to 800.
   Shade the 4-digit numbers that can be rounded to 9,000.

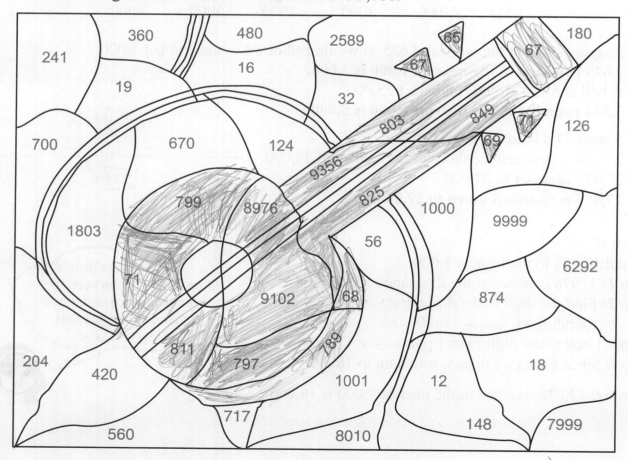

Number Patterns

1. Consecutive numbers

Numbers that come one after the other on the number line are consecutive numbers.
This pattern has been made by changing 2-digit numbers to 1-digit numbers. Can you see how? Complete the pattern.

〔1+0〕 〔1+1〕

1	2	3	4	5	6	7	8	9	10	11	12	13	14	15	16
1	2	3	4	5	6	7	8	9	1	2	3	4	5	6	7

17	18	19	20	21	22	23	24	25	26	27	28	29
8	9	10	2	3	4	5	6	7	8	9	10	11
		1									1	2

Add only till you see a pattern, then complete.

2. Consecutive even numbers

2	4	6	8	10	12	14	16	18	20	22	24
2	4	6	8	1	3	5	7	9	2	4	6

26	28	30	32	34	36	38	40	42	44	46	48
8	10	3	5	7	9	11	4	6	8	10	12
	1					2				1	3

3. Consecutive odd numbers

1	3	5	7	9	11	13	15	17	19	21	23	25	27	29
1	3	5	7	9	2	4	6	8	10	3	5	7	9	11
									1					2

Pascal's Triangle

Look for a pattern. Extend the triangle by another two rows.

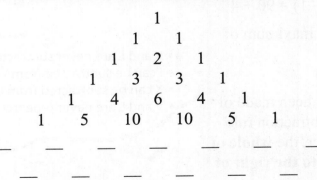

```
              1
           1     1
        1     2     1
     1     3     3     1
   1     4     6     4     1
 1    5    10    10    5    1
 __   __   __   __   __   __   __
 __   __   __   __   __   __   __   __
```

There are many patterns in this triangle. Can you spot at least three?
Refer Maths Lab Activity on page 24.

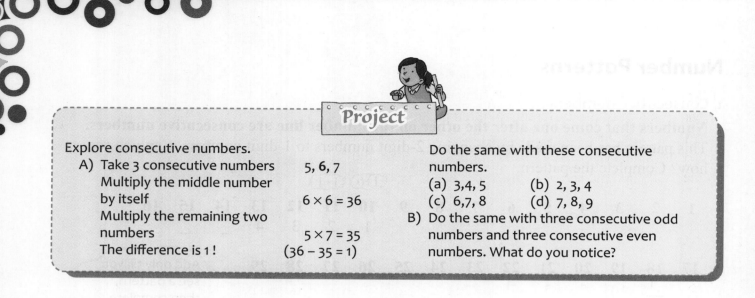

Explore consecutive numbers.
  A) Take 3 consecutive numbers   5, **6**, 7
     Multiply the middle number
     by itself   6 × 6 = 36
     Multiply the remaining two
     numbers   5 × 7 = 35
     The difference is 1 !   (36 − 35 = 1)

Do the same with these consecutive numbers.
  (a) 3, 4, 5   (b) 2, 3, 4
  (c) 6, 7, 8   (d) 7, 8, 9
  B) Do the same with three consecutive odd numbers and three consecutive even numbers. What do you notice?

Roman Numbers

You are familiar with Roman numbers up to 39. Let us look back at the rules of forming Roman numerals and apply it to numbers up to 100. Remember that the Romans did not have '0', so they did not use place value.

They had seven basic symbols represented by these letters.

Roman Number	I	V	X	L	C	D	M
Hindu-Arabic	1	5	10	50	100	500	1,000

They formed other numbers by combining these letters and following certain rules.

- Putting a letter **after** one of bigger value means you **add** it.
  (a) 75 = LXXV (50 + 10 + 10 + 5)
  (b) 60 = LX (50 + 10)

- Putting a letter **before** one of bigger value means you **subtract** it.
  (a) 40 = XL (50 − 10)
  (b) 94 = XCIV (100 − 10) + (5 − 1) = 90 + 4

- A letter can be **repeated** up to a maximum of **three times** only.
  80 = LXXX (50 + 10 + 10 + 10)

- When a smaller number that has been made of two letters using the addition/subtraction rule is combined with a larger number, the **whole of the smaller number is written to the right of the larger one.**
  (a) 59 = LIX
  (b) 74 = 70 + 4 = LXX + IV = LXXIV

- V and L are never subtracted.
- I can be subtracted from V and X only.
- X can be subtracted from L and C only.
- V and L are never repeated.

20

Play a Game

Take turns drawing the strokes of Roman Numbers with a friend. Each must use different coloured pencil and each is allowed 1, 2 or 3 strokes or lines at one time. The person who draws the last stroke/line to complete 'X' loses the game. In the example below, green has lost the game.

I II III IV V VI VII VIII IX X

Try This

Write the ages of the members of your family using Roman Numbers.

Exercise 1.4

1. Fill in the boxes with Hindu-Arabic numerals.

XL	X	LXX	XXX	XC	XX	LX	LXXX	C	L
40									

2. Write the Hindu-Arabic numerals.
   (a) XXIV 24 (b) XC (c) LVII (d) XLIV (e) LXXV (f) LXXXII

3. Write the numbers from 41 to 100 in your exercise book using Roman numerals.

4. Compare using <, >, or =.
   (a) XC $<$ XL
   (b) XLIV ◯ LXIV
   (c) XXVII ◯ LX
   (d) LVIII ◯ C

5. Give the answer in Roman numerals.
   (a) XXV + XL (b) LXII + XII (c) LXX + XXX (d) L – XXXIX

Challenge

Correct this Roman number sentence in three different ways.
(a) By moving one stick (b) By removing one stick (c) By not touching any stick

XI + I = X

Chapter Check-Up

1. Write the following numerals in word form and expanded notation.
   (a) 11,00,948   (b) 78,98,001   (c) 5,67,03,670

2. Write in figures.
   (a) Thirty lakh, seventy thousand, three hundred six
   (b) Four crore, seventeen lakh, one hundred ninety-five
   (c) Forty-eight lakh, three hundred five

3. Give the place value of the coloured digit.
   (a) 4,56,78,923   (b) 54,69,345   (c) 9,76,13,984

4. What are the greatest and the smallest 7-digit numbers you can make using the digits 3, 5, 7, 1, 2? (digits may be repeated)

5. Write the number after: (a) 79,98,999   (b) 15,09,999

6. Write the number before: (a) 5,10,000   (b) 13,80,970

7. Compare using >, <, or =.
   (a) 5,67,98,345 ◯ 5,76,98,435   (b) 67,83,009 ◯ 67,08,900
   (c) LVIII ◯ C   (d) LXXI ◯ XLIX

8. Put the commas using the international system and rewrite these statements using the word form of the number.
   (a) A 15-year-old boy would have lived for 131400 hours.
   (b) 2401596 people travelled by planes this year.

9. Rewrite these news headlines by rounding.
   (a) The flight carrying the cricketers from South Africa landed at 8:18 p.m. (Round to the nearest half hour.)
   (b) The stolen collection had 13,078 precious stamps and first-day covers. (Round to the nearest 1000.)

10. Write the Roman numerals for:
    (a) 29   (b) 12   (c) 81   (d) 95

11. Solve using Roman numerals.
    (a) XCIII – LXV   (b) XLVII + XXXIX   (c) LXXX – XXXI

Given below are the land areas of the ten largest countries of the world. Study the list and answer the questions below.

Country	Area in sq. km
Argentina	27,66,890
Australia	76,86,850
Brazil	85,11,965
Canada	3,28,05,000
China	95,96,960
India	32,87,590
Kazakhstan	27,17,300
Russia	1,70,75,200
Sudan	25,05,810
United States of America	96,29,091

Did you know that Vatican city is the smallest country in the world with an area of 1 sq. km?

Solve.

1. Rewrite the list in order of largest to smallest land area.

2. Which is the largest country?

3. Which is the smallest country in the list?

4. Rewrite the area of the largest and smallest countries using the international system in figures and words.

5. Write the area of India in words.

6. What is the value of '3' in the number giving the area of Canada?

7. Read out aloud the list made by you for question 1.

Maths Lab Activity

Number Patterns

Objective: To explore number patterns—triangular and square numbers.

Material Required: Bindis, sheet of paper

Preparation: Students may work in pairs.

Steps:

Triangular Number

1. One student sticks the bindis on paper into triangles as shown.
2. The other student counts and records the number of bindis needed for each triangle.
3. Then they find all the triangular numbers up to 50 using bindis or dots.
4. Next, one students sticks the bindis into squares as shown.
5. The other student counts and records the number of bindis needed for each square.
6. They then find all the square numbers up to 50 using bindis or dots.
7. Then each student finds the triangular and square numbers up to 100 using the pattern.

Record the Activity:

Triangular numbers:
1, 3, _5, 7, 9_

Square numbers:
1, 4, _____

Try this out:

Colour all the triangular numbers on this grid.

1	2	3	4	5	6	7	8	9	10
11	12	13	14	15	16	17	18	19	20
21	22	23	24	25	26	27	28	29	30
31	32	33	34	35	36	37	38	39	40
41	42	43	44	45	46	47	38	49	50
51	52	53	54	55	56	57	58	59	60
61	62	63	64	65	66	67	68	69	70
71	72	73	74	75	76	77	78	79	80
81	82	83	84	85	86	87	88	89	90
91	92	93	94	95	96	97	98	99	100

Count the boxes between the coloured numbers. Do you see a pattern?

Colour all the square numbers on this grid.

1	2	3	4	5	6	7	8	9	10
11	12	13	14	15	16	17	18	19	20
21	22	23	24	25	26	27	28	29	30
31	32	33	34	35	36	37	38	39	40
41	42	43	44	45	46	47	48	49	50
51	52	53	54	55	56	57	58	59	60
61	62	63	64	65	66	67	68	69	70
71	72	73	74	75	76	77	78	79	80
81	82	83	84	85	86	87	88	89	90
91	92	93	94	95	96	97	98	99	100

Count the boxes between the coloured numbers. Do you see a pattern?

Enrichment Time

The ancient Egyptians did not have a place value system, and neither did they have a symbol for zero. This is how they wrote their numbers.

Stick	|	1
Heel bone	∩	10
Coiled rope	ℰ	100
Lotus flower		1000
Pointing finger		10,000
Tadpole		1,00,000
Astonished man		10,00,000

Since they did not have a place value system, they simply combined the symbols and added their values. So they could write the symbols in any order.

18   ∩ \|\|\|\|\|\|\|\|

350   ℰℰℰ ∩∩∩∩∩

4186   \|\|\|\| ℰ ∩∩∩∩∩∩∩∩ \|\|\|\|\|\|

- How will you write these numbers using Egyptian numerals?
  46
  793
  5201
- Write your age in standard numerals and Egyptian numbers.
- Write the year of your birth in standard numerals and Egyptian numerals.
- Write the year of our independence in standard numerals and Egyptian numerals.

I am glad the Indians invented zero. These numbers are too long!

Activity Bag

This game can be played by the class as two teams. Two sets of digit cards from 0 to 9 are to be made. Two sets of place value charts are drawn on the board one for each team. A child from each team comes up and selects one digit card each and writes the digit he has picked in order starting from the crores place. The card is then placed back in the pile. The next two children come up and do the same thing writing their digits in the ten lakhs place. This continues till both teams have built a number. The team that makes the bigger number wins.

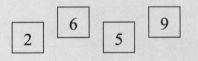

Addition, Subtraction and its Applications

Looking Back

Addition

Addition of large numbers is the same as addition of smaller numbers.
You **start from the ones place and regroup if necessary.**

(a)

L	TTh	Th	H	T	O
	①	①		①	
	6	1	3	2	7
+	3	9	8	5	5
1	0	1	1	8	2

(b)

L	TTh	Th	H	T	O
		②	①		
	1	2	7	5	3
	2	6	9	3	2
+	1	4	7	8	4	1
1	7	7	5	2	6

The numbers you add are called **addends**.

Subtraction

Subtraction of large numbers is the same as subtraction of smaller numbers.
You **start from the ones place and regroup if necessary.**
You can check your subtraction with addition.

L	TTh	Th	H	T	O
		10			
	6	0̶	14		
3	5	7̶	1̶	4̶	3
− 1	5	3	8	5	2
2	0	3	2	9	1

Check:

```
  2 0 3 2 9 1
+ 1 5 3 8 5 2
  3 5 7 1 4 3
```

The number you subtract from is called the **minuend**. The number you subtract is called the **subtrahend**.

Watch out for the zeros.

(a)

Th	H	T	O
	9	9	
5	1̶0̶	1̶0̶	16
6̶	0̶	0̶	6̶
− 2	7	5	8
3	2	4	8

(b)

TTH	Th	H	T	O
	14			
1	4̶	10	8	10
2̶	5̶	0̶	9̶	0̶
−		8	2	3	4
1	6	8	5	6

Use a shortcut!

Subtract: 4000 − 2847

Reduce both numbers by 1 and then **subtract**.

This helps avoid regrouping.

$$
\begin{array}{ll}
(4000-1) & 3\ 9\ 9\ 9 \\
(2847-1) & -2\ 8\ 4\ 6 \\
\hline
 & 1\ 1\ 5\ 3
\end{array}
$$

You can try this method for large numbers also.

Try This

$$
\begin{array}{ll}
50000 & (-1) \ = \\
-29846 & (-1) \ = - \underline{\hspace{2cm}}
\end{array}
$$

Exercise 2.1

1. Rewrite in columns using place value and add.

   (a) 5087 + 26542
   (b) 65875 + 75842
   (c) 45735 + 69046
   (d) 93485 + 48294
   (e) 54567 + 45765 + 12635
   (f) 287635 + 1198
   (g) 51487 + 456 + 239601
   (h) 111321 + 56789 + 45987
   (i) 108162 + 59346 + 18992

2. Subtract. Check your answers with addition.

   (a) 8765 − 2984
   (b) 93542 − 78645
   (c) 938743 − 78243
   (d) 439235 − 145987
   (e) 30000 − 18603
   (f) 21976 − 8756
   (g) 50001 − 39846
   (h) 20106 − 15302
   (i) 81065 − 21952

3. Fill in the boxes.

   (a)
   $$
   \begin{array}{r}
   2\ \square\ 4\ 5\ 6 \\
   +\ \square\ 8\ \square\ \square\ \square \\
   \hline
   8\ 2\ 0\ 1\ 3
   \end{array}
   $$

   (b)
   $$
   \begin{array}{r}
   7\ \square\ 7\ \square\ \square \\
   -\ 1\ 5\ \square\ 4\ 6 \\
   \hline
   \square\ 2\ 2\ 8\ 0
   \end{array}
   $$

4. Do this activity.

   • Choose a 3-digit number with the first digit greater than the third digit
   • Reverse the digits
   • Subtract
   • Reverse the digits
   • Add

   $$
   \begin{array}{r}
   6\ 7\ 2 \\
   -\ 2\ 7\ 6 \\
   \hline
   3\ 9\ 6 \\
   +\ 6\ 9\ 3 \\
   \hline
   1\ 0\ 8\ 9
   \end{array}
   $$

   Try with these numbers. What do you notice?

   (i) 3 2 1
   (ii) 7 8 2
   (iii) 8 4 4
   (iv) 7 7 5

Challenge

Complete the magic square.

44		
99		
58		90

Using Compensation for Addition and Subtraction

We can change numbers into multiples of 10 or 100 to make it easier to subtract.

Addition

(a)
$$\begin{array}{r} 3\ 8 \\ +2\ 6 \\ \hline 6\ 4 \end{array}$$
gives you the same answer as
$$\begin{array}{r} 3\ 8\ (+2) = \ \ 4\ 0 \\ +2\ 6\ (-2) = +2\ 4 \\ \hline 6\ 4 \end{array}$$

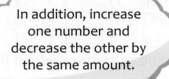

In addition, increase one number and decrease the other by the same amount.

(b) In this example it is easier to make the second number into a multiple of 10.

$$\begin{array}{r} 4\ 5 \\ +8\ 7 \\ \hline ? \end{array}$$
$\longrightarrow$
$$\begin{array}{r} 4\ 5 \\ +8\ 7\ \textbf{(+3)} \end{array}$$
$\longrightarrow$
$$\begin{array}{r} 4\ 5(-3) = \ \ 4\ 2 \\ 8\ 7(+3) = +9\ 0 \\ \hline 1\ 3\ 2 \end{array}$$

Subtraction

While subtracting we always change the number being subtracted into a multiple of 10 or 100.

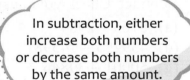

In subtraction, either increase both numbers or decrease both numbers by the same amount.

(a)
$$\begin{array}{r} 4\ 3 \\ -2\ 8 \\ \hline 1\ 5 \end{array}$$
gives you the same answer as
$$\begin{array}{r} 4\ 3\ (+2) = \ \ 4\ 5 \\ -2\ 8\ (+2) = -3\ 0 \\ \hline 1\ 5 \end{array}$$

(b)
$$\begin{array}{r} 7\ 7 \\ -3\ 3 \\ \hline ? \end{array}$$
$\longrightarrow$
$$\begin{array}{r} 7\ 7 \\ -3\ 3\ \textbf{(-3)} \end{array}$$
$\longrightarrow$
$$\begin{array}{r} 7\ 7\ (-3) = \ \ 7\ 4 \\ -3\ 3\ (-3) = -3\ 0 \\ \hline 4\ 4 \end{array}$$

 **Exercise 2.2**

Solve using compensation.

1. (a) 21 + 37   (b) 28 + 86   (c) 39 + 63   (d) 72 + 46
   (e) 63 + 94   (f) 47 + 86   (g) 51 + 39   (h) 93 + 47

2. (a) 56 − 38   (b) 80 − 27   (c) 97 − 29   (d) 63 − 31
   (e) 84 − 39   (f) 96 − 63   (g) 70 − 58   (h) 64 − 42

Profit and Loss

It costs me ₹ 363 to make this lamp in my factory.

I will sell it for ₹ 450 in my shop.

₹ 363 is the **cost price (C.P.)** of the lamp.

₹ 450 is the **selling price (S.P.)** of the lamp.

When the selling price is more than the cost price, the difference is the 'profit'.

I will earn ₹ 87 on each lamp I sell.

$$\begin{array}{ll} \text{Selling price} & = ₹\ 4\ 5\ 0 \\ \text{Cost price} & = ₹\ 3\ 6\ 3 \\ \hline & ₹\ 8\ 7 \leftarrow \text{Profit} \end{array}$$

These models will help you remember the relationship between these three terms.

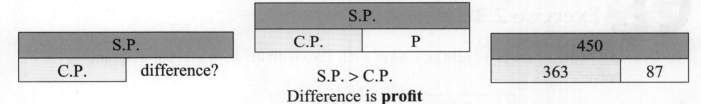

S.P.	
C.P.	difference?

S.P.	
C.P.	P

S.P. > C.P.
Difference is profit

450	
363	87

When the cost price is more than the selling price, the difference is the 'loss'.

This lamp was slightly damaged. So I sold it for ₹ 300.

$$\begin{array}{ll} \text{Cost price} & = ₹\ 3\ 6\ 3 \\ \text{Selling price} & = ₹\ 3\ 0\ 0 \\ \hline & ₹\ 6\ 3 \leftarrow \text{Loss} \end{array}$$

I lost ₹ 63 on this lamp.

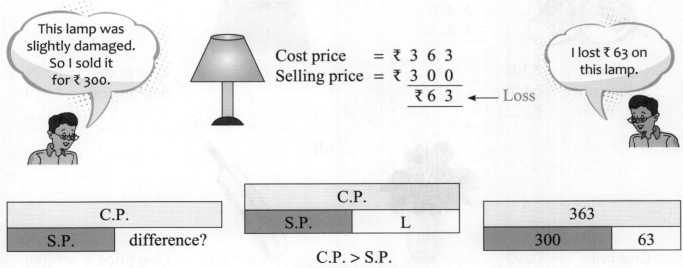

C.P.	
S.P.	difference?

C.P.	
S.P.	L

C.P. > S.P.
Difference is loss

363	
300	63

Sometimes the price of an object increases due to other expenses like transportation, shop rent, salaries, etc. **These are called overheads and are added to the cost price.**

It costs me ₹75 to deliver this lamp to a customer's home.

C.P. = ₹ 3 6 3
+   7 5
₹ 4 3 8   ← Final cost price

I will now sell it at ₹ 500.

S.P. > C.P.
So, difference is profit

S.P.	
C.P.	Profit

₹ 500	
₹ 438	?
C.P.	Profit

→

5 0 0
− 4 3 8
6 2

→

S.P.

₹ 500	
₹ 438	₹ 62
C.P.	Profit

Exercise 2.3

1. Decide whether there is a profit or loss in each case with the help of a bar diagram. Then solve.

(a)

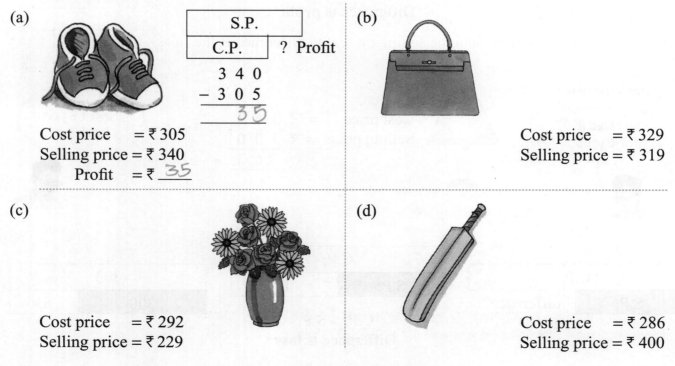

S.P.		
C.P.		? Profit

3 4 0
− 3 0 5
35

Cost price   = ₹ 305
Selling price = ₹ 340
Profit   = ₹ _35_

(b)

Cost price   = ₹ 329
Selling price = ₹ 319

(c)

Cost price   = ₹ 292
Selling price = ₹ 229

(d)

Cost price   = ₹ 286
Selling price = ₹ 400

2. Find out the profit or loss in each of these. You may use diagrams if you wish.

	Cost price	Selling price	Profit/Loss	Amount
(a)	₹ 2,090	₹ 2,100	C.P. < S.P. = Profit	₹ 2100 − ₹ 2090 = ₹ 10
(b)	₹ 8,395	₹ 8,935		
(c)	₹ 14,060	₹ 14,600		
(d)	₹ 9,319	₹ 9,139		
(e)	₹ 11,190	₹ 11,865		

3. First find the final cost of each item. Then calculate profit or loss using diagrams if you wish.

	Cost price	Overheads	Final cost (CP + Overheads)	SP	Profit/Loss amount
(a)	₹ 645	₹ 80	₹ 725	₹ 800	₹ 800 − ₹ 725 = ₹ 75 profit
(b)	₹ 909	₹ 162		₹ 1235	
(c)	₹ 2100	₹ 395		₹ 2300	
(d)	₹ 7213	₹ 520		₹ 9818	
(e)	₹ 9127	₹ 2061		₹ 10,050	

4. Solve.

(a) A collector buys a painting for ₹ 3,500 but sells it for ₹ 2,750. Find the gain or loss.

(b) A second-hand furniture dealer buys a used table for ₹ 3,250. He spends ₹ 500 on polishing and repairing it. If he sells it at ₹ 4,000, what is his profit?

(c) A calculator that costs ₹ 517 is sold at ₹ 575. What is the profit that is made?

(d) A used dining set is sold for ₹ 9,390. It had been bought for ₹ 11,500. What is the loss that is incurred?

(e) A furniture mart buys an old sofa set for ₹ 5,380. They spend ₹ 1,840 to put new covers on it and sell it for ₹ 8,000. What is the profit or loss?

Finding Cost Price or Selling Price

The same bar diagrams you used in the previous pages can help you find the cost price or selling price when you know the profit or loss.

Model A (for profit)

S.P.	
C.P.	P

If you know any two values you can find the third.

Model B (for loss)

C.P.	
S.P.	L

To Find the Cost Price

(a) Akshay sold a book for ₹ 315 at a loss of ₹ 23. What was the cost of the book?

Selling price = ₹ 315

Loss = ₹ 23

Cost price = ?

You know SP and L, so use Model B.

C.P.

?	
₹ 315	₹ 23

S.P.　　　　　L

Add to find C.P.
S.P. + L = C.P.

$$\begin{array}{r} ₹3\;1\;5 \\ +\quad 2\;3 \\ \hline ₹3\;3\;8 \end{array} \leftarrow \text{C.P.}$$

Check your answer:
C.P. – S.P. = L
338 – 315 = 23 ✓

Answer: The cost price of the book was ₹ 338.

(b) Ananya made a profit of ₹ 281 on a necklace she sold for ₹ 5,389. What had the necklace cost her?

Selling price = ₹ 5,389

Profit = ₹ 281

Cost price = ?

S.P.

₹ 5389	
?	₹ 281

C.P.　　　　　P

You know S.P. and P, so use Model A.

Subtract to find C.P.
S.P. – P = C.P.

$$\begin{array}{r} ₹5\;3\;8\;9 \\ -\quad 2\;8\;1 \\ \hline ₹5\;1\;0\;8 \end{array} \leftarrow \text{C.P.}$$

Check your answer:
S.P. – C.P. = P
5389 – 5108 = 281 ✓

Answer: The cost price of the necklace was ₹ 5108.

Try This

S.P. = ₹ 1205　　S.P. = ₹ 1900
P = ₹ 213　　　　L = ₹ 190
C.P. = ?　　　　　C.P. = ?

To Find the Selling Price

(a) A stamp collector bought a rare stamp for ₹ 21,380 and sold it at a profit of ₹ 1,500. What was the selling price of the stamp?

Cost price = ₹ 21,380

Profit = ₹ 1,500

Selling price = ?

You know C.P. and P, so use Model A.

S.P.	
?	
₹ 21380	₹ 1500
C.P.	P

Add to find S.P.
C.P. + P = S.P.

```
₹ 2 1 3 8 0
+   1 5 0 0
  2 2 8 8 0
```

Check your answer:
S.P. − C.P. = P
22880 − 21380 = 1500 ✓

Answer: The selling price of the stamp was ₹ 22,880.

(b) A man bought an encyclopaedia set for ₹ 8,350 and sold it after a few years for ₹ 550 less than what he paid for it. How much did he sell the set for?

Cost price = ₹ 8,350

Loss = ₹ 550

Selling price = ?

You know C.P. and L, so use Model B.

C.P.	
₹ 8350	
?	₹ 550
S.P.	L

Subtract to find S.P.
C.P. − L = S.P.

```
₹ 8 3 5 0
−   5 5 0
  7 8 0 0
```

Check your answer:
C.P. − S.P. = L
8350 − 7800 = 550 ✓

Answer: The selling price of the encyclopaedia was ₹ 7800.

Try This

C.P. = ₹ 1631   C.P. = ₹ 9060
P = ₹ 413   L = ₹ 1285
S.P. = ?   S.P. = ?

Challenge

Solve this famous puzzle!

I sold goods worth ₹ 20 to a customer who paid for it with a ₹ 100 note. As I didn't have change, I gave the ₹ 100 note to my neighbour and got change from him. I gave ₹ 80 to the customer and kept ₹ 20 with me. Later my neighbour returned the ₹ 100 note to me saying that it was fake. I gave him back his money. What was my loss?

Exercise 2.4

1. Find the selling price or cost price as required with the help of a model.

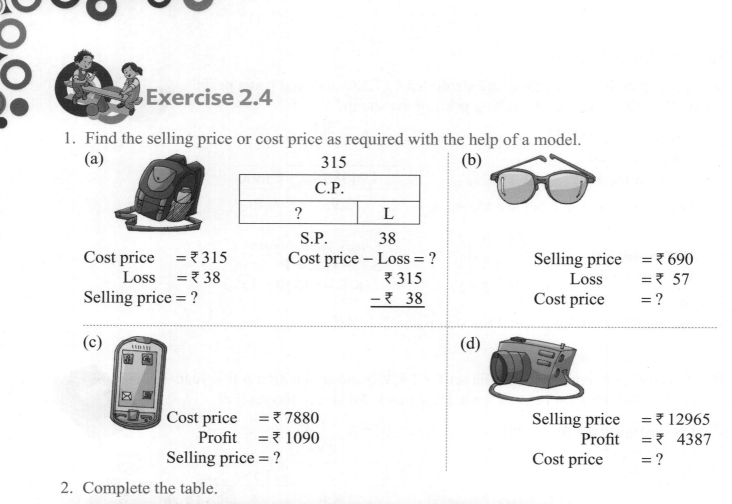

(a)

315	
C.P.	
?	L
S.P.	38

Cost price   = ₹ 315
　　Loss   = ₹ 38
Selling price = ?

Cost price – Loss = ?
　　　　₹ 315
　　　– ₹ 38

(b)

Selling price = ₹ 690
　　Loss   = ₹ 57
Cost price   = ?

(c)

Cost price   = ₹ 7880
　Profit   = ₹ 1090
Selling price = ?

(d)

Selling price = ₹ 12965
　Profit   = ₹ 4387
Cost price   = ?

2. Complete the table.

	Selling price	Profit	Loss	Cost price
(a)	₹ 2,385	₹ 195	—	
(b)	₹ 1,900	—	₹ 628	
(c)	₹ 8,630	—	₹ 1,020	
(d)	₹ 74,365	₹ 2,315	—	

3. Complete the table.

	Cost price	Profit	Loss	Selling price
(a)	₹ 1,095	—	₹ 89	
(b)	₹ 3,586	₹ 369	—	
(c)	₹ 9,980	—	₹ 351	
(d)	₹ 15,381	₹ 1,395	—	

4. (a) Rashid incurred a loss of ₹ 590 on a chair he sold at ₹ 1280. What was the cost price of the chair?
   (b) Ali made a profit of ₹ 3200 on a sofa set he bought for ₹ 15,290. At what price did he sell it?
   (c) A dozen books are sold at ₹ 1648 at a profit of ₹ 120. What is the cost price of the books?

Steps of Problem Solving

The steps of problem solving help you think in an organised way to help you decide how to solve a problem.

Alisha, the school cricket captain has made 1231 runs in interschool matches so far. Anita, the vice captain needs 125 runs to equal Alisha's record. How many runs has Anita made so far?

Step 1: Read the problem and understand the question
We have to find how many runs Anita has made so far

Step 2: Find the important information in the problem
- Alisha has made 1231 runs
- Anita has made 125 runs less than that

Step 3: Decide what to do
If we subtract the runs that Anita needs from Alisha's total runs, we can find how many runs Anita has made so far.

Step 4: Solve the problem and answer the question

$$\begin{array}{r} 1231 \\ -\ 125 \\ \hline 1106 \end{array}$$

Answer: Anita has made 1106 runs.

Step 5: Check your answer
  (a) *Is the calculation correct?*
      Yes, I have checked the calculation.
      $1106 + 125 = 1231$
  (b) *Have you answered the questions correctly?*
      Yes, I have found how many runs Anita has made.
      I have answered in a complete sentence.
  (c) *Does your answer make sense?*
      Yes, Anita's runs are less than Alisha's runs.

Read	R
Find	F
Decide	D
Solve	S
Check	C

Make a sentence to remember the steps.

Exercise 2.5

1. Solve using addition, subtraction, multiplication or division.

   (a) The Sunshine Club newspaper printed 33,530 copies in a year. Of these 28,395 copies were distributed. How many were not distributed?

   (b) The milometer on a van showed 53,811 km in October. After being used for three months it showed 84,209 km in December. If it had done 21,614 km in October and November, how much did it do in the month of December?

   (c)  Sushil's car did 25,384 km in one year and Suraj's car did 30,001 km in the same year. How many kilometres less did Sushil's car run?

   (d) Mr Shenoy had ₹ 3,25,765 to buy a new car. He borrowed ₹ 1,12,700. How much did the car cost?

   (e) Sriram won 75 tournaments. The prize money totalled up to ₹ 2,25,000. If he recieved the same amount for every tournament, how much had he earned per tournament?

   (f) A school needs 24,510 pencils a year. How many boxes of 25 must the school buy?

   (g)  The toy store had 20 boxes of dolls and 25 boxes of teddy bears. Each box holds 24 toys. How many toys did the toy store have in all?

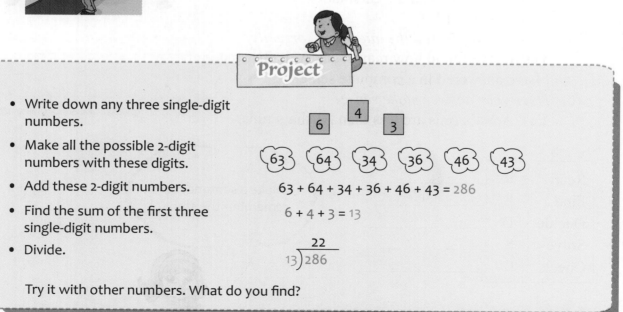

Project

- Write down any three single-digit numbers.

  6   4   3

- Make all the possible 2-digit numbers with these digits.

  63   64   34   36   46   43

- Add these 2-digit numbers.

  63 + 64 + 34 + 36 + 46 + 43 = 286

- Find the sum of the first three single-digit numbers.

  6 + 4 + 3 = 13

- Divide.

  $$13\overline{)286}22$$

Try it with other numbers. What do you find?

Using Models to Find Missing Numbers

Missing Addends

A pen drive can hold 530 songs. So far 391 songs have been copied on to it. How many more songs can be copied on to the pen drive?

In other words, what must you add to 391 to make it 530?

391 + ? = 530

Total songs	
530	
391	? difference

↓ | ↓

Songs already copied | *Songs yet to be copied*

Subtract to find the difference:

```
   5 3 0
 − 3 9 1
   1 3 9
```

Try This

What must you add to 7382 to make it 14095?

14095	
7382	? difference

Answer: 139 more songs can be copied on to the pen drive.

Missing Minuends

Devyani was playing a maths game on her computer. She made some points in the beginning but lost 128 points after a while. She now has 318 points left with her. How many points had Devyani made in the beginning?

In other words, from what can you take away 128 and leave 318?

? − 128 = 318

Total points	
?	
128	318

Points lost | *Points left*

Add to find the total points:

```
   1 2 8
 + 3 1 8
   4 4 6
```

Try This

Find the number from which 8913 must be subtracted to leave 11238.

?	
8913	11238

Answer: Devyani had made 446 points at the beginning.

Challenge

The stars all stand for different digits.
What is the only digit that can be put in the thousands place of the sum?

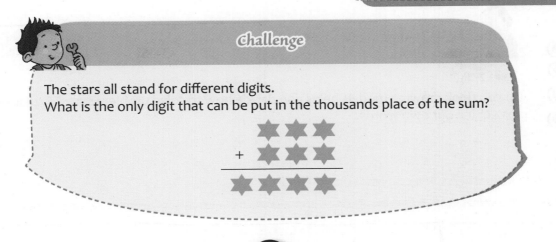

Missing Subtrahends

Dipti's laptop had 738 files. She deleted some of them, but still had 239 left on the laptop. How many files had she deleted?

In other words, what do you take away from 738 to leave 239?

738 – ? = 239

Total files

738	
239	? difference

↓   ↓

Files left   *Files deleted*

Subtract to find the difference:

$$\begin{array}{r} 7\,3\,8 \\ -\ 2\,3\,9 \\ \hline 4\,9\,9 \end{array}$$

Answer: Dipti had deleted 499 files from her laptop.

Try This

Find the number which when subtracted from 182934 leaves 92872?

	182934	
92872		? difference

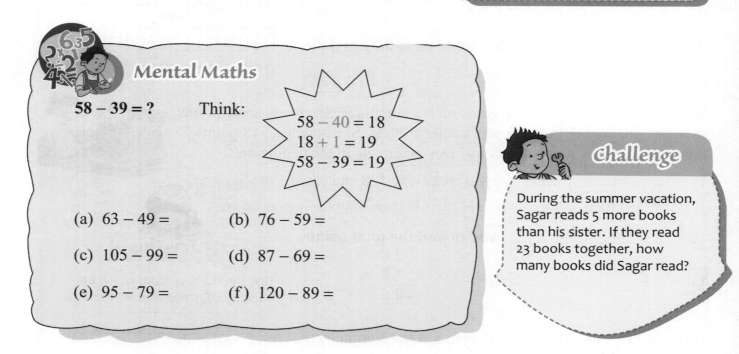

Mental Maths

58 – 39 = ?   Think:

58 – 40 = 18
18 + 1 = 19
58 – 39 = 19

(a) 63 – 49 =

(b) 76 – 59 =

(c) 105 – 99 =

(d) 87 – 69 =

(e) 95 – 79 =

(f) 120 – 89 =

Challenge

During the summer vacation, Sagar reads 5 more books than his sister. If they read 23 books together, how many books did Sagar read?

Journal

Do you think drawing models helps you decide how to solve problem sums? Explain your answer in your own words.

Exercise 2.6

Solve. Use models to help you.

1. (a) $612 + \underline{\hspace{1.5cm}} = 948$ (b) $7394 + \underline{\hspace{1.5cm}} = 12642$

   (c) $\underline{\hspace{1.5cm}} - 847 = 1238$ (d) $\underline{\hspace{1.5cm}} - 9162 = 1811$

   (e) $9408 - \underline{\hspace{1.5cm}} = 1138$ (f) $49584 - \underline{\hspace{1.5cm}} = 23175$

2. (a) What must you add to 18345 to make it 19624?

   (b) If you subtract 23146 from a number, you are left with 35906. Find the number.

   (c) Find the number which must be subtracted from 83196 to leave 11422.

   (d) The sum of two numbers is 40132. If one number is 29184, find the other number.

3. (a) Khalid wants to buy a board game that costs ₹ 501. He has ₹ 479. How much more money does he need?

   (b) Harshita's stamp album can hold 1500 stamps. So far she has pasted 785 stamps in it. How many more stamps can she paste in it?

   (c) A large library has lent out 1785 books. It has 7816 books left. How many books does the library have in all?

   (d) An art exhibition had 915 piece of art on show. Some of them got sold but there were 211 unsold pieces. How many pieces were sold?

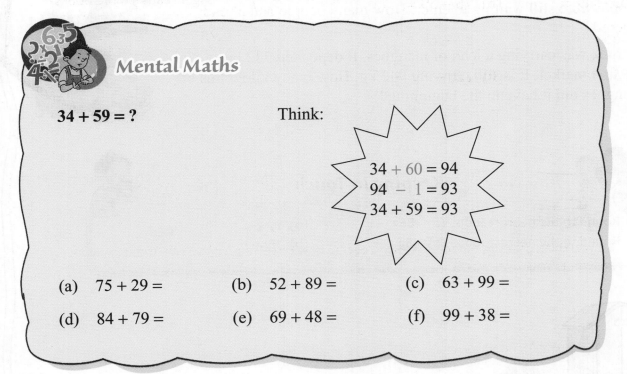

Mental Maths

$34 + 59 = ?$ Think:

$34 + 60 = 94$
$94 - 1 = 93$
$34 + 59 = 93$

(a) $75 + 29 =$ (b) $52 + 89 =$ (c) $63 + 99 =$

(d) $84 + 79 =$ (e) $69 + 48 =$ (f) $99 + 38 =$

Chapter Check-Up

1. Solve.
   - (a) 45673 + 3452 + 456
   - (b) 434476 + 365432
   - (c) 36542 − 27543
   - (d) 849007 − 256324
   - (e) 45631 + 7654 − 36542
   - (f) 65213 − 4532 − 5643

2. Solve using compensation.
   - (a) 41 + 34
   - (b) 73 − 58
   - (c) 24 + 48
   - (d) 92 − 39

3. Solve.
   - (a) A painting was bought for ₹ 45895. The frame was changed for ₹ 2060. It was finally sold for ₹ 51080. What was the loss or gain?
   - (b) A factory makes car wheels. If it sells each wheel at ₹ 5925 at a profit of ₹ 398, what is the cost price of the wheel?
   - (c) A chair costs ₹ 1046. If it is sold at a loss of ₹ 191, what is its selling price?

4. Solve with the help of models.
   - (a) What number should be added to 78,543 to get 87,653?
   - (b) The sum of two numbers is 93,861. If one number is 21,981, what is the other number?
   - (c) 1328 people were waiting to enter an exhibition. At noon 737 people were still waiting to enter. How many people had already entered?
   - (d) A truck was carrying a load of mangoes. It deposited 302 kg at the first market. It is still carrying 942 kg. How many kilograms of mangoes did it have in the beginning?

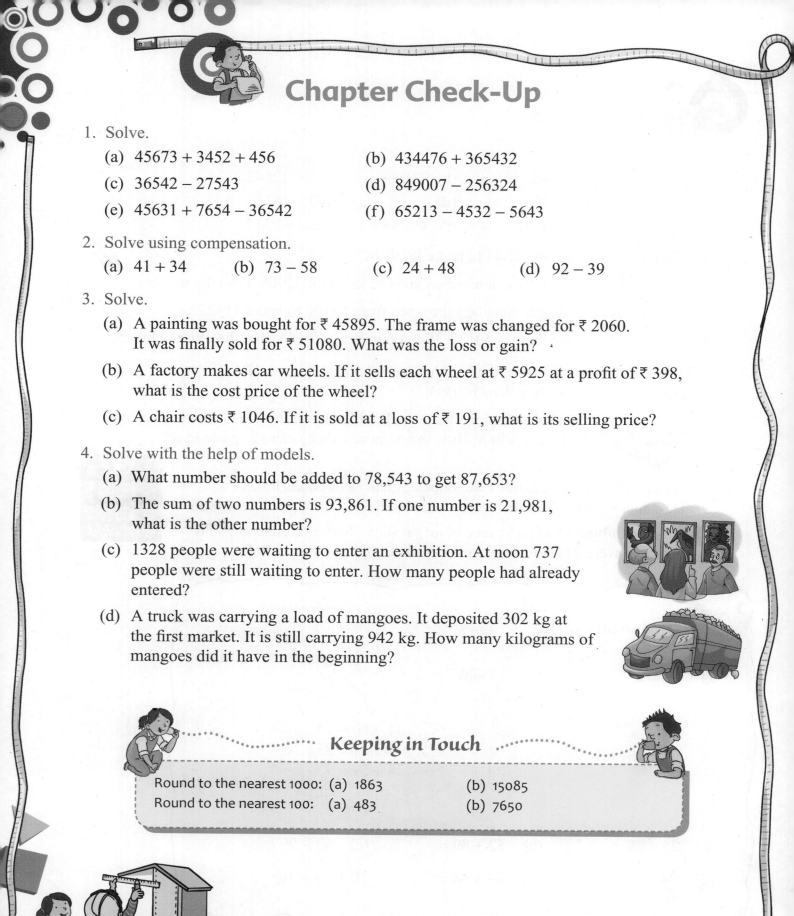

······· **Keeping in Touch** ·······

Round to the nearest 1000: (a) 1863   (b) 15085
Round to the nearest 100: (a) 483   (b) 7650

WHAT DID THE BEACH SAY WHEN THE TIDE CAME IN?

To find the answer, first find each sum or difference. Use the decoder to find the letter that matches the answer and write the letter in the space below.

93582 + 67158 160740	141286 + 183192 324478	568952 + 405458 974410	201020 − 98562 102458
L	O	N	G

Watch out for the signs.

70000 − 8316 61684	25879 − 9856 16023	131051 − 86152 44899	87385 + 69852 157237
T	I	M	E

958628 + 15782 974410	137027 + 187451 324478
N	O

"

362000 − 120050 241950	35895 + 121342 157237	831952 − 97060 734892
S	e	a

"

Decoder

A – 734892
E – 157237
G – 102458
I – 16023
L – 160740
M – 44899
N – 974410
O – 324478
S – 241950
T – 61684

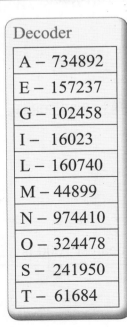

Mental Maths

Learn

32 → 30 + 2   +   44 → 40 + 4

30 + 40 = 70
2 + 4 = 6
70 + 6 = 76

Break up both numbers according to place value to add.

45 → 40 + 5   +   28 → 20 + 8

40 + 20 = 60
5 + 8 = 13
60 + 13 = 73

Practice

(a) 32 + 65   (b) 55 + 33   (c) 44 + 18   (d) 57 + 23
(e) 48 + 29   (f) 23 + 76   (g) 39 + 42   (h) 36 + 56

Use

(a) 799 + 51 = _850_

(b) 583 + 17 = _600_

(c) 21395, 31395, 41395, _51395_

(d) 105 + 37 = _142_

(e) 50,00,000 is 1 less than _50,00,001_.

(f) 7,00,000 is 1 more than _6,99,999_.

(g) 25,550 + 450 = _26,000_

(h) 80000 + 5000 − 4000 = _81,000_

(i) 60, 51, 42, 33, _22_

(j) Take away 599 from 6000: _5401_

(k) 16,76,500 = _16,76,500_ + 16,70,000

(l) 50,000 − 100 = _49,900_

(m) 29365 − 8000 = _21,365_

(n) 296 − 42 = _254_

(o) Sum of place values of 8 in 8,39,508 is _8 Million_

(p) 57 + 43 = _100_

(q) 99 + 67 = _166_

(r) 250 − 49 = _201_

(s) 1789 + 11 = _18,000_

(t) 12890 rounded to the nearest 1000 is _10900_.

Multiplication, Division and its Applications

Looking Back

Multiplication

- The numbers that are multiplied are called the **factors** and the answer is called the **product**.

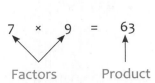

$$7 \times 9 = 63$$

Factors   Product

Division

- The terms to be remembered in division are **dividend**, **divisor**, **quotient** and **remainder**.

  Remember, division is the inverse of multiplication. *You can check your division with multiplication.*
  Quotient × Divisor + Remainder = Dividend

Divisor

```
      5  ←── Quotient
3) 1 6  ←── Dividend
  −1 5
  ─────
      1  ←── Remainder
```

1. Solve.

   (a)
   ```
        2 1
      7 5 2 3
    ×       4
    ─────────
    30 0,3 20
   ```

   (b)
   ```
        2 2
      5 6 8
    ×   3 1
    ─────────
    17,0 40
    # 5 68
   = 17,6 08
   ```

   (c)
   ```
      5 6 0
    ×   7 0 6
    ──────────
    #71 00
    +0 00
    #3 3 20
    ──────────
    4 0,9 20
   ```

2. Solve and check your answer.

   (a)
   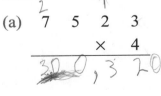
   ```
         2 2 9
      9) 2 0 6 5
        −1 8 ↓
        ─────
         0 2 6
        −0 1 8 ↓
        ─────
         0 0 8 5
        −0 0 8 1
        ─────
         0 0 0 4
   ```

   (b)

   ```
            1
      18) 2 6 1
         −1 8 ↓
         ─────
          0 8 1
   ```

   (c)
   ```
      23) 2 4 0 8
   ```

Multiplication

Multiplying by a 2-Digit Number

A factory makes 4375 soaps a day. How many soaps will it make in 47 days?

$4375 \times 47 = ?$

Step 1: Multiply by ones

```
    4 3 7 5
  ×     4 7
  ─────────
  3 0 6 2 5  ──→ (4375 × 7)
```

Step 2: Multiply by tens

```
    4 3 7 5
  ×     4 7
  ─────────
  3 0 6 2 5  ──→ (4375 × 7)
1 7 5 0 0 0  ──→ (4375 × 40)
```

Step 3: Add

```
    4 3 7 5
  ×     4 7
  ─────────
  3 0 6 2 5  ──→ (4375 × 7)
+ 1 7 5 0 0 0 ──→ (4375 × 40)
  ─────────
  2 0 5 6 2 5 ──→ (4375 × 47)
```

Answer: 2,05,625 soaps will be made in 47 days.

Multiplying by a 3-Digit Number

$6945 \times 427 = ?$

Step 1: Multiply by ones

```
    6 9 4 5
  ×   4 2 7
  ─────────
  4 8 6 1 5  ──→ (6945 × 7)
```

Step 2: Multiply by tens

```
      6 9 4 5
    ×   4 2 7
  ───────────
    4 8 6 1 5  ──→ (6945 × 7)
  1 3 8 9 0 0  ──→ (6945 × 20)
```

Step 3: Multiply by hundreds

```
        6 9 4 5
      ×   4 2 7
  ─────────────
      4 8 6 1 5  ──→ (6945 × 7)
    1 3 8 9 0 0  ──→ (6945 × 20)
  2 7 7 8 0 0 0  ──→ (6945 × 400)
```

Step 4: Add

```
        6 9 4 5
      ×   4 2 7
  ─────────────
      4 8 6 1 5
    1 3 8 9 0 0
  + 2 7 7 8 0 0 0
  ─────────────
  2 9 6 5 5 1 5
```

Mental Maths

```
      83 × 102
        /\
    100  +  2
  83 × 100 = 8300
  83 × 2 = +166
           ─────
            8466
```

Solve:

(a) 48×102 (b) 73×102

(c) 101×36 (d) 101×62

Multiplying with Zeros

When you multiply by multiples of 10, 100 and 1000 the product will have **at least the same number of zeros** as the factors. Pay special attention to **example (c).**

(a) $40 \times 70 = 2800$

(b) $3300 \times 900 = 2970000$

(c) $6800 \times 5000 = 3{,}4000000$

Multiplying with Zeros in the Factors

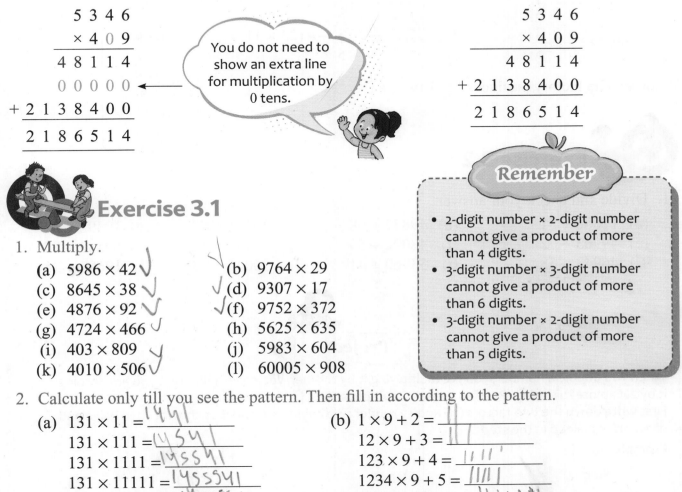

$$\begin{array}{r} 5\ 3\ 4\ 6 \\ \times\ 4\ 0\ 9 \\ \hline 4\ 8\ 1\ 1\ 4 \\ 0\ 0\ 0\ 0\ 0 \\ +\ 2\ 1\ 3\ 8\ 4\ 0\ 0 \\ \hline 2\ 1\ 8\ 6\ 5\ 1\ 4 \end{array}$$

You do not need to show an extra line for multiplication by 0 tens.

$$\begin{array}{r} 5\ 3\ 4\ 6 \\ \times\ 4\ 0\ 9 \\ \hline 4\ 8\ 1\ 1\ 4 \\ +\ 2\ 1\ 3\ 8\ 4\ 0\ 0 \\ \hline 2\ 1\ 8\ 6\ 5\ 1\ 4 \end{array}$$

Exercise 3.1

Remember

- 2-digit number × 2-digit number cannot give a product of more than 4 digits.
- 3-digit number × 3-digit number cannot give a product of more than 6 digits.
- 3-digit number × 2-digit number cannot give a product of more than 5 digits.

1. Multiply.

(a) 5986×42 (b) 9764×29

(c) 8645×38 (d) 9307×17

(e) 4876×92 (f) 9752×372

(g) 4724×466 (h) 5625×635

(i) 403×809 (j) 5983×604

(k) 4010×506 (l) 60005×908

2. Calculate only till you see the pattern. Then fill in according to the pattern.

(a) $131 \times 11 = \underline{1441}$

    $131 \times 111 = \underline{14541}$

    $131 \times 1111 = \underline{145541}$

    $131 \times 11111 = \underline{1455541}$

    $131 \times 111111 = \underline{14555541}$

(b) $1 \times 9 + 2 = \underline{11}$

    $12 \times 9 + 3 = \underline{111}$

    $123 \times 9 + 4 = \underline{1111}$

    $1234 \times 9 + 5 = \underline{11111}$

    $12345 \times 9 + 6 = \underline{111111}$

(c) $101 \times 33 = \underline{3333}$

    $101 \times 333 = \underline{33633}$

    $101 \times 3333 = \underline{336633}$

    $101 \times 33333 = \underline{3366653}$

(d) $101 \times 22 = \underline{2222}$

    $101 \times 222 = \underline{22422}$

    $101 \times 2222 = \underline{224422}$

    $101 \times 22222 = \underline{2244422}$

Division

Dividing a 5-Digit Number

A factory produces 59,598 tyres in 23 days. How many tyres does it produce in one day?

$59598 \div 23 = ?$

Method 1:

$$2591$$
$$23\overline{)59598}$$
$$-46$$
$$135$$
$$-115$$
$$209$$
$$-207$$
$$28$$
$$-23$$
$$5$$

Method 2:

$$2591$$
$$23\overline{)59598}$$
$$-46000 \rightarrow (23 \times 2000)$$
$$13598$$
$$-11500 \rightarrow (23 \times 500)$$
$$2098$$
$$-2070 \rightarrow (23 \times 90)$$
$$28$$
$$-23 \rightarrow (23 \times 1)$$
$$5$$

Use any method you find easier!

Check:
2591
× 23
59593
+ 5
59598

Answer: The factory produces 2591 tyres a day.

Exercise 3.2

1. Divide and check your answer.

(a) 12686 ÷ 51   (b) 49872 ÷ 68   (c) 86243 ÷ 89   (d) 19498 ÷ 49
(e) 49903 ÷ 72   (f) 48091 ÷ 59   (g) 18468 ÷ 22   (h) 60582 ÷ 87
(i) 46943 ÷ 58   (j) 53960 ÷ 41   (k) 30045 ÷ 25   (l) 19687 ÷ 35

Project

When you double a number, you are multiplying it by 2. When you halve a number, you are dividing it by 2. Explore this using **'Russian peasant multiplication.'**
First write down the two factors (26 and 42) under two coloums A and B as shown. Then halve and divide as explained in the steps.

Example: 26 × 42

Step 1:

A Half	B Double
26	42
13	84
6	168
3	336
1	672

Step 2:

A Half	B Double
~~26~~	~~42~~
13	84
~~6~~	~~168~~
3	336
1	672

Step 3:

84
336
+ 672
―――
1092

26 × 42 = 1092

- Ignore remainders when you have to halve an odd number.
- Stop when you reach 1 in column A.

- Cross out all the even numbers from column A and its pair from B.

- Add the numbers that are not crossed out in coloumn B.

Try these on your own: a) 32 × 53   b) 43 × 28

Averages

I studied for an average of 2 hours every day last week.

I scored an average of 60 runs over the last 3 matches.

To understand the meaning of the word 'average' look at the examples below.

(a)

Score

Match 1 – 25
Match 2 – 80
Match 3 – 75
—————
180 ⟶ Total runs in 3 matches

If we divide the total number of runs with the total number of matches, we find the **average** number of runs of each match.

$$\begin{array}{r} 6\ 0 \\ 3\overline{)1\ 8\ 0} \\ -1\ 8\ 0 \\ \hline 0 \end{array}$$

Average = sum of quantities ÷ number of quantities
Average run rate = 60 runs

The cricketer did not score 60 runs in each match. The average number does not have to be one of the numbers in the group.
Look at the next example.

(b)

Hours of study

Mon	–	2 hours
Tue	–	4 hours
Wed	–	3 hours
Thu	–	0 hours
Fri	–	0 hours
Sat	–	3 hours
Sun	–	2 hours
7 days		14 hours

$$\begin{array}{r} 2 \\ 7\overline{)1\ 4} \\ -1\ 4 \\ \hline 0\ 0 \end{array}$$

Average number of hours studied daily –2 hours

(c) An average of 123 umbrellas per month were sold over the monsoon months of June, July and August. How many umbrellas were sold in all?

Each month has an average sale of 123 umbrellas. So,
June + July + August
123 + 123 + 123 OR 123 × 3 = 369
Answer: 369 umbrellas were sold in all.

Refer Maths Lab Activity on page 54.

Exercise 3.3

1. Find the average of these numbers.
   (a) 15, 14, 21, 30
   (b) ₹ 15, ₹ 8, ₹ 14, ₹ 6, ₹ 12
   (c) 124 cm, 137 cm, 114 cm, 125 cm
   (d) 20 minutes, 15 minutes, 13 minutes, 12 minutes

2. Find the average number of fish.

27   44   22

3. This table shows the number of newspapers collected by students of classes 1, 2, 3, 4 and 5 to donate to the animal shelter over the month of December.

Classes	1st week	2nd week	3rd week	4th week	Total Collection	Average Collection
Class 1	38	49	75	62		
Class 2	71	63	88	90		
Class 3	45	54	52	61		
Class 4	90	85	110	99		
Class 5	148	130	171	119		

(a) Find the total collection of each class. Then find their average collection.

(b) Which class has the highest average?

(c) Which class has the lowest average?

(d) Find the average of all the 5 classes.

4. Suraj, Azim, Jo and Aastha got an average of 95 points in a spelling competition. What was their total score?

5. Make a list of 4 different numbers whose average works up to 50.

6. A travelling salesman travelled 75 km, 49 km, 81 km, 36 km and 59 km in the first 5 days of a week. What was the average distance travelled by him?

Problem Solving

Building Skills—Ask the Question

In this section you will learn how to frame a question when you know the facts and the answer.

Mrs Kumar had ₹ 11,250 in the beginning of the month. She spent ₹ 5,080 on food and groceries and ₹ 2,110 on school fees, clothes and entertainment.
Answer: ₹ 4,060

What is the question?

On reading the problem and the answer, we realise that the figure of ₹ 4,060 is arrived at by first adding the amount spent (5080 + 2110 = 7190) and then subtracting it from the amount at the beginning (11250 – 7190 = 4060).
So the question must be:
'How much money was left over with Mrs Kumar?'

 Exercise 3.4

1. The problems given below have the answers but not the question. Write a question that fits the answer.

   (a) Dhruv sold one secondhand car for ₹ 1,10,500 and two secondhand scooters for ₹ 7,500 each.
   How man rupees did he get in all?
   Answer: ₹ 1,25,500

   (b) Sahil buys a washing machine for ₹ 11,580 and a television set for ₹ 15,860.

   _____?
   Answer: ₹ 4280

   (c)  A group of 16 students went on a trip. The trip cost them ₹ 16,384 altogether.
   _____?
   Answer: ₹ 1,024

   (d) A factory produced 99,400 balloons a month and put them into packets of 50 balloons each.
   _____?
   Answer: 1988 packets

Problem Solving Using Models

Just like you modelled the quantities in problems relating to addition and subtraction, you can do the same for multiplication and division.

Multiplication Models

(a) Giant bamboos grow very fast. Sometimes they can grow even at the rate of 6 metres a week. At that rate, how much would a bamboo grow in 5 weeks?

Take one bar to be one week.

The bamboo grows 6 m in one week. | 6 m |

So in 5 weeks we will have: | 6 m | 6 m | 6 m | 6 m | 6 m |

Repeated addition is the same as multiplication.

So multiply, 5 × 6 metres = 30 metres.

Answer: The bamboo can grow 30 metres in 5 weeks.

(b) Priya practiced her guitar for 2 hours every day during the month of June. How many hours did she practice in the month?
June has 30 days.

In one day she practiced | 2 hours |

So for 30 days she practised:

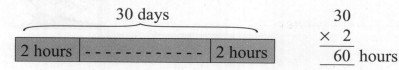

30 days

| 2 hours | - - - - - - - - - - - - - | 2 hours |

$$\begin{array}{r} 30 \\ \times\ 2 \\ \hline 60 \end{array} \text{ hours}$$

When there are too many boxes to show, we can use such models.

Answer: Priya practised 60 hours in the month of June.

Try This

Model with a bar diagram.

(a) Ashutosh weighs 28 kg. His older brother weighs twice that. What is their combined weight?

(b) Biju earns ₹ 55 a day selling popcorn. How much would he earn over 92 days?

(c) Sujith made 53 flags for Independence Day. His friend Pranay made 6 times that number. How many flags did they make altogether?

We can represent Sujith's flags with one bar.

Sujith's flags ⟶ 53

So Pranay would have made 6 times that represented by six bars.

Pranay's flags ⟶ | 53 | 53 | 53 | 53 | 53 | 53 |

We have to find how many flags were made in all.

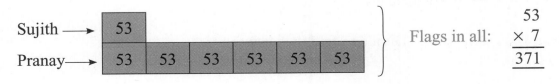

Sujith ⟶ 53
Pranay ⟶ | 53 | 53 | 53 | 53 | 53 | 53 |

Flags in all:
```
    53
  ×  7
  ───
   371
```

Answers: They made 371 flags in all.

Division Models

(a) A mobile phone shop had 168 phones on display. If they were displayed equally in 6 glass cases, how many phones were in each case?

This bar represents all the phones on display.

Total phones
| 168 |

The second bar has been put into 6 equal parts showing that the phones were shared equally.

Total phones

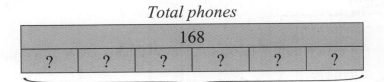

In each glass case

Divide to find the answer: 168 ÷ 6 = 28

Answer: Each glass case has 28 mobile phones on display.

Try This

Draw a bar model to solve. A teacher had 60 books to correct. If she can correct 12 books in one hour, how many hours does she need to correct all the books?

(b) A flower seller has 216 strings of flowers. He wants to sell them in bunches of 8 strings. How many bunches can he make?

Total number of strings

216

We need to find how many equal parts of 8 are in 216. So we can ask the question— 'How many 8s in 216'?

Total number of strings

216

| 8 | → ? bunches |

↓
Strings in a bunch

Divide to find the answer
216 ÷ 8 = 27

Answer: The flower seller can make 27 bunches of 8 strings each.

Exercise 3.5

Solve with the help of models.

1. Shirin can read 27 pages of her book in one hour. How many pages can she read in 7 hours?
   Answer: 189 pages

2. Shagufta's mother drives 17 km every day to and from work. If she works 23 days a month, how many kilometres does she drive in a month?
   Answer: 391 km

3. An office paid ₹ 6260 for 5 new desks. How much did each desk cost?
   Answer: ₹ 1252

4. A newspaper delivery man delivers 72 newspapers every day. If he delivers 3 papers to each house, how many houses does he deliver to?
   Answer: 24 news papers

5. Anaida finishes her homework in 45 minutes on Sunday. On Saturday she needs 4 times that amount of time. How much time does she spend on homework on both days together?
   Answer: 225 minutes.

Chapter Check-Up

1. Multiply.
   - (a) 345×907
   - (b) 4654×45
   - (c) 3487×398

2. Divide and check your answer.
   - (a) $5476 \div 23$
   - (b) $26590 \div 65$
   - (c) $77218 \div 35$

3. Find the average of the following.
   - (a) 24 kg, 32 kg, 43 kg, 16 kg, 75 kg
   - (b) 18 days, 20 days, 22 days, 32 days

4. Solve.
   - (a) A plane flies 1620 km in 4 hours. What is the average distance it files per hour?
   - (b) Sohail got 23, 18, 21, 25 and 28 marks on maths tests in the first term. Find his average marks.

5. Solve with the help of models if you like.
   - (a) Aslam does social service for 2 hours every day. How much time does he spend on social service in a week?
   - (b) A sack holds 560 onions. How many onions can fit in 114 such sacks?
   - (c) A tile factory had to pack 1825 tiles in boxes of 25 tiles each. How many boxes did it need?
   - (d) Suraksha donated ₹ 75 to the Red Cross. Varun donated 5 times that amount. How much did they donate together?

Keeping in Touch

Write these numbers in Roman numerals.
   - (a) 99: _____
   - (b) 56: _____
   - (c) 84: _____

Maths Lab Activity

Averages

Objective: To find the average of 4, 8 and 9.

Material required: Square-lined paper, 3 different colours of crayons, sello tape and scissors

Preparation: Students may work in pairs.

Method:

1. One student cuts strips of 4, 8 and 9 squares.

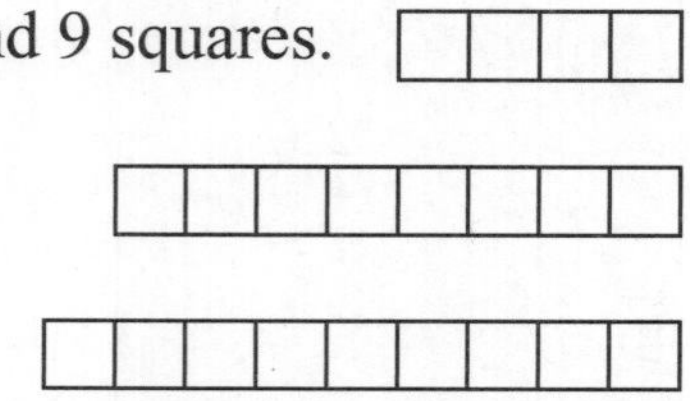

2. The second student colours the strips in 3 different colours.

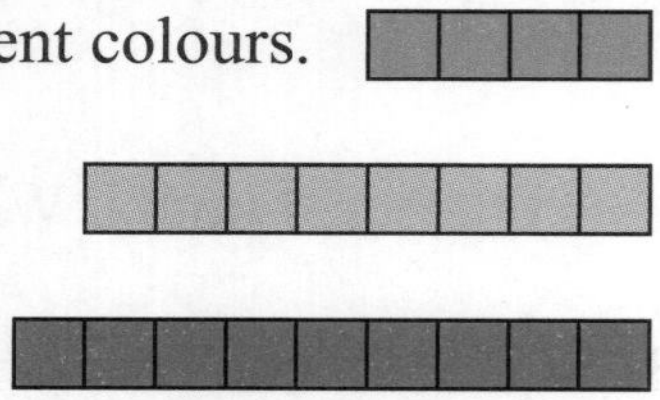

3. The first student now sticks the 3 strips with the help of sello tape to make one long strip.

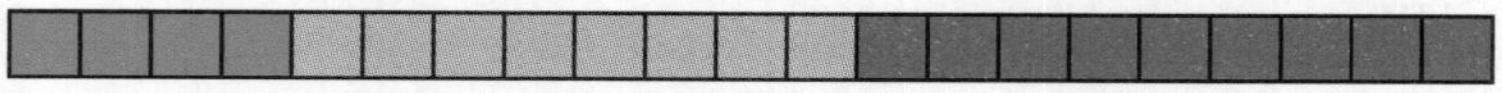

4. The second student then folds and cuts the long strip into **3 equal parts.**

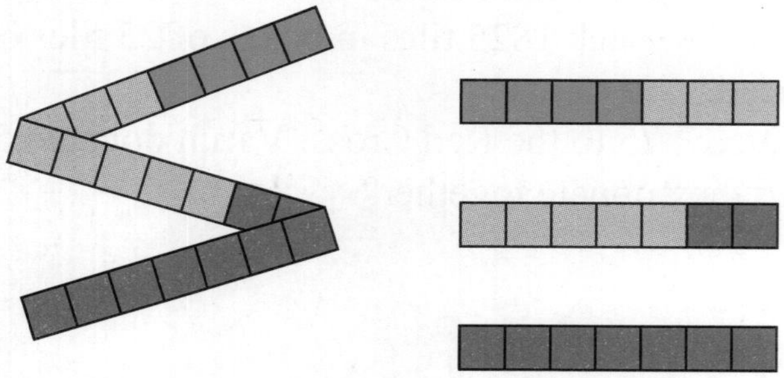

5. They record the length of each strip. Each strip is 7 squares long.
   So, the average of 4, 8 and 9 is 7.

Try this out

Find the average of 3, 7, 8 and 10 with square-lined paper.

Mental Maths

Learn

9×19

$20 - 1$

$9 \times 20 = 180$

$9 \times 1 \;\; = -9$

$\overline{171}$

$9 \times 19 = 171$

8×29

$30 - 1$

$8 \times 30 = 240$

$8 \times 1 \;\; = -8$

$\overline{232}$

$8 \times 29 = 232$

You can use the multiples of 10 to multiply mentally.

Practice

(a) 7×19 (b) 6×19 (c) 5×19 (d) 8×19

(e) 5×29 (f) 6×29 (g) 7×29 (h) 9×29

Use

(a) $34 \times 30 = $ _____

(b) Add the product of 5 and 5 to 275.

(c) $91 \times 101 = $ _____

(d) _____ $- 5000 = 15000$

(e) _____ $+ 9000 = 18864$

(f) How many times 50 is 2500?

(g) $5000 \div 50 = $ _____

(h) 1200 eggs = _____ dozen eggs

(i) How many 6s in 6666?

(j) $58350 - 6000 = $ _____

(k) $97 + 39 = $ _____

(l) $150 - 89 = $ _____

(m) If $13 \times 9 = 117$, then $13 \times 18 = $ _____

(n) CP = ₹ 1000, SP is half of CP. What is the loss?

(o) $4 \times 19 = $ _____

(p) _____ $\div 5 = 80$

(q) If $28 \times 5 = 140$, then $14 \times 5 = $ _____

(r) _____ $\times 20 = 160$

(s) What is twice the product of 10 and 10? _____

(t) What is half the sum of 23 and 23? _____

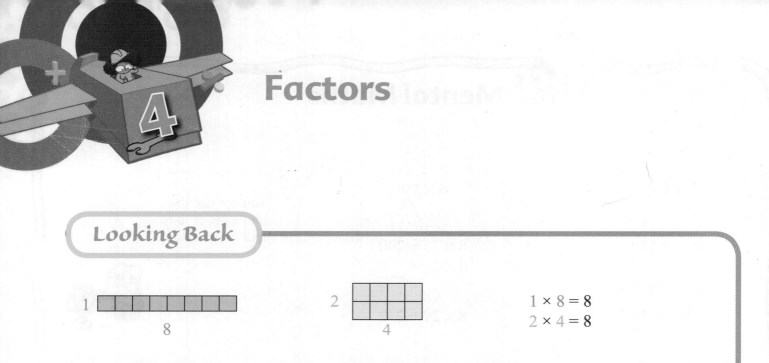

Factors

Looking Back

$$1 \times 8 = 8$$
$$2 \times 4 = 8$$

1, 2, 4 and 8 are all factors of 8. The numbers that are multiplied to find a product are called its **factors**.

Factors of 8 = ① ② ④ 8

Factors of 12 = ① ② 3 ④ 6 12

Common Factors of 8 and 12 are 1, 2 and 4.
You can find factors by multiplication or division.

Factors of 20:

① × ⑳ = 20   20 ÷ ① = ⑳

② × ⑩ = 20   20 ÷ ② = ⑩

3 × _____   20 ÷ 3 = _____

④ × ⑤ = 20   20 ÷ ④ = ⑤

Factors of 20 are 1, 2, 4, 5, 10 and 20.

Factors trees help us find different ways of making a number by multiplying.

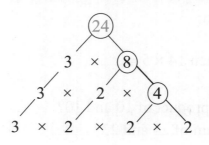

- The circled numbers are further broken up
- Stop when you need to use 1 as a factor
- $24 = 3 \times 2 \times 2 \times 2$

Remember

- 1 is a factor of every number. It is also the smallest factor of a number.
- Every number is a factor of itself. It is also the greatest factor of that number.
- The factor of a number is less than or equal to the number.
- Every number (other than 1) has at least 2 factors— 1 and the number itself.

Exercise 4.1

1. Find the factors of the following.
   (a) 10 1, 2, 5, 10   (b) 16 1, 2, 4, 8, 16 (c) 30 1, 2, 3, 5, 6, 30, 10, 15,

2. Use question 1 to find the common factors of the following.
   (a) 10, 16 1, 2   (b) 10, 30 1, 2, 5, 10 (c) 16, 30 1, 2

   2 ⟌ 10, 30   2 ⟌ 8, 12
   3 ⟌ 5, 15   2 ⟌ 4, 6
   5 . 5   3 ⟌ 2, 3

3. Make factor trees for the following.
   (a) 18   (b) 36   (c) 48

   6 × 3

Rules of Divisibility

The rules of divisibility will help you find which numbers divide others without leaving any remainder.

A number is divisible by

 if the last digit is 0, 2, 4, 6, 8 ⟶ 32 90 116

 if the last digit is 0, 5 ⟶ 40 75 920

 if the last digit is 0 ⟶ 20 130 500

We learn the rules of divisibility also because it helps us find factors easily.

A number is divisible by

 if the sum of the digits is divisible by 3 ⟶ 84 (8 + 4 = 12)

if the sum of the digits is divisible by 9 ⟶ 81 (8 + 1 = 9)

A number is divisible by

if the number formed by the last two digits is divisible by 4 or ends with '00' ⟶ 84 216 800

if the number is divisible by both 2 and 3 ⟶ 24 72 384

Exercise 4.2

1. Circle the numbers:
   (a) Divisible by 2: 11 (24) (38) 49 (160)
   (b) Divisible by 5: 51 (75) 37 (190) (300)
   (c) Divisible by 10: (90) 63 25 (200) 101

2. Circle the numbers:
   (a) Divisible by 3: (72) (63) 92 (60) 130
   (b) Divisible by 9: (36) (45) 56 118 919

3. Circle the numbers:
   (a) Divisible by 4: 56 (92) (104) 414 (700)
   (b) Divisible by 6: (42) (32) (120) 28 200

4. Complete the table. One has been done for you.

Number	Divisible by						
	2	3	4	5	6	9	10
12	✓	✓	✓	✗	✓	✗	✗
79	✗	✗	✗	✗	✗	✗	✗
98	✓	✗	✗	✗	✗	✗	✗
65	✗	✗	✗	✓	✗	✗	✗
60	✓	✓	✓	✓	✓	✗	✓
120	✓	✓	✓	✓	✓	✗	✓
313	✗	✗	✗	✗	✗	✗	✗
504	✓	✓	✓	✗	✓	✓	✗
600	✓	✓	✗	✓	✓	✗	✓

Journal

All numbers that are divisible by 10 are also divisible by 5. But all numbers that are divisible by 5 are not divisible by 10!

Explain why this is so in your own words. 10 is divisible if the number has 0 at the end. 5 is divisible if the number has 5 or 0 at the end.

Exploring Factors

Put a cross mark (✘) in the adjacent box to show the factors of the numbers.

The number 1 has only **1** as a factor.

The number 2 has **1** and **2** as factors.

The factors of 3 are **1** and **3**.

Complete the rest.

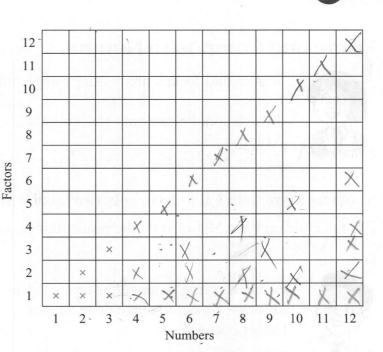

Use the completed grid to answer the following questions.

(a) Complete the table on the right.

(b) Which number is the factor of every number? 1

(c) How many factors does 10 have? 4

(d) Which factors are common between 5 and 10? 1, 5

(e) Which factors are common between 6 and 12? Which is the highest of these? 2 and 3 and 1

(f) Which are the numbers that have only two factors? Shade those numbers on the table. 2, 3, 5, 7, 11

Numbers	Factors
1	1
2	1, 2
3	1, 3
4	1, 2, 4
5	1, 5
6	1, 2, 3, 6
7	1, 7
8	1, 2, 4, 8
9	1, 3, 9
10	1, 2, 5, 10
11	1, 11
12	1, 2, 3, 4, 6, 12

Project

Did you know that 6 is called a 'perfect number'?
That is because the factors of 6 (excluding 6 itself) are 1, 2 and 3;
1 + 2 + 3 = 6. The sum of the factors is also 6.
Find the next perfect number.
(**Hint:** It is less than 30. Remember, do not include the number itself as a factor while adding.)

I am a perfect number.

Prime and Composite Numbers

Jessica and Joseph are making cubes and cuboids using blocks.

Jessica could make only two cuboidal shapes using 5 blocks.

That is because the number 5 has only two factors — 1 and 5 itself.

Numbers more than 1 that have only two factors are called prime numbers.

Use the table on Page 59 to list all the prime numbers up to 12.

Joseph is trying to make the shapes using 4 blocks. He could make three shapes.

That is because 4 has three factors — 1, 2 and 4.

Numbers more than 1 that have more than two factors are called composite numbers.

Use the table on Page 59 to list the composite numbers up to 12.

The number 1 has only one factor. It is neither prime nor composite.

Try This

1. Make rectangles on the first grid to show the factors of 13. How many rectangles could you make? Is it prime or composite?
2. Do the same with 14 on the second grid. Is it prime or composite?

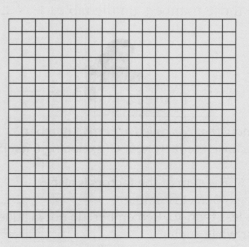

Primes between 1 and 100

A Greek mathematician, named Eratosthenes, long ago found a simple method of locating prime numbers from 1 to 100. This is called the Sieve of Eratosthenes.

1	2	3	4	5	6	7	8	9	10
11	12	13	14	15	16	17	18	19	20
21	22	23	24	25	26	27	28	29	30
31	32	33	34	35	36	37	38	39	40
41	42	43	44	45	46	47	48	49	50
51	52	53	54	55	56	57	58	59	60
61	62	63	64	65	66	67	68	69	70
71	72	73	74	75	76	77	78	79	80
81	82	83	84	85	86	87	88	89	90
91	92	93	94	95	96	97	98	99	100

- Cross 1 as it is neither prime nor composite.
- Leave 2 as it is a prime number but cross out all the multiples of 2.
- Leave 3 as it is prime, but cross out all its multiples.
- Leave 5, but cross out all its multiples.
- Leave 7, but cross out all its multiples.

All the numbers that are not crossed out are prime numbers.

Use the grid above to answer these questions.

(a) List all the prime numbers from 1 to 100.

(b) Which is the only even prime number?

(c) Which are the only prime numbers that end with 2 and 5?

(d) Which is the greatest prime number less than 50?

(e) Which is the greatest prime number less than 100?

Challenge

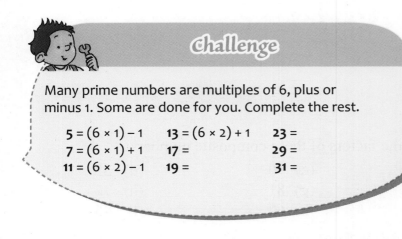

Many prime numbers are multiples of 6, plus or minus 1. Some are done for you. Complete the rest.

$5 = (6 \times 1) - 1$	$13 = (6 \times 2) + 1$	$23 =$
$7 = (6 \times 1) + 1$	$17 =$	$29 =$
$11 = (6 \times 2) - 1$	$19 =$	$31 =$

Project

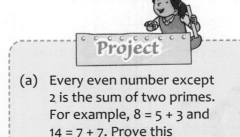

(a) Every even number except 2 is the sum of two primes. For example, $8 = 5 + 3$ and $14 = 7 + 7$. Prove this for 12, 18, 24, 32 and 40.

(b) Every odd number greater than 7 is the sum of three primes. For example, $9 = 3 + 3 + 3$ and $21 = 11 + 3 + 7$. Prove this for 11, 15, 19, 23 and 33.

Prime Factorisation

All composite numbers can be broken up into their factors.

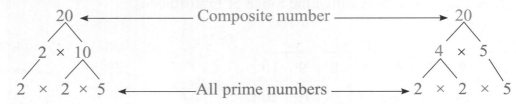

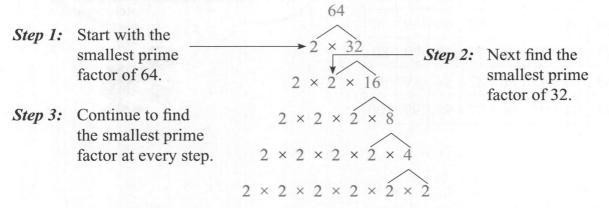

When the factors are all prime, it is called the **prime factorisation** of the number.
Prime factorisation of 20 = 2 × 2 × 5

Prime Factorisation Method

(a) Find the prime factors of 64.

Step 1: Start with the smallest prime factor of 64.

Step 2: Next find the smallest prime factor of 32.

Step 3: Continue to find the smallest prime factor at every step.

$$64$$
$$2 \times 32$$
$$2 \times 2 \times 16$$
$$2 \times 2 \times 2 \times 8$$
$$2 \times 2 \times 2 \times 2 \times 4$$
$$2 \times 2 \times 2 \times 2 \times 2 \times 2$$

Stop when the last row has only prime numbers.

Check: 2 × 2 × 2 × 2 × 2 × 2 = 64

(b) Find the prime factors of 56 using prime factorisation method.

$$56 = 2 \times 28$$
$$= 2 \times 2 \times 14$$
$$= 2 \times 2 \times 2 \times 7$$

Answer: The prime factorisation of 56 = 2 × 2 × 2 × 7.

Exercise 4.3

1. Use prime factorisation to find the prime factors of these composite numbers.

   (a) 51   (b) 60   (c) 90   (d) 32
   (e) 24   (f) 63   (g) 81   (h) 72
   (i) 28   (j) 88   (k) 62   (l) 45

Highest Common Factor

Diksha and Shabnam were exploring number rectangles.

Diksha cut these rectangles using 12 squares.

Shabnam cut these rectangles using 18 squares.

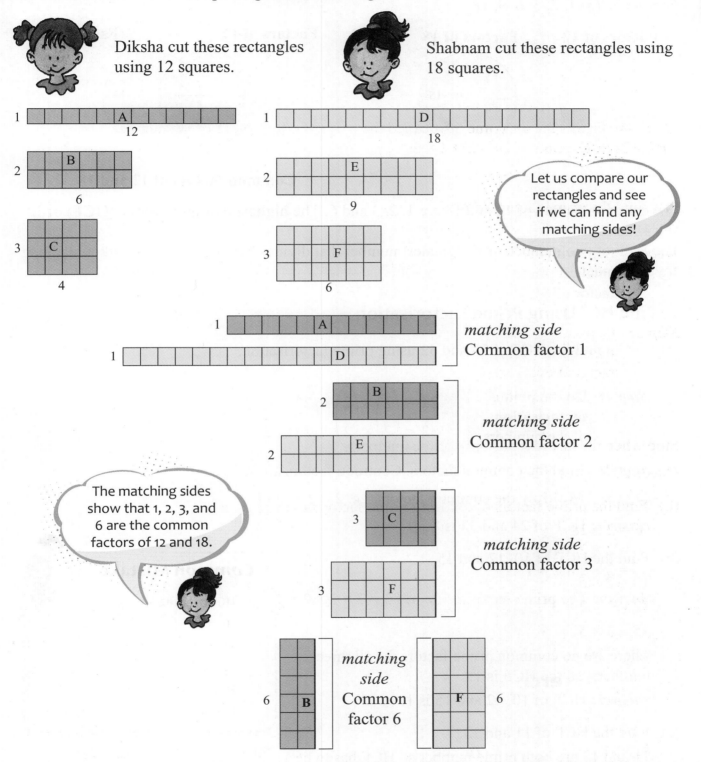

Let us compare our rectangles and see if we can find any matching sides!

matching side
Common factor 1

matching side
Common factor 2

The matching sides show that 1, 2, 3, and 6 are the common factors of 12 and 18.

matching side
Common factor 3

matching side
Common factor 6

If you look at all the matching sides, we find that the biggest matching side between the two sets of rectangles is the side that shows the factor 6. We call this the **highest common factor (HCF)** of 12 and 18.

To Find HCF Using Factors

Factors of 12: 1, 2, 3, 4, 6, 12
Factors of 18: 1, 2, 3, 6, 9, 18

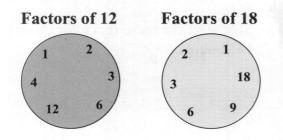

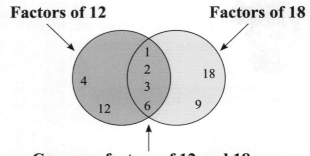

Common factors of 12 and 18

The common factors of 12 and 18 are 1, 2, 3 and 6. The **highest common factor (HCF)** of 12 and 18 is 6.

The HCF of two numbers is the greatest number that divides both the numbers without leaving any remainder.

To Find HCF Using Prime Factorisation

(a) Let us find the HCF of 24 and 32 using prime factorisation.

Step 1: Do the **prime factorisation** of the numbers.

$24 = 2 \times 2 \times 2 \times 3$
$32 = 2 \times 2 \times 2 \times 2 \times 2$

Step 2: Find the common factors. Common factors are 2, 2, 2

Step 3: **Multiply** the common factors, i.e. $2 \times 2 \times 2 = 8$

Answer: HCF of 24 and 32 is 8.

(b) Find the HCF of 10, 12 and 15.

$10 = 2 \times 5$
$12 = 2 \times 2 \times 3$
$15 = 3 \times 5$

There are no common prime factors for all three numbers, so the HCF is 1.

Answer: HCF of 10, 12 and 15 is 1.

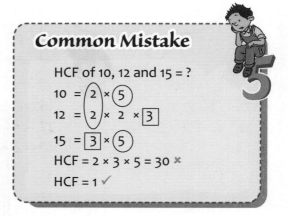

Common Mistake

HCF of 10, 12 and 15 = ?

$10 = 2 \times 5$
$12 = 2 \times 2 \times 3$
$15 = 3 \times 5$
HCF = $2 \times 3 \times 5 = 30$ ✗
HCF = 1 ✓

(c) Find the HCF of 11 and 13.

11 and 13 are both prime number so HCF has to be 1.

Answer: HCF of 11 and 13 is 1.

Exercise 4.4

1. Find the common factors of these numbers. Then find their HCF.

Numbers		Factors	Common factors	Highest common factor
(a)	9			
	15			
(b)	8			
	16			
(c)	4			
	18			
(d)	28			
	32			
(e)	40			
	24			

2. Complete the HCF chart. Some are done for you.

HCF	12	15	18	30	36
3					
6					
9			9		
12					
24				6	

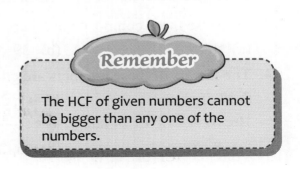

Remember

The HCF of given numbers cannot be bigger than any one of the numbers.

3. These numbers have already been factorised for you. Find the HCF of the given pairs.

20 – 2 × 2 × 5   **36** – 2 × 2 × 3 × 3
16 – 2 × 2 × 2 × 2   **27** – 3 × 3 × 3
14 – 2 × 7   **40** – 2 × 2 × 2 × 5

(a) 20, 40   (b) 20, 36   (c) 27, 40
(d) 14, 36   (e) 14, 16   (f) 16, 36

4. Find the HCF of these numbers using the prime factorisation method.

(a) 6, 10   (b) 16, 8   (c) 15, 25   (d) 16, 48
(e) 28, 36   (f) 36, 45   (g) 27, 36   (h) 28, 33

Chapter Check-Up

1. Complete the table.

Number	Divisible by						
	2	3	4	5	6	9	10
93							
84							
35							
450							
700							

2. (a) List all the prime numbers up to 20.

   _____

   (b) List the composite numbers from 21 to 30.

   _____

3. Factorise these composite numbers into prime factors.

   (a) 48   (b) 39   (c) 60

4. The factors of these numbers are given. Find the HCF of the pairs.

   8→1, 2, 4, 8   16→1, 2, 4, 8, 16
   15→1, 3, 5, 15   20→1, 2, 4, 5, 10, 20

   (a) 8, 20: _____ (b) 15, 20: _____ (c) 16, 8: _____

5. Find the HCF using prime factorisation.

   (a) 16, 24   (b) 14, 56   (c) 36, 28

Keeping in Touch

(a) 3592 + 16847   (b) 9010 + 3462   (c) 8957 + 6384

(d) 8016 – 1234   (e) 10500 – 8629   (f) 6001 – 3842

Test Your Skills

(For Chapters 1, 2, 3, 4)

1. Solve.
   (a) 463892 + 13965
   (b) 80100 – 42346
   (c) 193 × 408
   (d) 3462 ÷ 25

2. (a) What are the greatest and smallest 7-digit numbers you can make with 3, 8, 0, 5, 2? (Digits may be repeated)
   (b) Give the numbers that you have built in word form and expanded notation.

3. Find the HCF of 24 and 18 using prime factorisation.

4. Solve. You may use models if you wish.
   (a) 178, 322, 168 and 295 craftsmen participated in the first four days of the annual crafts mela. What was the average number of craftsmen who participated daily?
   (b) A book of 512 pages had equal chapters of 32 pages each. How many chapters are there in the book?
   (c) A restaurant used 175 forks one evening. It used 3 times that many spoons. How many pieces of cutlery did it use in all?

5. Fill in the blanks.
   (a) The roman numeral for 91 is _____.
   (b) 83226 rounded to the nearest 1000 is _____.
   (c) A number is divisible by 6 when _____.
   (d) _____ is the only even prime number.
   (e) 2781201 in words using the international system is:
   _____.

6. ✓ the correct answer.

(a) Profit = ₹ 1289	(b) The prime factorisation of 48 is	(c) What should be added to 18395 to get 67326?
S.P. = ₹ 6085	(i) 2 × 2 × 2 × 6	(i) 48931
C.P. = ?	(ii) 2 × 2 × 2 × 3 × 3	(ii) 57942
(i) ₹ 7374	(iii) 2 × 2 × 12	(iii) 85721
(ii) ₹ 7264	(iv) 2 × 2 × 2 × 2 × 3	(iv) 96620
(iii) ₹ 4796		
(iv) ₹ 4804		

Multiples

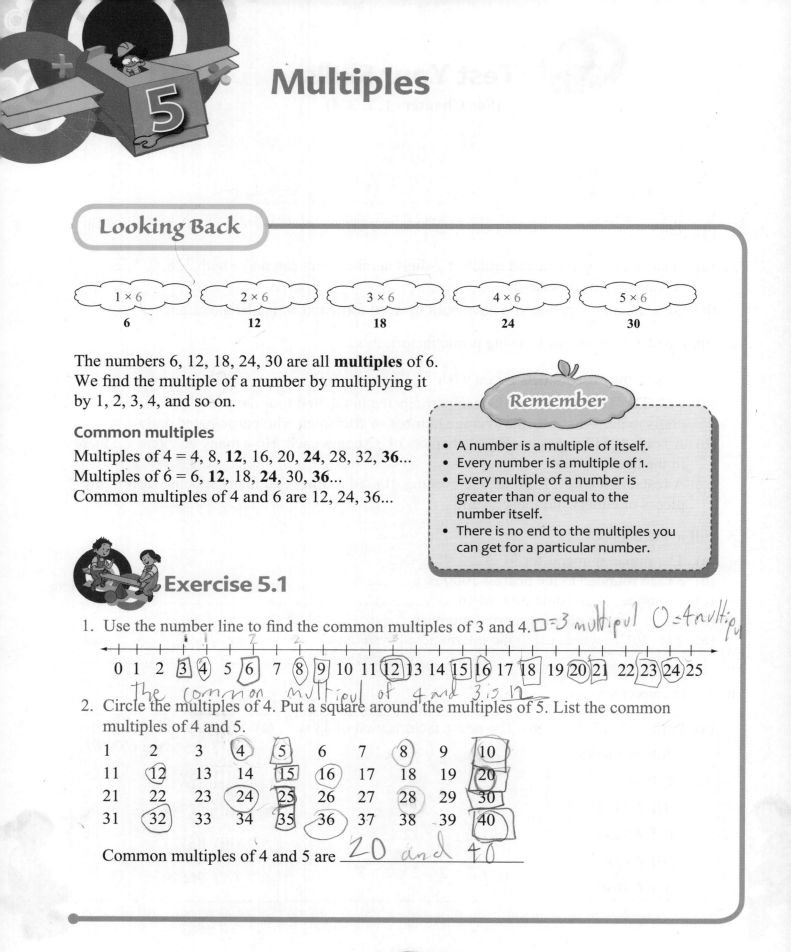

1 × 6	2 × 6	3 × 6	4 × 6	5 × 6
6	12	18	24	30

The numbers 6, 12, 18, 24, 30 are all **multiples** of 6.
We find the multiple of a number by multiplying it
by 1, 2, 3, 4, and so on.

Common multiples

Multiples of 4 = 4, 8, **12**, 16, 20, **24**, 28, 32, **36**...
Multiples of 6 = 6, **12**, 18, **24**, 30, **36**...
Common multiples of 4 and 6 are 12, 24, 36...

> **Remember**
>
> - A number is a multiple of itself.
> - Every number is a multiple of 1.
> - Every multiple of a number is greater than or equal to the number itself.
> - There is no end to the multiples you can get for a particular number.

Exercise 5.1

1. Use the number line to find the common multiples of 3 and 4. □=3 multipul O=4 multip

```
0 1 2 ③ ④ 5 ⑥ 7 ⑧ ⑨ 10 11 ⑫ 13 14 ⑮ ⑯ 17 ⑱ 19 ⑳ ㉑ 22 23 ㉔ 25
```

the common multipul of 4 and 3 is 12

2. Circle the multiples of 4. Put a square around the multiples of 5. List the common multiples of 4 and 5.

1	2	3	④	⑤	6	7	⑧	9	⑩
11	⑫	13	14	⑮	⑯	17	18	19	⑳
21	22	23	㉔	㉕	26	27	㉘	29	㉚
31	㉜	33	34	㉟	㊱	37	38	39	㊵

Common multiples of 4 and 5 are _____ 20 and 40

Lowest Common Multiple

Amudha was making a special 'THANK YOU' poster to put up in class for Teacher's Day.

T	H	A	N	K	T	H	A	N	K	T	H	A	N	K
Y	O	U	Y	O	U	Y	O	U	Y	O	U	Y	O	U

This was the shortest possible poster she could make with complete words. There are 15 boxes in each row.

We could have found this using another method.

THANK – 5 letters   YOU – 3 letters

Multiples of 5 – 5, 10, 15, 20, 25, 30, ...
Multiples of 3 – 3, 6, 9, 12, 15, 18, 21, 24, 27, 30, ...

Common multiples of 3 and 5 are 15, 30, and so on.

Lowest common multiple of 3 and 5 is **15**

Therefore the shortest possible poster that could have been made was 15 squares long.

Look at the number line that shows the multiples of 2 on top and the multiples of 3 below:

The places where the two multiples meet are the common multiples.
They are 6, 12, 18, 24, ...
The smallest of these is the first place where both multiples meet, that is at 6.
6 is the **lowest common multiple (LCM)** of 2 and 3.

The LCM of two or more numbers is the smallest number that can be divided by those numbers without leaving a remainder.

Challenge

Four friends go to a park for a walk in the morning. Praneeta goes every day, Sunita goes every second day, Sheila goes every third day, and Ramila goes every fourth day. If Praneeta starts her walk on October 01, Sunita on October 02, Sheila on October 03, and Ramila on October 04, on which date will all four friends meet at the park?

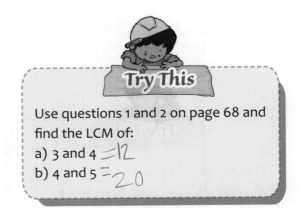

Try This

Use questions 1 and 2 on page 68 and find the LCM of:
a) 3 and 4 = 12
b) 4 and 5 = 20

To Find LCM by Prime Factorisation

(a) Let us find the LCM of 20 and 16 by prime factorisation.

Step 1: Find the prime factors of 20.

Step 2: Find the prime factors of 16.

Step 3: Multiply the common factors and the factors that are not common.

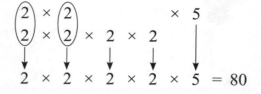

$2 \times 2 \times 2 \times 2 \times 5 = 80$

Answer: LCM = 80

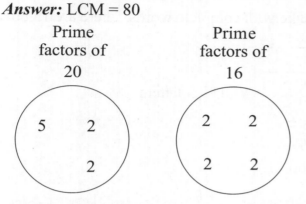

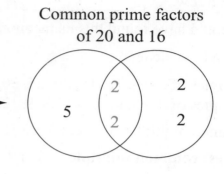

To find the LCM multiply $5 \times 2 \times 2 \times 2 \times 2 = 80$

(b) Find the LCM of 18, 30 and 50.

Prime factorisation of 18 = $2 \times 3 \times 3$

Prime factorisation of 30 = $2 \times 3 \times 5$

Prime factorisation of 50 = $2 \times 5 \times 5$

$2 \times 3 \times 3 \times 5 \times 5 = 450$

Answer: LCM = 450

(c) Find the LCM of 3, 7 and 8.

$3 = 3 \times 1$

$7 = 7 \times 1$

$8 = 2 \times 2 \times 2$

LCM = $3 \times 7 \times 2 \times 2 \times 2$

LCM = 168

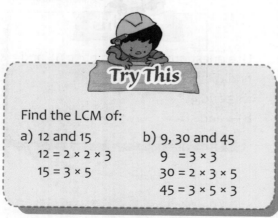

Try This

Find the LCM of:

a) 12 and 15
   $12 = 2 \times 2 \times 3$
   $15 = 3 \times 5$

b) 9, 30 and 45
   $9 = 3 \times 3$
   $30 = 2 \times 3 \times 5$
   $45 = 3 \times 5 \times 3$

Common Mistake

LCM of 6 and 30 = ?

$6 = 2 \times 3$

$30 = 2 \times 3 \times 5$

LCM = $2 \times 2 \times 3 \times 3 \times 5$ ✗

LCM = $2 \times 3 \times 5$ ✓

Exercise 5.2

1. First find 6 multiples of each of these numbers and then find 3 common multiples. Finally, find the LCM.

Numbers	Common multiples	LCM
(a) 6, 9	18, 36, and	18
(b) 5, 10		
(c) 3, 6		
(d) 3, 2, 4		

2. Use the number line to find the common multiples and lowest common multiple of 3 and 5.

1 2 3 4 5 6 7 8 9 10 11 12 13 14 15 16 17 18 19 20 21 22 23 24 25

3. These numbers have already been factorised for you. Find the LCM of the pairs given.

8 − 2 × 2 × 2   **25** − 5 × 5   **16** − 2 × 2 × 2 × 2   **10** − 2 × 5

(a) 8, 16   (b) 25, 10   (c) 8, 10   (d) 8, 25   (e) 16, 10   (f) 25, 16

4. Find the LCM of these numbers using prime factorisation.

(a) 16, 24   (b) 18, 20   (c) 10, 18   (d) 15, 35
(e) 25, 30   (f) 18, 32   (g) 10, 15, 20   (h) 16, 12, 32

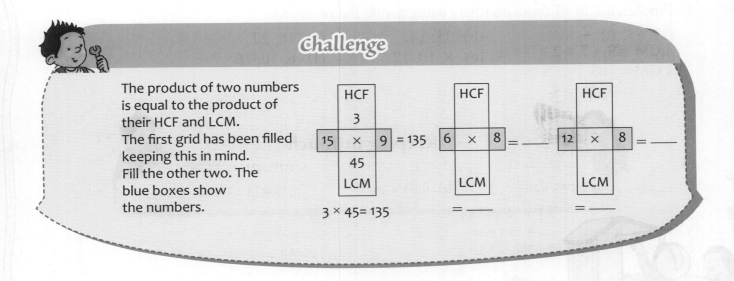

Challenge

The product of two numbers is equal to the product of their HCF and LCM. The first grid has been filled keeping this in mind. Fill the other two. The blue boxes show the numbers.

HCF
3
15 × 9 = 135
45
LCM
3 × 45 = 135

HCF
6 × 8 = ___
LCM
= ___

HCF
12 × 8 = ___
LCM
= ___

Chapter Check-Up

1. Make a poster which says 'BEST WISHES'. What is the length of the shortest poster you can make?

Words	No. of letters
BEST	4
WISHES	6

Multiples
4, 8, 12, 16, 20, 24, 28, 32, 36, 40, 44, 48
6, 12, 18, 24, 30, 36, 42, 48, 54

Common multiples 12 36 48

Lowest common multiple 12

Check to see if you are right.

B	E	S	T	B	e	s	t	B	e	s	t				
W	I	S	H	E	S	w	i	s	h	e	s				

2. Use the number line to find the common multiples and lowest common multiple of 4 and 5.

1 2 3 4 5 6 7 8 9 10 11 12 13 14 15 16 17 18 19 20 21 22 23 24 25

3. Complete the LCM chart. Some are done for you.

LCM	1	2	3	4	5	6	7	8	9
1	1								
2		2							
3									
4							28		
5									

4. Find the LCM of these numbers using prime factorisation.

(a) 15, 12
(b) 35, 14
(c) 18, 27
(d) 5, 9, 15
(e) 8, 10, 12
(f) 6, 10, 16

Keeping in Touch

(a) 735 × 202
(b) 1864 × 39
(c) 16423 ÷ 28

Maths Lab Activity

Lowest Common Multiple

Objective: To explore the concept of LCM.

Materials Required: Square-lined paper, crayons of two colours

Preparation: Students work in pairs.

Method:

Steps:

1. The students use the square-lined paper to colour (build) a brick wall. They colour rectangles of three squares length and 4 squares length to represent the bricks.

light   **dark**

Square-lined paper

2. The wall is made of two layers only. The lower layer has bricks of 4 squares only and the upper layer has bricks of 3 squares only.

3. The students colour the bricks one at a time (taking turns) to make the **shortest** complete wall possible with no brick jutting out. What is the length of the wall?

4. They then discuss and record their observation.

Record the activity:

Length of bricks	Shortest complete wall
3 squares, 4 squares	_____ squares

Try this out:

Repeat the same activity with bricks of lengths 4 squares and 5 squares.

Mental Maths

Learn

Find the LCM of 4 and 12.
12 is a multiple of 4, so 12 is the LCM of 4 and 12.

> Of two numbers, if one is a multiple of the other the greater number is the LCM.

Find the LCM of 9 and 72.
72 is a multiple of 9, so LCM of 9 and 72 is 72.

2, 4, 6, 8, 9,

Practice

Find the LCM of
- (a) 2 and 18: __9__
- (b) 7 and 49: __7__
- (c) 3 and 15: __5__
- (d) 9 and 108: __12__
- (e) 5 and 65: __13__
- (f) 6 and 54: __9__

Use

1. HCF of 17 and 19 = _____
2. LCM of 8 and 64 = __8__
3. 53 × 101 = __5353__
4. S.P. = ₹ 700, profit ₹ 70, C.P. = _____
5. C.P. – _____ = S.P.
6. S.P. + _____ = C.P.
7. Roman numeral for 83 is _____ .
8. Prime factors of 67 is _____ .
9. 450 – 39 = _____
10. __30__ × 30 = 900

101
× 53
5050
× 303
5353

11. How much more is 450 than 415?
12. Average of 3, 6, 9 = __6__
13. HCF of 4 and 5 is 1, so HCF of 40 and 50 is __10__ .
14. 73984 rounded to the nearest 1000 is __74000__
15. 760 – 59 = __701__
16. 64 + 28 = __92__
17. 60000 – 100 = __50900__
18. 169 + 31 __200__
19. Prime factors of 27 = __6__
20. C.P. = ₹ 5000, Loss = ₹ 500, S.P. = _____

Fractions

Looking Back

A fraction shows part of a whole. A whole can be a region or a collection.

$\dfrac{1}{4}$ $\dfrac{\text{Numerator}}{\text{Denominator}}$ $\dfrac{3}{5}$

A fraction that has 1 as the numerator is called a unit fraction.

You are familiar with the following types of fractions.

Like fractions have a same denominator: $\dfrac{3}{7}, \dfrac{5}{7}, \dfrac{1}{7}$

Unlike fractions have different denominators: $\dfrac{4}{7}, \dfrac{5}{10}, \dfrac{5}{9}$

Proper fractions have a value of less than one and have the numerator smaller than the denominator: $\dfrac{1}{8}, \dfrac{4}{9}, \dfrac{6}{11}$

Improper fractions have a value of more than one and have the numerator greater than the denominator: $\dfrac{5}{2}, \dfrac{12}{7}, \dfrac{8}{3}$

A mixed number combines a whole number and a fraction:

3    $\dfrac{1}{2}$ $= 3\dfrac{1}{2}$

1. Compare the following like fractions using < or >.

   (a) $\dfrac{7}{12}$ < $\dfrac{9}{12}$ (b) $\dfrac{8}{11}$ > $\dfrac{3}{11}$ (c) $\dfrac{6}{8}$ > $\dfrac{3}{8}$

2. (a) Change into mixed numbers.   (i) $\dfrac{17}{8}$: ____   (ii) $\dfrac{26}{13}$: ____

   (b) Change into improper fractions.   (i) $2\dfrac{3}{7}$: ____   (ii) $5\dfrac{8}{9}$: ____

3. Colour to show equivalent fractions.

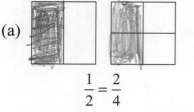

(a)

$$\frac{1}{2} = \frac{2}{4}$$

(b)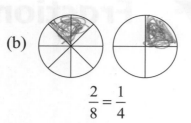

$$\frac{2}{8} = \frac{1}{4}$$

4. Of the ₹ 2400 Mr Krishnan earned, he spent $\frac{3}{8}$ on food, $\frac{1}{3}$ on taxes and $\frac{1}{6}$ on other expenses. Find out how much all this is in rupees. Then find out how much he saved.

Finding Equivalent Fractions

Mrs Shah baked 2 cakes of the same size.

She divided one cake into 2 equal parts and gave 1 part or $\frac{1}{2}$ the cake to her daughter.

She divided the other cake into 4 equal parts and gave 2 parts or $\frac{2}{4}$ the cake to her son.

$$\frac{1}{2} = \frac{2}{4}$$ → Both got the same amount

So, $\frac{1}{2}$ and $\frac{2}{4}$ are equivalent fractions. Equivalent fractions have the same value.

We can find equivalent fractions by multiplying the numerator and denominator by the same number.

(a) $\dfrac{1\,(\times 4)}{2\,(\times 4)} = \dfrac{4}{8}$

(b) $\dfrac{2\,(\times 2)}{3\,(\times 2)} = \dfrac{4}{6}$

(c) $\dfrac{3}{7} = \dfrac{15}{?}$

$$\dfrac{3\,(\times 5)}{7\,(\times 5)} = \dfrac{15}{35}$$

Think 3 × ? = 15
3 × 5 = 15
7 × 5 = ?

Try This

$$\frac{1}{2} = \frac{\square}{6}$$

Answer: $\dfrac{3}{7} = \dfrac{15}{35}$

We can also find equivalent fractions by dividing the numerator and denominator by the same number.

(a) 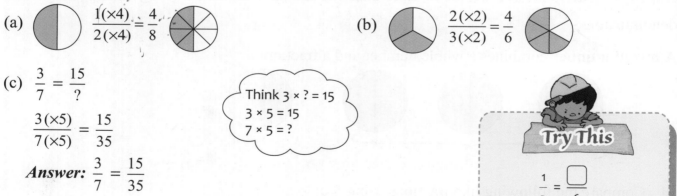 Piyush painted $\dfrac{4}{6}$ of a wall.

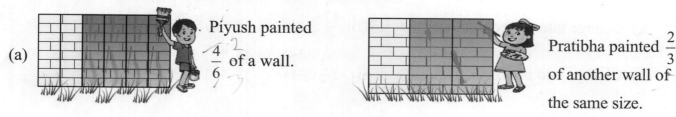 Pratibha painted $\dfrac{2}{3}$ of another wall of the same size.

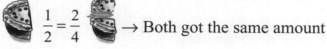

Take Piyush's fraction $\dfrac{4}{6}$ and divide both the numerator and the denominator by any common factor other than 1.

$$\frac{4\,(\div 2)}{6\,(\div 2)} = \frac{2}{3}$$

$\dfrac{4}{6}$ and $\dfrac{2}{3}$ are equivalent fractions. So both Piyush and Pratibha painted the same amount.

(b) $\dfrac{6\,(\div 3)}{9\,(\div 3)} = \dfrac{2}{3}$ $\dfrac{14\,(\div 7)}{21\,(\div 7)} = \dfrac{2}{3}$ $\left[\dfrac{2}{3} = \dfrac{6}{9} = \dfrac{14}{21}\right]$

Try This

$$\frac{4}{10} = \frac{2}{\boxed{\ }}$$

(c) $\dfrac{18}{45} = \dfrac{?}{5}$ Think $45 \div ? = 5$
$45 \div 9 = 5$
$18 \div 9 = ?$

$\dfrac{18\,(\div 9)}{45\,(\div 9)} = \dfrac{2}{5}$

Answer: $\dfrac{18}{45} = \dfrac{2}{5}$

Checking Equivalent Fractions

(a) Rahul studied for $\dfrac{2}{5}$ of an hour and Raju studied for $\dfrac{6}{15}$ of an hour. Did they both study for the same amount of time?

If we want to check whether two fractions are equivalent, we must **cross-multiply**.

$$\frac{2}{5} \times \frac{6}{15} \rightarrow 5 \times 6 = 30$$
$$\rightarrow 2 \times 15 = 30$$

Since the cross-products are equal, the fractions are equivalent.
Answer: Rahul and Raju both studied for the same amount of time.

(b) Are $\dfrac{2}{5}$ and $\dfrac{4}{7}$ equivalent?

$$\frac{2}{5} \times \frac{4}{7} \rightarrow 5 \times 4 = 20$$
$$\rightarrow 2 \times 7 = 14$$

Since the cross-products are not equal, the fractions are not equivalent.

Answer: $\dfrac{2}{5}$ and $\dfrac{4}{7}$ are not equivalent.

Exercise 6.1

1. Multiply the numerator and the denominator by 3 in each of these to get an equivalent fraction.

   (a) $\frac{1}{4}$ (b) $\frac{3}{5}$ (c) $\frac{1}{6}$ (d) $\frac{1}{5}$ (e) $\frac{2}{5}$ (f) $\frac{4}{5}$

2. Multiply the <u>numerator and the denominator</u> by 2, 3 and 4 in each of these to get a set of equivalent fractions. The first one has been done for you.

   (a) $\frac{1}{5} = \frac{2}{10} = \frac{3}{15} = \frac{4}{20}$ (b) $\frac{1}{4}$ (c) $\frac{2}{3}$ (d) $\frac{2}{5}$ (e) $\frac{3}{4}$

3. Divide by a common factor to get an equivalent fraction.

   (a) $\frac{6}{24}$ (b) $\frac{14}{49}$ (c) $\frac{28}{32}$ (d) $\frac{10}{30}$ (e) $\frac{17}{34}$ (f) $\frac{88}{120}$

4. Fill in the empty boxes.

   (a) $\frac{2}{5} = \frac{\boxed{6}}{15}$ (b) $\frac{5}{7} = \frac{10}{\boxed{14}}$ (c) $\frac{\boxed{10}}{5} = \frac{20}{25}$ (d) $\frac{5}{\boxed{7}} = \frac{15}{21}$

   (e) $\frac{8}{15} = \frac{40}{\boxed{?}}$ (f) $\frac{6}{7} = \frac{42}{\boxed{49}}$ (g) $\frac{\boxed{3}}{7} = \frac{15}{35}$ (h) $\frac{3}{\boxed{4}} = \frac{18}{24}$

5. Cross-multiply to find whether the fractions are equivalent. Write E if they are and NE if they are not.

   (a) $\frac{4}{5}$ $\frac{8}{10}$ $\boxed{NE}$ (b) $\frac{6}{9}$ $\frac{3}{2}$ $\boxed{E}$ (c) $\frac{1}{6}$ $\frac{2}{3}$ $\boxed{E}$

   (d) $\frac{4}{5}$ $\frac{6}{8}$ $\boxed{NE}$ (e) $\frac{2}{6}$ $\frac{4}{12}$ $\boxed{NE}$ (f) $\frac{2}{4}$ $\frac{3}{6}$ $\boxed{NE}$

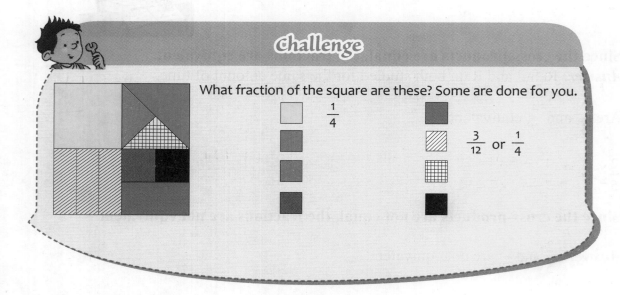

Challenge

What fraction of the square are these? Some are done for you.

$\frac{1}{4}$

$\frac{3}{12}$ or $\frac{1}{4}$

A Fraction in its Lowest Term

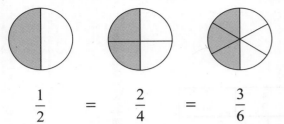

$\dfrac{1}{2}$ = $\dfrac{2}{4}$ = $\dfrac{3}{6}$

$\dfrac{1}{2}, \dfrac{2}{4}, \dfrac{3}{6}$ are all equivalent fractions, but $\dfrac{1}{2}$ is the fraction in its **lowest term**.

A fraction is in the lowest term when the only common factor between the numerator and the denominator is 1.

A fraction can be reduced to its lowest term by the following methods.

Abu and Amina were trying to reduce the fraction $\dfrac{18}{30}$ to its lowest term.

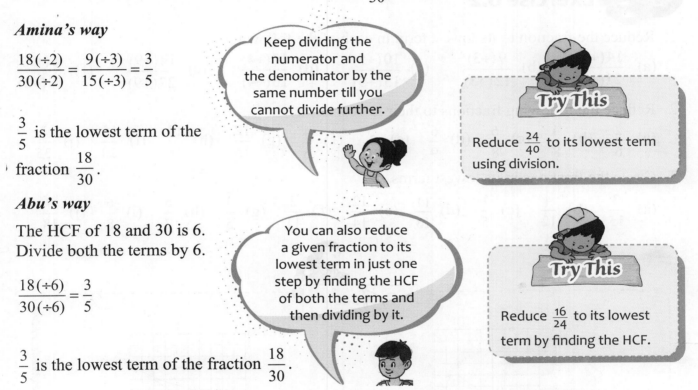

Amina's way

$$\dfrac{18\,(\div 2)}{30\,(\div 2)} = \dfrac{9\,(\div 3)}{15\,(\div 3)} = \dfrac{3}{5}$$

$\dfrac{3}{5}$ is the lowest term of the fraction $\dfrac{18}{30}$.

Keep dividing the numerator and the denominator by the same number till you cannot divide further.

Try This

Reduce $\dfrac{24}{40}$ to its lowest term using division.

Abu's way

The HCF of 18 and 30 is 6.
Divide both the terms by 6.

$$\dfrac{18\,(\div 6)}{30\,(\div 6)} = \dfrac{3}{5}$$

You can also reduce a given fraction to its lowest term in just one step by finding the HCF of both the terms and then dividing by it.

Try This

Reduce $\dfrac{16}{24}$ to its lowest term by finding the HCF.

$\dfrac{3}{5}$ is the lowest term of the fraction $\dfrac{18}{30}$.

You can also use the HCF method to find out whether a fraction is in its lowest term.

(a) Is $\dfrac{7}{12}$ in the lowest term?

The HCF of 7 and 12 is 1. So, $\dfrac{7}{12}$ is the lowest term of the fraction.

(b) Is $\dfrac{9}{27}$ in the lowest term?

The HCF of 9 and 27 is 9. So $\dfrac{9}{27}$ does not have 1 as its HCF. So, $\dfrac{9}{27}$ is not in the lowest term.

Shade the fraction in the lowest term.

$\frac{2}{3}$	$\frac{12}{16}$	$\frac{3}{9}$	$\frac{2}{5}$	$\frac{4}{9}$	$\frac{7}{14}$
$\frac{2}{12}$	$\frac{1}{2}$	$\frac{8}{16}$	$\frac{4}{9}$	$\frac{6}{12}$	$\frac{6}{7}$	
$\frac{5}{10}$	$\frac{3}{4}$	$\frac{3}{7}$	$\frac{18}{21}$	$\frac{16}{24}$	$\frac{3}{5}$

Exercise 6.2

1. Reduce the fraction to its lowest term in each of the following.

   (a) $\frac{14(\div 7)}{21(\div 7)}$ (b) $\frac{9(\div 3)}{12(\div 3)}$ (c) $\frac{10(\div 5)}{15(\div 5)}$ (d) $\frac{12(\div 4)}{16(\div 4)}$ (e) $\frac{18(\div 9)}{27(\div 9)}$ (f) $\frac{6(\div 2)}{10(\div 2)}$

2. Reduce the following fractions to their lowest terms.

   (a) $\frac{2}{6}$ (b) $\frac{4}{8}$ (c) $\frac{6}{8}$ (d) $\frac{6}{9}$ (e) $\frac{5}{10}$ (f) $\frac{4}{6}$ (g) $\frac{12}{15}$ (h) $\frac{12}{18}$ (i) $\frac{16}{20}$ (j) $\frac{7}{35}$

3. Circle the fractions in its lowest terms.

   (a) $\frac{3}{15}$ (b) $\frac{4}{12}$ (c) $\frac{1}{5}$ (d) $\frac{11}{13}$ (e) $\frac{12}{14}$ (f) $\frac{2}{11}$ (g) $\frac{3}{5}$ (h) $\frac{5}{7}$ (i) $\frac{6}{8}$ (j) $\frac{9}{18}$

Project

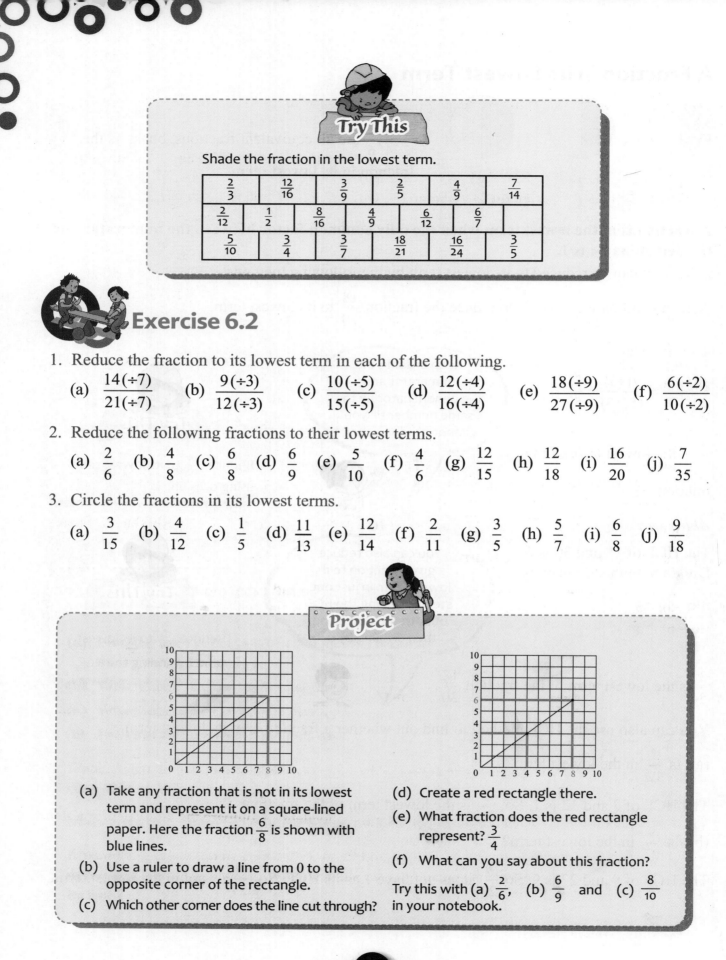

(a) Take any fraction that is not in its lowest term and represent it on a square-lined paper. Here the fraction $\frac{6}{8}$ is shown with blue lines.

(b) Use a ruler to draw a line from 0 to the opposite corner of the rectangle.

(c) Which other corner does the line cut through?

(d) Create a red rectangle there.

(e) What fraction does the red rectangle represent? $\frac{3}{4}$

(f) What can you say about this fraction?

Try this with (a) $\frac{2}{6}$, (b) $\frac{6}{9}$ and (c) $\frac{8}{10}$ in your notebook.

Comparing Unlike Fractions

To compare unlike fractions we must first change them to like fractions.

Fractions with the Same Numerator

(a) Shikha ate $\frac{1}{3}$ of her pizza. Susie ate $\frac{1}{4}$ of her pizza. Shikha,
Who ate more?

Find equivalent fractions of $\frac{1}{3}$ and $\frac{1}{4}$ such that they are **like fractions.**

$$\frac{1}{3} = \frac{2}{6} = \frac{3}{9} = \frac{4}{12} \qquad \frac{1}{4} = \frac{2}{8} = \frac{3}{12}$$

$$\frac{4}{12} > \frac{3}{12} \qquad \textit{Answer:}\ \frac{1}{3} > \frac{1}{4}\text{; so Shikha ate more.}$$

In unlike fractions with the same numerator, the fraction with the greater denominator is the smaller fraction.

(a) Rearrange these fractions in descending order.

$$\frac{5}{6}, \frac{5}{12}, \frac{5}{7}, \frac{5}{16}, \frac{5}{13} \longrightarrow \frac{5}{6} > \frac{5}{7} > \frac{5}{12} > \frac{5}{13} > \frac{5}{16}$$

(b) Rearrange these fractions in ascending order.

$$\frac{7}{11}, \frac{7}{17}, \frac{7}{9}, \frac{7}{15}, \frac{7}{10} \longrightarrow \frac{7}{17} < \frac{7}{15} < \frac{7}{11} < \frac{7}{10} < \frac{7}{9}$$

Fractions with Different Numerators

(a) Later Shikha ate $\frac{3}{4}$ of her pizza and Susie ate $\frac{5}{6}$. Who had eaten more? Susie $\frac{3}{4}$ $\frac{5}{6}$

Change the unlike fractions into like fractions.

$$\frac{3}{4} = \frac{6}{8} = \frac{9}{12} \qquad \frac{5}{6} = \frac{10}{12}$$

$$\frac{9}{12} < \frac{10}{12} \qquad \textit{Answer:}\ \frac{3}{4} < \frac{5}{6}\text{; so Susie ate more.}$$

Use a shortcut!

$$\frac{2}{3} \ ? \ \frac{4}{5}$$

Step 1:
Find the LCM of the two denominators.
LCM of 3 and 5 is 15

Answer: $\frac{2}{3} < \frac{4}{5}$

Step 2:
Convert the fractions into equivalent fractions with denominator 15.

$$\frac{2(\times 5)}{3(\times 5)} = \frac{10}{15}, \ \frac{4(\times 3)}{5(\times 3)} = \frac{12}{15}$$

Step 3:
Compare the equivalent fractions.

$$\frac{10}{15} < \frac{12}{15}$$

So, $\frac{2}{3} < \frac{4}{5}$

(b) Rearrange the following fractions into both ascending and descending orders.

$$\frac{1}{2}, \frac{2}{3}, \frac{5}{6}, \frac{3}{8}$$

Step 1: LCM of denominators 2, 3, 6, 8 = 24

Step 2: Convert them into like fractions

$$\frac{1}{2} = \frac{1 \times 12}{2 \times 12} = \frac{12}{24} \qquad \frac{2}{3} = \frac{2 \times 8}{3 \times 8} = \frac{16}{24} \qquad \frac{5}{6} = \frac{5 \times 4}{6 \times 4} = \frac{20}{24} \qquad \frac{3}{8} = \frac{3 \times 3}{8 \times 3} = \frac{9}{24}$$

Step 3: Compare the equivalent fractions: $\frac{12}{24}, \frac{16}{24}, \frac{20}{24}, \frac{9}{24}$

Step 4: (i) In ascending order

$$\frac{9}{24}, \frac{12}{24}, \frac{16}{24}, \frac{20}{24} \longrightarrow \frac{3}{8} < \frac{1}{2} < \frac{2}{3} < \frac{5}{6}$$

(ii) In descending order

$$\frac{20}{24}, \frac{16}{24}, \frac{12}{24}, \frac{9}{24} \longrightarrow \frac{5}{6} > \frac{2}{3} > \frac{1}{2} > \frac{3}{8}$$

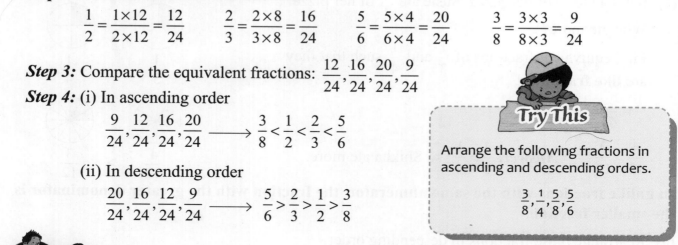

Try This

Arrange the following fractions in ascending and descending orders.

$$\frac{3}{8}, \frac{1}{4}, \frac{5}{8}, \frac{5}{6}$$

Exercise 6.3

1. Put the >, < or = sign without changing into equivalent fractions.
   Apply the rules you have learnt so far.

   (a) $\frac{2}{5} \bigcirc \frac{2}{7}$ (b) $\frac{1}{7} \bigcirc \frac{1}{9}$ (c) $\frac{5}{12} \bigcirc \frac{5}{11}$ (d) $\frac{1}{11} \bigcirc \frac{1}{13}$

   (e) $\frac{3}{13} \bigcirc \frac{3}{7}$ (f) $\frac{6}{15} \bigcirc \frac{6}{13}$ (g) $\frac{4}{7} \bigcirc \frac{4}{9}$ (h) $\frac{8}{19} \bigcirc \frac{8}{11}$

2. Compare using >, < or = .

   (a) $\frac{3}{4} \bigcirc \frac{1}{5}$ (b) $\frac{7}{8} \bigcirc \frac{2}{3}$ (c) $\frac{3}{4} \bigcirc \frac{2}{3}$ (d) $\frac{1}{12} \bigcirc \frac{5}{7}$

   (e) $\frac{7}{10} \bigcirc \frac{3}{4}$ (f) $\frac{9}{10} \bigcirc \frac{7}{8}$ (g) $\frac{2}{8} \bigcirc \frac{3}{5}$ (h) $\frac{4}{5} \bigcirc \frac{3}{4}$

3. Rearrange in ascending order.

   (a) $\frac{9}{10}, \frac{9}{15}, \frac{9}{21}, \frac{9}{16}, \frac{9}{19}$ (b) $\frac{3}{15}, \frac{14}{15}, \frac{12}{15}, \frac{1}{15}, \frac{6}{15}$ (c) $\frac{7}{8}, \frac{1}{6}, \frac{3}{4}, \frac{2}{3}$

   (d) $\frac{3}{12}, \frac{7}{8}, \frac{2}{4}, \frac{2}{6}$ (e) $\frac{1}{2}, \frac{2}{3}, \frac{3}{4}, \frac{1}{3}$ (f) $\frac{4}{5}, \frac{2}{3}, \frac{1}{2}, \frac{5}{6}, \frac{6}{10}$

4. Rearrange in descending order.

   (a) $\frac{10}{14}, \frac{10}{20}, \frac{10}{15}, \frac{10}{35}, \frac{10}{22}$ (b) $\frac{11}{19}, \frac{9}{19}, \frac{10}{19}, \frac{8}{19}, \frac{15}{19}$ (c) $\frac{2}{3}, \frac{1}{5}, \frac{1}{2}, \frac{5}{6}$

   (d) $\frac{1}{8}, \frac{5}{12}, \frac{2}{6}, \frac{3}{4}$ (e) $\frac{2}{3}, \frac{3}{5}, \frac{5}{6}, \frac{3}{4}$ (f) $\frac{3}{4}, \frac{2}{3}, \frac{5}{8}, \frac{7}{9}, \frac{11}{12}$

Addition

Adding Unlike Fractions

(a) Bholu, the farmer, planted rice on $\frac{1}{2}$ of his farm and corn on $\frac{1}{4}$ of it. What fraction of the farm has rice and corn?

$$\frac{1}{2} + \frac{1}{4} = ?$$

To add unlike fractions we must first change them to like fractions

- Find the equivalent fraction of $\frac{1}{2}$.

$$\frac{1 (\times 2)}{2 (\times 2)} = \frac{2}{4}$$

- Add the like fractions.

$$\frac{2}{4} + \frac{1}{4} = \frac{3}{4}$$

- $\frac{3}{4}$ of the farm is planted with corn and rice.

Common Mistake

$$\frac{1}{2} + \frac{1}{4} = \frac{2}{6} \ \text{✗}$$

$$\frac{1}{2} + \frac{1}{4} = \frac{3}{4} \ \text{✓}$$

(b) $\frac{2}{5} + \frac{1}{4} = ?$

$$\frac{2}{5} = \frac{4}{10} = \frac{6}{15} = \frac{8}{20} \qquad \frac{1}{4} = \frac{2}{8} = \frac{3}{12} = \frac{4}{16} = \frac{5}{20}$$

$\frac{8}{20}$ and $\frac{5}{20}$ are like fractions

$$\frac{8}{20} + \frac{5}{20} = \frac{13}{20}$$

Answer: $\frac{2}{5} + \frac{1}{4} = \frac{13}{20}$

Learn these well!

$$\frac{1}{2} + \frac{1}{2} = 1 \qquad \frac{1}{3} + \frac{2}{3} = 1$$

$$\frac{1}{4} + \frac{3}{4} = 1$$

(c) You can also use the LCM method to find equivalent fractions.

$$\frac{1}{6} + \frac{3}{4} = ?$$

Step 1:

Find the LCM of both denominators.
LCM of 6 and 4 is 12

Step 2:

Find the equivalent fractions with denominator 12.

$$\frac{1 (\times 2)}{6 (\times 2)} = \frac{2}{12}$$

$$\frac{3 (\times 3)}{4 (\times 3)} = \frac{9}{12}$$

Step 3:

Add the fractions. Reduce to lowest term if required.

$$\frac{2}{12} + \frac{9}{12} = \frac{11}{12}$$

Common Mistake

$$\frac{2}{5} + \frac{1}{2} = \frac{3}{7} \ \text{✗}$$

$$\frac{2}{5} + \frac{1}{2} = \frac{4+5}{10} = \frac{9}{10} \ \text{✓}$$

Answer: $\frac{1}{6} + \frac{3}{4} = \frac{11}{12}$

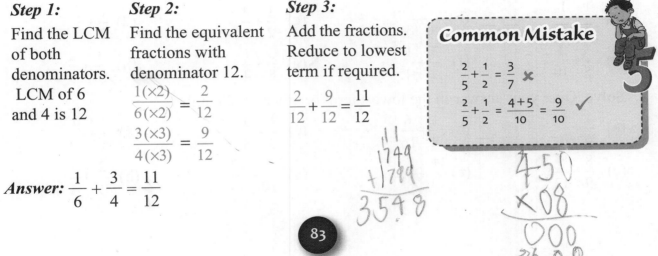

83

(d) Uday walked $\frac{2}{5}$ of a km and jogged $\frac{1}{10}$ of a km. How far did he go?

$$\frac{2}{5}+\frac{1}{10}=?$$

Step 1: LCM of 5 and 10 is 10.

Step 2: $\frac{2\times2}{5\times2}=\frac{4}{10}$

Step 3: $\frac{4}{10}+\frac{1}{10}=\frac{5}{10}$

$\frac{5}{10}=\frac{1}{2}$ (lowest term)

Answer: Uday went $\frac{1}{2}$ km.

If the sum of two or more fractions is not in its lowest term, reduce it to its lowest term.

(e) Vineeta walked $\frac{3}{4}$ of a km and jogged $\frac{2}{3}$ of a km. How far did she go?

$$\frac{3}{4}+\frac{2}{3}=?$$

LCM of 4 and 3 = 12

$$\frac{9}{12}+\frac{8}{12}=\frac{17}{12}=1\frac{5}{12}$$

Answer: Vineeta went $1\frac{5}{12}$ km.

If the sum of two or more fractions is an improper fraction, change the improper fraction to a mixed number.

Exercise 6.4

1. Solve.

   (a) $\frac{1}{8}+\frac{1}{4}$

   (b) $\frac{1}{9}+\frac{2}{3}$

   (c) $\frac{1}{2}+\frac{3}{8}$

   (d) $\frac{1}{2}+\frac{1}{6}$

   (e) $\frac{3}{5}+\frac{1}{10}$

   (f) $\frac{1}{2}+\frac{1}{4}$

   (g) $\frac{3}{8}+\frac{1}{4}$

   (h) $\frac{3}{10}+\frac{2}{5}$

2. Solve. Give your answer in the lowest term or as a mixed number.

   (a) $\frac{1}{6}+\frac{1}{3}$

   (b) $\frac{1}{8}+\frac{6}{16}$

   (c) $\frac{1}{2}+\frac{5}{8}$

   (d) $\frac{2}{5}+\frac{9}{10}$

   (e) $\frac{8}{9}+\frac{5}{12}$

   (f) $\frac{1}{2}+\frac{7}{8}$

   (g) $\frac{9}{10}+\frac{13}{15}$

   (h) $\frac{2}{12}+\frac{3}{4}$

Adding Mixed Numbers

The painter used $3\frac{1}{2}\ \ell$ of white paint and $2\frac{1}{4}\ \ell$ of blue paint to paint the wall.

How much paint did he use in all?

$$3\frac{1}{2}+2\frac{1}{4}=?$$

Method 1:

Step 1: Add the fractions $\frac{1}{2}+\frac{1}{4}=\frac{2+1}{4}=\frac{3}{4}$

Step 2: Add the whole numbers $3+2=5$

Step 3: Add the fractions and whole numbers

$$5+\frac{3}{4}=5\frac{3}{4}$$

Answer: $3\frac{1}{2}+2\frac{1}{4}=5\frac{3}{4}$

Method 2:

Step 1: Convert the mixed numbers into improper fractions

$$3\frac{1}{2}=\frac{7}{2},\ 2\frac{1}{4}=\frac{9}{4}$$

Step 2: Add the fractions

$$\frac{7}{2}+\frac{9}{4}=\frac{14+9}{4}=\frac{23}{4}$$

Step 3: Convert to a mixed number

$$\frac{23}{4}=5\frac{3}{4}$$

 **Exercise 6.5**

1. Add.

   (a) $5+3\frac{1}{2}$ (b) $3\frac{3}{7}+2\frac{2}{7}$ (c) $1\frac{1}{4}+2\frac{1}{4}$ (d) $1\frac{3}{4}+2\frac{2}{3}$ (e) $1\frac{3}{8}+\frac{2}{7}$

   (f) $1\frac{3}{10}+4\frac{1}{2}$ (g) $2\frac{3}{4}+2\frac{2}{3}$ (h) $3\frac{2}{5}+2\frac{1}{2}$ (i) $1\frac{7}{9}+4\frac{5}{6}$ (j) $4\frac{1}{2}+2\frac{3}{4}$

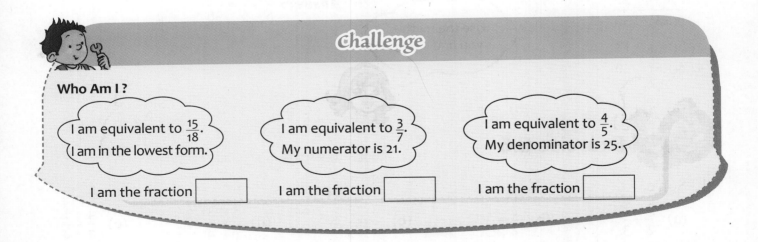

Challenge

Who Am I?

I am equivalent to $\frac{15}{18}$.
I am in the lowest form.

I am the fraction ☐

I am equivalent to $\frac{3}{7}$.
My numerator is 21.

I am the fraction ☐

I am equivalent to $\frac{4}{5}$.
My denominator is 25.

I am the fraction ☐

Subtracting Unlike Fractions

Subtracting Proper Fractions

(a) Aparna ate $\frac{1}{2}$ of a chocolate bar. Vishu ate $\frac{1}{3}$ of a chocolate bar. How much more did Aparna eat than Vishu?

$\frac{1}{2} - \frac{1}{3} = ?$

To subtract unlike fractions, change them to equivalent fractions first.

$\frac{1}{2} = \frac{2}{4} = \frac{3}{6}$

$\frac{1}{3} = \frac{2}{6}$

$\frac{3}{6} - \frac{2}{6} = \frac{1}{6}$

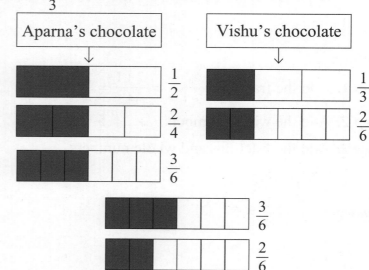

Answer: Aparna ate $\frac{1}{6}$ of a chocolate bar more than Vishu.

You can also use the LCM method to find the equivalent denominator.

(b) $\frac{5}{6} - \frac{3}{5} = ?$

Step 1: Find the LCM of the two denominators.
LCM of 6 and 5 is 30

Step 2: Find the equivalent fractions with denominator 30.

$\frac{5(\times 5)}{6(\times 5)} = \frac{25}{30}$

$\frac{3(\times 6)}{5(\times 6)} = \frac{18}{30}$

Step 3: Subtract. Reduce to the lowest term if needed.

$\frac{25}{30} - \frac{18}{30} = \frac{7}{30}$

Answer: $\frac{5}{6} - \frac{3}{5} = \frac{7}{30}$

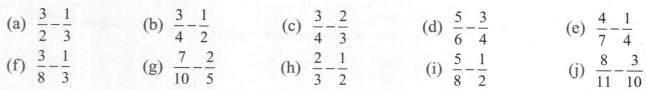

Use the method you find easier.

 **Exercise 6.6**

1. Solve.

(a) $\frac{3}{2} - \frac{1}{3}$

(b) $\frac{3}{4} - \frac{1}{2}$

(c) $\frac{3}{4} - \frac{2}{3}$

(d) $\frac{5}{6} - \frac{3}{4}$

(e) $\frac{4}{7} - \frac{1}{4}$

(f) $\frac{3}{8} - \frac{1}{3}$

(g) $\frac{7}{10} - \frac{2}{5}$

(h) $\frac{2}{3} - \frac{1}{2}$

(i) $\frac{5}{8} - \frac{1}{2}$

(j) $\frac{8}{11} - \frac{3}{10}$

Subtracting Mixed Numbers

(a) The milkman had $2\frac{2}{3}$ litres of milk in the can. He sold $1\frac{1}{4}\,\ell$ to a customer. How much is left in the can?

$$2\frac{2}{3} - 1\frac{1}{4} = ?$$

To subtract mixed numbers, change them to improper fractions first.

Step 1: Change to **improper fractions** $\rightarrow \dfrac{8}{3} - \dfrac{5}{4}$ $\left(2\frac{2}{3} = \dfrac{8}{3} \text{ and } 1\frac{1}{4} = \dfrac{5}{4}\right)$

Step 2: Change to **equivalent fractions** $\rightarrow \dfrac{32}{12} - \dfrac{15}{12} = \dfrac{17}{12}$ $\left(\dfrac{8}{3} = \dfrac{8(\times 4)}{3(\times 4)} = \dfrac{32}{12} \text{ and } \dfrac{5}{4} = \dfrac{5(\times 3)}{4(\times 3)} = \dfrac{15}{12}\right)$

Step 3: Change the difference obtained to a **mixed number** $\rightarrow \dfrac{17}{12} = 1\dfrac{5}{12}$

Answer: There is $1\dfrac{5}{12}\,\ell$ milk left in the can.

(b) $7 - 1\dfrac{3}{6} = ?$

$$7 - 1\frac{3}{6} = \frac{7}{1} - \frac{9}{6} = \frac{42}{6} - \frac{9}{6} = \frac{33}{6} = \frac{11}{2} = 5\frac{1}{2}$$

Answer: $5\dfrac{1}{2}$

> Before you change an improper fraction to a mixed number in the answer first change it to its lowest terms.

Exercise 6.7

1. Solve.

(a) $3\dfrac{5}{6} - 1\dfrac{3}{6}$

(b) $7\dfrac{4}{5} - 2\dfrac{3}{5}$

(c) $9\dfrac{3}{7} - \dfrac{2}{7}$

(d) $4\dfrac{1}{2} - 2\dfrac{3}{5}$

(e) $6\dfrac{3}{4} - 2\dfrac{1}{2}$

(f) $5 - 4\dfrac{1}{3}$

(g) $8 - \dfrac{2}{3}$

(h) $5\dfrac{2}{3} - 3$

(i) $4\dfrac{3}{4} - \dfrac{1}{2}$

(j) $7\dfrac{1}{5} - 2$

(k) $4\dfrac{2}{5} - 3\dfrac{1}{2}$

(l) $3\dfrac{2}{3} - 1\dfrac{1}{6}$

(m) $6\dfrac{1}{3} - 2\dfrac{1}{4}$

(n) $5\dfrac{1}{4} - 2\dfrac{2}{3}$

(o) $9\dfrac{3}{7} - \dfrac{5}{8}$

Problem Solving

Decide whether to add or subtract

(a) Vedika spent $\frac{1}{2}$ of her pocket money on a movie and $\frac{1}{4}$ on a new pen. What fraction of her total pocket money did she spend?

(b) Ankana did $\frac{3}{8}$ of her homework on Saturday and $\frac{1}{4}$ of the homework on Sunday. How much of the homework did she do over the weekend?

(c) Mrs Kumar bought 3 litres of milk in the morning. There was $\frac{5}{8}$ litres left in the evening. How much was used during the day?

(d) If $3\frac{2}{3}$ metres is cut from a ribbon which is $5\frac{1}{2}$ metres long, how much ribbon is left?

(e) A recipe needs $\frac{2}{5}$ cup of milk and $\frac{1}{3}$ cup of cream. How much more milk than cream is required?

Multiplication of Fractions

Multiplying Fractions by Whole Numbers

(a) Eight families went on a picnic. Each family had carried a cake for the picnic. $\frac{3}{4}$ of each cake was eaten. How much cake was eaten in all?

We want to find out how much cake was eaten in all. We could find out using **repeated addition**.

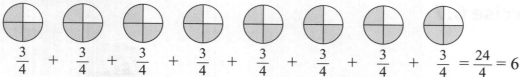

$$\frac{3}{4} + \frac{3}{4} + \frac{3}{4} + \frac{3}{4} + \frac{3}{4} + \frac{3}{4} + \frac{3}{4} + \frac{3}{4} = \frac{24}{4} = 6$$

Or we could multiply

$8 \times \frac{3}{4} = ?$

To multiply a whole number and a fraction:

Step 1: Write the **whole number as a fraction** $\longrightarrow$ $\frac{8}{1} \times \frac{3}{4}$

Step 2: (a) **Multiply** the numerators

(b) **Multiply** the denominators $\longrightarrow$ $\frac{8}{1} \times \frac{3}{4} = \frac{24}{4}$

Step 3: Simplify ⟶ $\dfrac{24}{4} = \dfrac{6}{1} = 6$

Answer: 6 cakes were eaten at the picnic.

(b) $\dfrac{5}{7} \times 0 = ?$

$= \dfrac{5}{7} \times \dfrac{0}{1} = \dfrac{5 \times 0}{7 \times 1}$

$= \dfrac{0}{7} = 0$

Answer: $\dfrac{5}{7} \times 0 = 0$

(c) $\dfrac{6}{7} \times 1 = ?$

$= \dfrac{6}{7} \times \dfrac{1}{1} = \dfrac{6 \times 1}{7 \times 1}$

$= \dfrac{6}{7}$

Answer: $\dfrac{6}{7} \times 1 = \dfrac{6}{7}$

- When we multiply a fraction by zero, we get zero as the answer.
- When we multiply a fraction by 1, we get the same fraction.

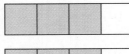 **Exercise 6.8**

1. Multiply. Give the answers in the lowest terms.

(a) $7 \times \dfrac{1}{2}$ (b) $8 \times \dfrac{4}{5}$ (c) $\dfrac{2}{7} \times 14$ (d) $5 \times \dfrac{2}{3}$ (e) $\dfrac{1}{20} \times 20$

(f) $\dfrac{3}{7} \times 0$ (g) $18 \times \dfrac{2}{3}$ (h) $\dfrac{3}{4} \times 32$ (i) $\dfrac{5}{12} \times 5$ (j) $\dfrac{8}{17} \times 1$

(k) $9 \times \dfrac{5}{6}$ (l) $4 \times \dfrac{1}{8}$ (m) $0 \times \dfrac{7}{12}$ (n) $1 \times \dfrac{3}{5}$ (o) $\dfrac{4}{5} \times 10$

Multiplying Fractions by Fractions

Pradeep's mother had made halwa and put it into a rectangular dish. This is the amount of halwa that Pradeep saw was left in the dish.

$\dfrac{3}{4}$ of the halwa was left in the dish.

Pradeep ate $\dfrac{1}{2}$ of it.

How much did Pradeep eat?

To find $\dfrac{1}{2}$ of $\dfrac{3}{4}$ we could also **multiply**.

$\dfrac{1}{2}$ of $\dfrac{3}{4}$ is the same as $\dfrac{1}{2} \times \dfrac{3}{4}$

$\dfrac{1}{2} \times \dfrac{3}{4} = ?$

To multiply a fraction by a fraction:

Step 1: **Multiply** the numerators
        Multiply the denominators
$$\frac{1\times3}{2\times4}=\frac{3}{8}$$

Step 2: **Simplify** if possible. The fraction $\frac{3}{8}$ is already in the lowest form.

Answer: Pradeep ate $\frac{3}{8}$ of the halwa.

Use a shortcut!

Sometimes it is possible to use a shortcut and **simplify before the last step**.

$$\frac{4}{5}\times\frac{7}{8}=?$$

$$=\frac{\overset{1}{\cancel{4}}\times7}{5\times\underset{2}{\cancel{8}}}$$

$$=\frac{7}{10}$$

Answer: $\frac{7}{10}$

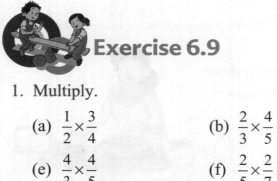

Look for common factors between the numerator and denominator and then divide. Here 4 divides both 4 and 8.

Refer Maths Lab Activity on page 98.

Refer Maths Lab Activity on page 98.

Common Mistake

$$\frac{2}{3}\times\frac{3}{5}=?$$

$$\frac{2}{3}\times\frac{3}{5}=\frac{6}{15}\quad\text{Answer is incomplete}$$

$$\frac{2}{3}\times\frac{3}{5}=\frac{6}{15}=\frac{2}{5}\quad\checkmark$$

Common Mistake

$$\frac{7}{10}\times\frac{14}{3}=\frac{\overset{1}{\cancel{7}}}{10}\times\frac{\overset{2}{\cancel{14}}}{3}=\frac{2}{30}\quad\times$$

$$\frac{7}{\underset{5}{\cancel{10}}}\times\frac{\overset{7}{\cancel{14}}}{3}=\frac{49}{15}\quad\checkmark$$

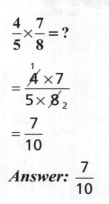

Exercise 6.9

1. Multiply.

   (a) $\frac{1}{2}\times\frac{3}{4}$ (b) $\frac{2}{3}\times\frac{4}{5}$ (c) $\frac{3}{2}\times\frac{1}{4}$ (d) $\frac{5}{3}\times\frac{7}{4}$

   (e) $\frac{4}{3}\times\frac{4}{5}$ (f) $\frac{2}{5}\times\frac{2}{7}$ (g) $\frac{1}{2}\times\frac{1}{2}$ (h) $\frac{2}{5}\times\frac{1}{3}$

2. Multiply. Use the shortcut.

   (a) $\frac{5}{12}\times\frac{7}{10}$ (b) $\frac{1}{6}\times\frac{9}{4}$ (c) $\frac{5}{33}\times\frac{11}{2}$ (d) $\frac{5}{8}\times\frac{8}{15}$

   (e) $\frac{6}{11}\times\frac{55}{42}$ (f) $\frac{7}{6}\times\frac{6}{21}$ (g) $\frac{3}{4}\times\frac{4}{3}$ (h) $\frac{2}{3}\times\frac{9}{14}$

Reciprocals

Two numbers whose product is 1 are called **reciprocals**. Another word for reciprocal is **multiplicative inverse.**

(a) $\frac{3}{4}$ and $\frac{4}{3}$ are reciprocals.

$$\frac{3}{4} \times \frac{4}{3} = \frac{12}{12} = 1$$

(b) 5 and $\frac{1}{5}$ are reciprocals.

$$5 \times \frac{1}{5} = \frac{5}{5} = 1$$

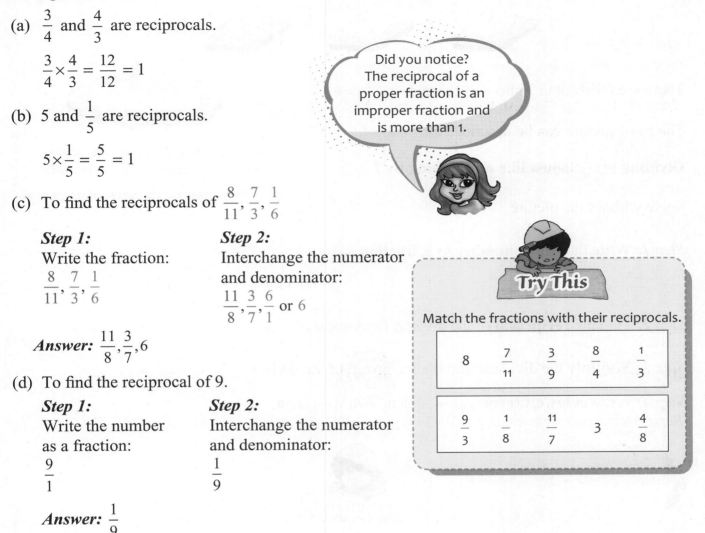

Did you notice? The reciprocal of a proper fraction is an improper fraction and is more than 1.

(c) To find the reciprocals of $\frac{8}{11}, \frac{7}{3}, \frac{1}{6}$

Step 1:
Write the fraction:
$\frac{8}{11}, \frac{7}{3}, \frac{1}{6}$

Step 2:
Interchange the numerator and denominator:
$\frac{11}{8}, \frac{3}{7}, \frac{6}{1}$ or 6

Answer: $\frac{11}{8}, \frac{3}{7}, 6$

(d) To find the reciprocal of 9.

Step 1:
Write the number as a fraction:
$\frac{9}{1}$

Step 2:
Interchange the numerator and denominator:
$\frac{1}{9}$

Answer: $\frac{1}{9}$

Try This

Match the fractions with their reciprocals.

8	$\frac{7}{11}$	$\frac{3}{9}$	$\frac{8}{4}$	$\frac{1}{3}$

$\frac{9}{3}$	$\frac{1}{8}$	$\frac{11}{7}$	3	$\frac{4}{8}$

Division of Fractions

To understand division of fractions let us look at division once more. Given below are 6 slices of bread.

If you had to solve $6 \div 2$, you could think of it as *"how many 2s are there in 6?"*

There are three 2s in 6.

Dividing a Whole Number by a Unit Fraction

To understand $3 \div \dfrac{1}{2}$, ask the question *"how many halves are there in 3?"*

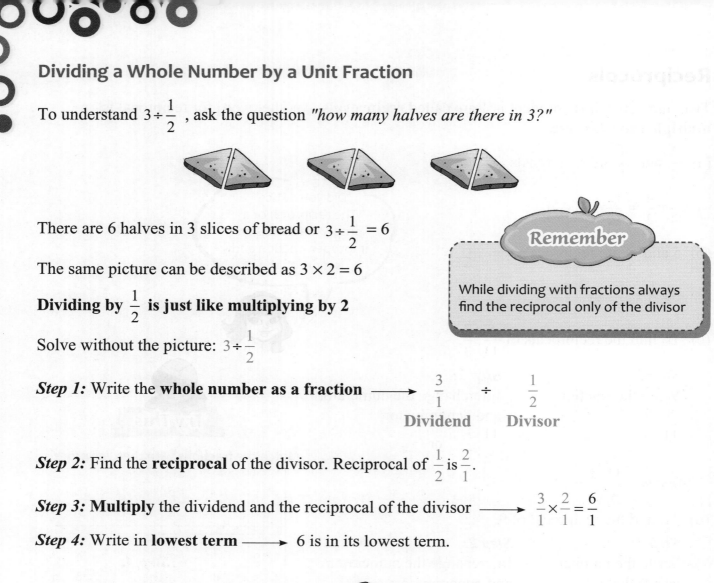

There are 6 halves in 3 slices of bread or $3 \div \dfrac{1}{2} = 6$

The same picture can be described as $3 \times 2 = 6$

Dividing by $\dfrac{1}{2}$ is just like multiplying by 2

Solve without the picture: $3 \div \dfrac{1}{2}$

> **Remember**
>
> While dividing with fractions always find the reciprocal only of the divisor

Step 1: Write the **whole number as a fraction** ⟶ $\quad \dfrac{3}{1} \quad \div \quad \dfrac{1}{2}$

Dividend   Divisor

Step 2: Find the **reciprocal** of the divisor. Reciprocal of $\dfrac{1}{2}$ is $\dfrac{2}{1}$.

Step 3: **Multiply** the dividend and the reciprocal of the divisor ⟶ $\dfrac{3}{1} \times \dfrac{2}{1} = \dfrac{6}{1}$

Step 4: Write in **lowest term** ⟶ 6 is in its lowest term.

Try This

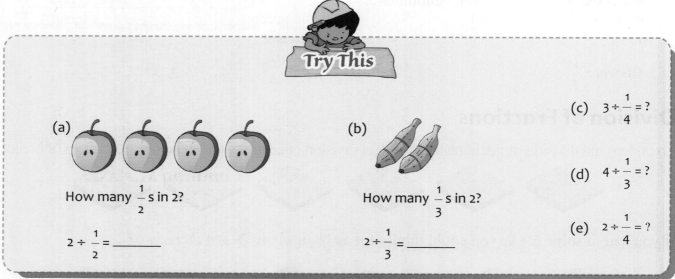

(a) How many $\dfrac{1}{2}$s in 2?

$2 \div \dfrac{1}{2} = $ _____

(b) How many $\dfrac{1}{3}$s in 2?

$2 \div \dfrac{1}{3} = $ _____

(c) $3 \div \dfrac{1}{4} = ?$

(d) $4 \div \dfrac{1}{3} = ?$

(e) $2 \div \dfrac{1}{4} = ?$

Dividing a Whole Number by a Fraction

How many $\frac{3}{4}$ pieces in 3 pizzas?

$3 \div \frac{3}{4} = ?$

Think: How many $\frac{3}{4}$ ths in 3?

Here are 3 pizzas:

How many $\frac{3}{4}$ ths in 3 pizzas?

First cut each pizza into $\frac{1}{4}$ ths.

Then separate them into $\frac{3}{4}$ ths

four $\frac{3}{4}$ ths

Answer: There are four $\frac{3}{4}$ th pieces in 3 pizzas.

Here is how you can solve this without pictures.

$3 \div \frac{3}{4} = ?$

Step 1:
Write the whole number as a fraction.

$3 \rightarrow \frac{3}{1}$

Answer: $3 \div \frac{3}{4} = 4$

Step 2:
Find the reciprocal of the divisor.

$\frac{3}{4} \rightarrow \frac{4}{3}$

Step 3:
Multiply the dividend and the reciprocal of the divisor.

$\frac{3}{1} \times \frac{4}{3} = \frac{12}{3}$

Step 4:
Write in the lowest term.

$\frac{12}{3} = 4$

Try This

$2 \div \frac{2}{3} = ?$

How many $\frac{2}{3}$ s in 2? Solve with the help of pictures first. Then solve with steps.

Common Mistake

$4 \div \frac{1}{8} = ?$

$\frac{4}{1} \div \frac{1}{8}$

$\frac{1}{4} \times \frac{1}{8} = \frac{1}{32}$ ✗

$4 \div \frac{1}{8} = ?$

$\frac{4}{1} \div \frac{1}{8}$

$\frac{4}{1} \times \frac{8}{1} = 32$ ✓

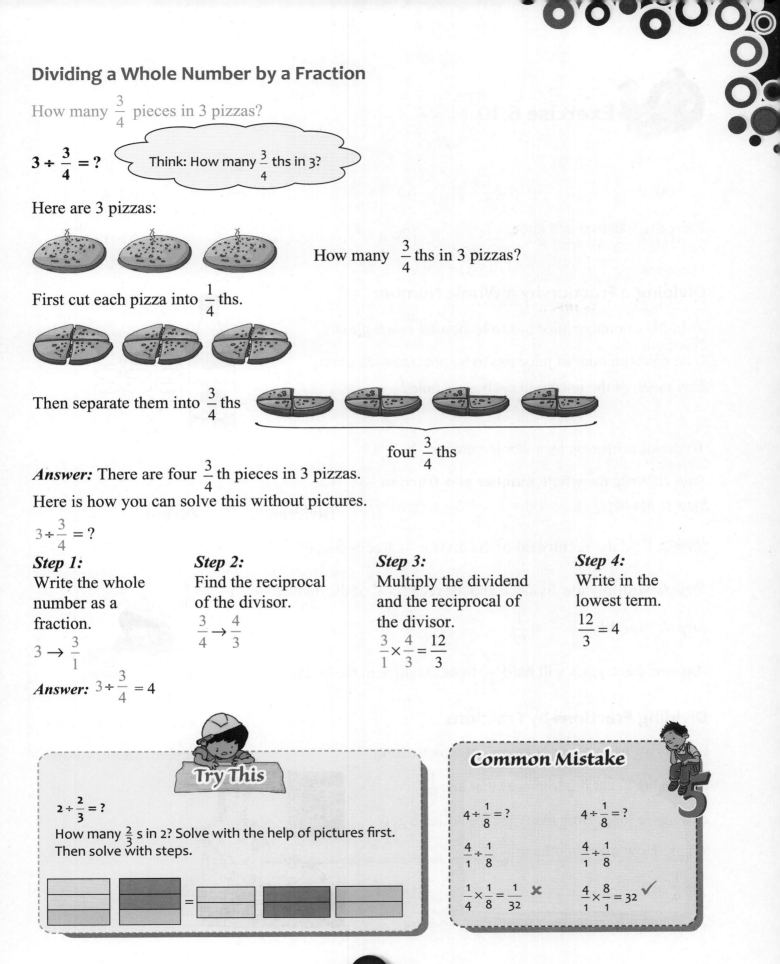

Exercise 6.10

1. Solve.

(a) $3 \div \dfrac{1}{5}$ (b) $7 \div \dfrac{1}{3}$ (c) $8 \div \dfrac{1}{6}$ (d) $6 \div \dfrac{1}{2}$ (e) $4 \div \dfrac{1}{3}$

(f) $6 \div \dfrac{3}{4}$ (g) $5 \div \dfrac{2}{5}$ (h) $4 \div \dfrac{2}{3}$ (i) $6 \div \dfrac{2}{3}$ (j) $1 \div \dfrac{1}{10}$

Dividing a Fraction by a Whole Number

$\dfrac{3}{4}$ bottle of orange juice has to be poured into 9 glasses.

If an equal amount of juice has to be put into each glass, how much of the juice will each glass hold?

$\dfrac{3}{4} \div 9 = ?$

To divide a fraction by a whole number:

Step 1: Write the **whole number as a fraction** → $\quad \dfrac{3}{4} \quad \div \quad \dfrac{9}{1}$

Dividend   **Divisor**

Step 2: Find the **reciprocal** of the divisor → Reciprocal of $\dfrac{9}{1}$ is $\dfrac{1}{9}$

Step 3: **Multiply** the dividend and the reciprocal of the divisor → $\dfrac{3}{4} \times \dfrac{1}{9} = \dfrac{3}{36}$

Step 4: **Simplify** → $\dfrac{3}{36} = \dfrac{1}{12}$

Answer: Each glass will hold $\dfrac{1}{12}$th of the juice in the bottle.

Try This

(a) $\dfrac{2}{3} \div 6 = ?$ (b) $\dfrac{3}{5} \div 2 = ?$

Dividing Fractions by Fractions

(a) Shristi has a piece of lace $\dfrac{8}{9}$ of a metre long.

She wants to cut it into pieces that are $\dfrac{1}{9}$ of a metre long. How many pieces will she get?

Think: How many ninths in $\dfrac{8}{9}$?

$\dfrac{8}{9} \div \dfrac{1}{9} = ?$

To divide a fraction by a fraction:

Step 1: Find the **reciprocal of the divisor** → Reciprocal of $\frac{1}{9}$ is $\frac{9}{1}$

Step 2: **Multiply** the dividend and the **reciprocal** of the divisor → $\frac{8}{9} \times \frac{9}{1} = \frac{72}{9}$

Step 3: **Simplify** → $\frac{72}{9} = \frac{8}{1} = 8$

Answer: Shristi will get 8 pieces of lace.

(b) $\frac{3}{7} \div \frac{2}{5} = ?$

$= \frac{3}{7} \times \frac{5}{2}$

$= \frac{15}{14}$

Answer: $\frac{3}{7} \div \frac{2}{5} = \frac{15}{21} = 1\frac{1}{14}$

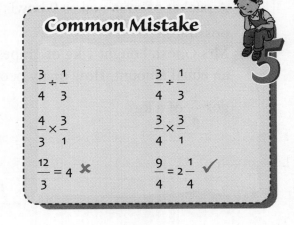

Common Mistake

$\frac{3}{4} \div \frac{1}{3}$ $\frac{3}{4} \div \frac{1}{3}$

$\frac{4}{3} \times \frac{3}{1}$ $\frac{3}{4} \times \frac{3}{1}$

$\frac{12}{3} = 4$ ✗ $\frac{9}{4} = 2\frac{1}{4}$ ✓

 **Exercise 6.11**

1. Divide.

  (a) $\frac{9}{7} \div 3$ (b) $\frac{4}{5} \div 12$ (c) $\frac{6}{7} \div 5$ (d) $\frac{1}{2} \div 7$ (e) $\frac{1}{3} \div 12$

  (f) $\frac{3}{8} \div 8$ (g) $\frac{2}{5} \div 2$ (h) $\frac{3}{7} \div 21$ (i) $\frac{4}{5} \div 10$ (j) $\frac{1}{6} \div 3$

2. Divide.

  (a) $\frac{1}{2} \div \frac{7}{12}$ (b) $\frac{5}{9} \div \frac{2}{3}$ (c) $\frac{1}{3} \div \frac{5}{9}$ (d) $0 \div \frac{3}{8}$ (e) $\frac{3}{8} \div \frac{3}{5}$

  (f) $\frac{6}{7} \div \frac{2}{3}$ (g) $\frac{1}{3} \div \frac{1}{3}$ (h) $\frac{3}{5} \div \frac{1}{5}$ (i) $\frac{2}{3} \div \frac{1}{4}$ (j) $\frac{3}{5} \div \frac{1}{2}$

3. Solve using multiplication or division.

  (a) A painter uses $\frac{3}{5}$ of a can of paint to cover one wall of a house.

     How many cans of paint will he need to cover 7 such walls?

  (b) Nandita used $\frac{1}{4}$ of a sheet of clear plastic to cover her book.

     How many sheets would she need to cover 12 books?

(c) Three children are sharing $\frac{2}{3}$ of a pizza. What fraction of the pizza will each child get?

(d) Kiran is giving away $\frac{1}{4}$ of his bookmark collection to 5 of his friends. If each friend gets the same number of bookmarks, what fraction of the collection has each child received?

(e) A packet of soup makes 9 bowls of servings. How many $\frac{3}{4}$ bowls of servings are possible?

(f) Mrs Ghosh bought 1 kg of grapes and served each member of her family an equal amount. How many people did she serve it to if each person got $\frac{1}{4}$ of a kg?

Project

Find a recipe for fruit salad that serves 4 people. Use cup and spoon measurements. Make the fruit salad. Rewrite the recipe for 8 people. Rewrite the recipe for 2 people.

Mental Maths

To solve $\frac{1}{8} + \frac{3}{4}$

Think $\frac{3}{4} = \frac{6}{8}$

So, $\frac{1}{8} + \frac{6}{8} = \frac{7}{8}$

To solve $\frac{1}{3} - \frac{3}{12}$

Think $\frac{1}{3} = \frac{4}{12}$

So, $\frac{4}{12} - \frac{3}{12} = \frac{1}{12}$

The denominators here are multiples of each other

Do these mentally: (a) $\frac{3}{10} + \frac{1}{5} = ?$ (b) $\frac{3}{4} - \frac{1}{2} = ?$

(c) $\frac{5}{8} + \frac{1}{4} = ?$ (d) $\frac{1}{3} - \frac{1}{6} = ?$

Chapter Check-Up

1. Find two equivalent fractions for each of the following.

   (a) $\dfrac{4}{5}$　　　(b) $\dfrac{7}{9}$　　　(c) $\dfrac{6}{11}$

2. Reduce to the lowest terms.

   (a) $\dfrac{16}{24}$　　　(b) $\dfrac{32}{48}$　　　(c) $\dfrac{81}{90}$

3. Compare using < or >.

   (a) $\dfrac{1}{7} \bigcirc \dfrac{1}{3}$　　(b) $\dfrac{2}{9} \bigcirc \dfrac{5}{9}$　　(c) $\dfrac{3}{5} \bigcirc \dfrac{2}{7}$　　(d) $\dfrac{6}{9} \bigcirc \dfrac{2}{5}$

4. Solve.

   (a) $\dfrac{3}{13} + \dfrac{7}{13}$　(b) $\dfrac{2}{4} + \dfrac{5}{5}$　(c) $\dfrac{8}{9} + \dfrac{2}{9} + \dfrac{3}{9}$　(d) $\dfrac{2}{7} + \dfrac{3}{5}$

   (e) $\dfrac{4}{5} + \dfrac{8}{9} + \dfrac{2}{3}$　(f) $\dfrac{7}{17} - \dfrac{4}{17}$　(g) $\dfrac{7}{9} - \dfrac{7}{12}$　(h) $3\dfrac{2}{5} - 2\dfrac{1}{10}$

5. Solve.

   (a) $\dfrac{5}{7} \times 2$　(b) $\dfrac{7}{3} \times \dfrac{4}{11}$　(c) $0 \times \dfrac{7}{13}$　(d) $\dfrac{3}{6} \times \dfrac{4}{12}$　(e) $\dfrac{2}{11} \times \dfrac{5}{6}$

   (f) $\dfrac{2}{7} \div \dfrac{3}{4}$　(g) $\dfrac{4}{7} \div 5$　(h) $\dfrac{4}{5} \div \dfrac{1}{2}$　(i) $16 \div \dfrac{3}{4}$　(j) $\dfrac{5}{11} \div \dfrac{3}{7}$

6. (a) Zeenat bought 5 kg of wax to make some decorative candles. If she needs $\dfrac{1}{10}$ kg per candle, how many candles can she make?

   (b) Divya spent $2\dfrac{1}{2}$ hours watching birds on Saturday and $1\dfrac{3}{4}$ hours watching birds on Sunday. How many hours over the weekend did Divya spend bird watching?

   (c) Prateek studied for $6\dfrac{1}{3}$ hours in one week and $4\dfrac{3}{4}$ hours the next week. How much longer did he study in the first week?

Keeping in Touch

1. Find the HCF of 56, 14 using prime factorisation.
2. Find the LCM of 32, 24 using prime factorisation.

Maths Lab Activity

Multiplication of Fractions

Objective: To build an understanding of multiplication of fractions.

Materials Required: Square-lined paper, crayons of two colours

Preparation: Students work independently or in pairs.

Steps:

To solve $\frac{1}{3} \times \frac{2}{5}$

1. Since the two denominators are 3 and 5, the students draw a rectangle of sides 3 squares by 5 squares on the square-lined paper.

Step 1

2. Then one student colours $\frac{1}{3}$ of the rectangle with blue horizontal lines.

Step 2

3. The second student colours $\frac{2}{5}$ of the blue squares with red vertical lines.

   What fraction of the sheet does have both vertical and horizontal lines?
   ($\frac{2}{15}$ of the sheet has both vertical and horizontal lines)

   This shows that $\frac{1}{3}$ of $\frac{2}{5} = \frac{2}{15}$

Step 3

So, $\frac{1}{3} \times \frac{2}{5} = \frac{2}{15}$

Try this out:

(a)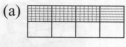

$\frac{1}{2} \times \frac{3}{4} = \boxed{}$

(b)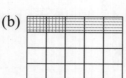

$\frac{2}{5} \times \frac{1}{4} = \boxed{}$

(c)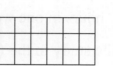

$\frac{4}{6} \times \frac{1}{3} = \boxed{}$

(d)

$\frac{2}{3} \times \frac{3}{4} = \boxed{}$

Mental Maths

Learn

Since 1 is the same as $\frac{1}{1}, \frac{2}{2}, \frac{3}{3}, \frac{4}{4}$, etc., 5 is the same as $4\frac{2}{2}, 4\frac{3}{3}, 4\frac{4}{4}$, etc.

To solve (mentally): $5 - \frac{3}{4}$

Think: $5 = 4\frac{4}{4}$

$4\frac{4}{4} - \frac{3}{4} = 4\frac{1}{4}$

To solve (mentally): $6 - 1\frac{2}{7}$

Think: $6 = 5\frac{7}{7}$

$5\frac{7}{7} - 1\frac{2}{7} = 4\frac{5}{7}$

Practice

(a) $3 - \frac{1}{3}$

(b) $4 - \frac{2}{3}$

(c) $2 - \frac{3}{4}$

(d) $5 - \frac{2}{3}$

(e) $6 - \frac{3}{8}$

Use

1. Write in descending order:

$\frac{5}{12}, \frac{5}{11}, \frac{5}{17}, \frac{5}{13}$

2. $\frac{8}{64}$ in lowest term is _____.

3. $\frac{15}{30} \boxed{\geq} \frac{4}{8}$ (Use <, > or =)

4. $\frac{16}{28} = \frac{\boxed{}}{7}$

5. $3\frac{1}{2} + 3\frac{1}{2} = $ _____

6. How many halves in 5? _____

7. Reciprocal of 1 is _____ .

8. $\frac{6}{18} \boxed{} \frac{6}{8}$ (Use > < or =)

9. $6 - \frac{3}{5} = $ _____

10. If $\frac{1}{4}$ th of a number is 100, what is the number?

11. $\frac{2}{3}$ of 21 = _____

12. $\frac{2}{5} \times \frac{8}{9} \times 0 = $ _____

13. $6\frac{2}{7} - 5\frac{2}{7}$ _____

14. $\frac{1}{4}$ of 2 rupees = _____

15. $\frac{4}{5} \boxed{=} \frac{16}{25}$ (Use > < or =)

16. $\frac{7}{\boxed{}} = \frac{42}{66}$

17. $7 - \frac{3}{4} = $ _____

18. $\frac{3}{17} + \frac{14}{17} = $ _____

19. $\frac{4}{3} \times \frac{3}{4} \times 1 = $ _____

20. $8 - 1\frac{1}{2} = $ _____

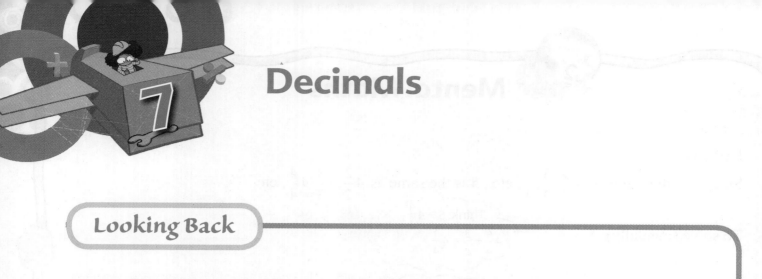

Decimals

Looking Back

When a digit moves to the right of the ones place it gets ten times smaller.
When 'one' is further divided into 10 equal parts, each part is called a tenth.

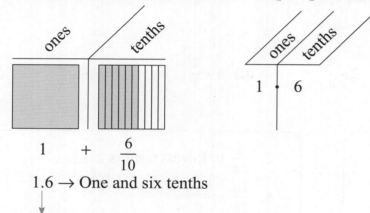

1.6 → One and six tenths

The decimal point separates the ones place and the tenths place.
When one tenth is further divided into 10 equal parts, each part is called a hundredth.

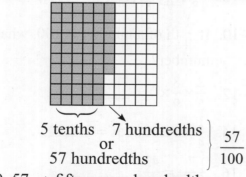

5 tenths   7 hundredths
or
57 hundredths $\frac{57}{100}$

0. 57 → fifty-seven hundredths

Fractions to Decimals

$$\frac{5}{10} = 0.5 \qquad \frac{36}{10} = 3.6 \qquad \frac{128}{10} = 12.8$$

$$\frac{5}{100} = 0.05 \qquad \frac{36}{100} = 0.36 \qquad \frac{128}{100} = 1.28$$

Decimals to Fractions

$$0.7 = \frac{7}{10} \qquad 5.2 = \frac{52}{10} \qquad 13.7 = \frac{137}{10}$$

$$0.07 = \frac{7}{100} \qquad 0.52 = \frac{52}{100} \qquad 1.37 = \frac{137}{100}$$

The number of decimal places is the same as the number of zeros in the denominator.

Exercise 7.1

1. Match.

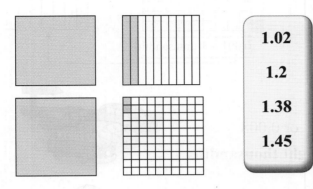 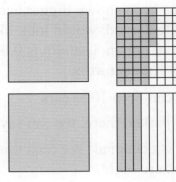

2. For the number 186.45 write the digit in the:

   (a) tens place   (b) tenths place   (c) hundreds place

   (d) hundredths place   (e) ones place

3. Build a decimal with:

   (a) 7 in the tenths place and 4 in the ones place.

   (b) 9 in the tenths place, 6 in the hundredths place, 8 in the ones place, 5 in the tens place.

   (c) 5 in the ones place, 7 in the tenths place, 8 in the hundredths place.

4. Express as a decimal.

   (a) $\dfrac{13}{10}$ (b) $\dfrac{27}{100}$ (c) $\dfrac{142}{10}$ (d) $\dfrac{843}{100}$ (e) $\dfrac{5}{100}$

5. Express as a fraction.

   (a) 0.11   (b) 0.8   (c) 1.1   (d) 3.07   (e) 5.84

6. Give the next three numbers.

   (a) 1.2, 1.3, 1.4 _____   (b) 5.92, 5.93, 5.94 _____

   (c) 11.8, 11.9, 12.0 _____   (d) 8.01, 8.02, 8.03 _____

   (e) 6.02, 6.03, 6.04 _____   (f) 4.23, 4.24, 4.25 _____

Project

Go through the newspaper and find different places where decimals are used. Copy these into your notebook and write them out in words.

Thousandths

- 1 hundredth is further divided into 10 equal parts. Each part is called 1 **thousandth.**
- The fractional form of one thousandth is $\dfrac{1}{1000}$.
  The corner box has been shown bigger here.
  All other boxes, if enlarged, would look like this.
- The decimal form of one thousandth is 0.001.
  1 hundredth = 10 thousandths

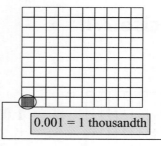

0.001 = 1 thousandth

A car park at a mall can hold 1000 cars.

- If there are 8 cars parked there, we can say $\dfrac{8}{1000}$ or 0.008 of the parking lot is occupied. We read this as **eight thousandths** or zero point zero zero eight.

- If there are 75 cars parked there, we can say $\dfrac{75}{1000}$ or 0.075 of the parking lot is occupied. We read this as **seventy-five thousandths** or zero point zero seven five.

- If there are 598 cars parked there we can say $\dfrac{598}{1000}$ or 0.598 of the car park is occupied. We read this as **five hundred ninety-eight thousandths** or zero point five nine eight.

Using the place value chart we would write it like this:

Try This

(a) Give as a decimal:
$\dfrac{5}{1000}$, $\dfrac{123}{1000}$

(b) Give as a fraction:
0.076, 1.529

ones	.	tenths	hundredths	thousandths
0	.	0	0	8
0	.	0	7	5
0	.	5	9	8

Eight thousandths

Seventy-five thousandths

Five hundred ninety-eight thousandths

Journal

Explain in your own words the difference it makes if '0' is placed before a decimal point or after it.

0.5   .05

Equivalent Decimals

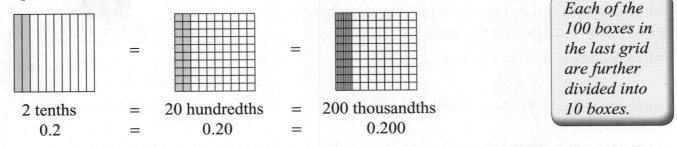

2 tenths	=	20 hundredths	=	200 thousandths
0.2	=	0.20	=	0.200

All three decimal numbers shown above have the same value and so they are called **equivalent decimals.**

This can also be checked by comparing the decimals with equivalent fractions:

$$\frac{2}{10} \quad = \quad \frac{20}{100} \quad = \quad \frac{200}{1000}$$
$$\downarrow \qquad\qquad \downarrow \qquad\qquad \downarrow$$
$$\textbf{0.2} \quad = \quad \textbf{0.20} \quad = \quad \textbf{0.200}$$
$$\downarrow \qquad\qquad \downarrow \qquad\qquad \downarrow$$
$$\textbf{0.2} \quad = \quad \textbf{0.2} \quad = \quad \textbf{0.2}$$

Writing or removing zeros at the end of a decimal number does not change its value.

Try This

(a) 0.6 = 0.60 = _____
(b) 1.7 = 1.70 = _____
(c) 2.40 = _____ = _____

> Each of the 100 boxes in the last grid are further divided into 10 boxes.

Like and Unlike Decimals

Decimals with the same number of decimal places are called like decimals.

(a) 0.3   4.5   8.7   (*one decimal place each*)
(b) 12.17   1.04   263.11   (*two decimal places each*)
(c) 1.093   0.847   11.970   (*three decimal places each*)

Decimals having different number of decimal places are called unlike decimals.

(a) 0.7   2.81
(b) 18.24   13.8
(c) 0.724   8.74

Unlike decimals can also be equivalent decimals.

0.7, 0.70, 0.700 are *unlike but equivalent decimals*.

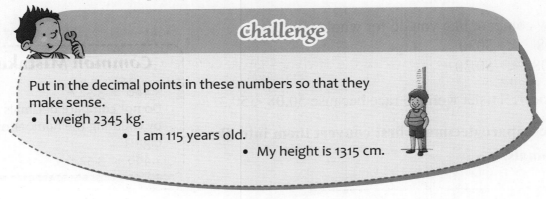

Challenge

Put in the decimal points in these numbers so that they make sense.
- I weigh 2345 kg.
- I am 115 years old.
- My height is 1315 cm.

Converting Unlike Decimals into Like Decimals

Unlike decimals can be converted into like decimals
by finding their equivalent decimals.

Unlike decimals	1.7	8.36	9.755
	↓	↓	↓
Like decimals	1.700	8.360	9.755

**To convert unlike decimals into like decimals find
their equivalent decimals up to the same number
of places.**

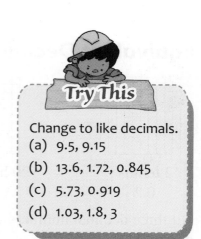

Try This

Change to like decimals.
(a) 9.5, 9.15
(b) 13.6, 1.72, 0.845
(c) 5.73, 0.919
(d) 1.03, 1.8, 3

Comparing and Ordering Decimals

Comparing Decimals

(a) Using mathematical models

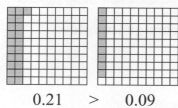 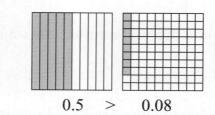

0.21	>	0.09		0.5	>	0.08		0.33	<	0.39

(b) Trisha and Tanay were having a roller-skating race.
Trisha finished in 50.08 seconds.
Tanay finished in 50.3 seconds.
Who won the race?
The child who took less time won the race. To find out which child
took less time, we need to compare:

50.08 ◯ 50.3
         ↓ } *Convert into like decimals*
50.08 ◯ 50.30

Now compare like you do for whole numbers.
5008 < 5030
50.08 < 50.30

Answer: Trisha won the race because 50.08 < 50.3.

**To compare decimals, first convert them into like
decimals.**

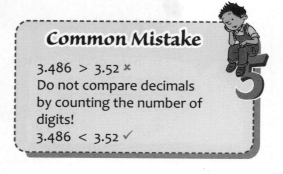

Common Mistake

3.486 > 3.52 ✗
Do not compare decimals
by counting the number of
digits!
3.486 < 3.52 ✓

Exercise 7.2

1. Colour to compare.

(a) 0.53 ◯ 0.07

(b) 0.1 ◯ 0.01

(c) 0.2 ◯ 0.6

(d) 0.42 ◯ 0.45

(e) 0.7 ◯ 0.72

(f) 0.38 ◯ 0.35

2. Compare using <, > or =.

(a) 9.099 ◯ 9.99

(b) 70.08 ◯ 70.7

(c) 6.6 ◯ 6.066

(d) 96.550 ◯ 96.55

(e) 5.091 ◯ 5.09

(f) 0.5 ◯ 0.15

(g) 6.4 ◯ 6.359

(h) 0.3 ◯ 2.895

(i) 0.76 ◯ 0.8

Ordering Decimals

(a) During a medical inspection, the weight of four children
was recorded as shown. Rewrite the list in descending order
(*Place the heaviest child first*)

Naren   43.17 kg
Natasha   43.7 kg
Vidya   42.09 kg
Varun   41.8 kg

To put them in descending order, convert into like decimals of two places each.

Naren	Natasha	Vidya	Varun
43.17	43.7	42.09	41.8
↓	↓	↓	↓
43.17	43.70	42.09	41.80

Now rearrange as you would do for
whole numbers.
(4370   4317   4209   4180)

Answer: Natasha   43.7 kg
          Naren   43.17 kg
          Vidya   42.09 kg   *placed in descending order*
          Varun   41.8 kg

(b) Rewrite in ascending order.

0.88   0.8   0.808

Step 1: Convert into like decimals → 0.880   0.800   0.808

Step 2: Write in ascending order → 0.800   0.808   0.880

Answer: 0.8,   0.808,   0.88

Exercise 7.3

1. Rewrite in descending order.

   (a) 8.06   8.059   8.013   8.3   (b) 3.48   4.2   3.8   4.02

   (c) 19.4   1.945   19.46   1.95   (d) 6.8   8.66   8.06   6.08

   (e) 8.63   80.002   8.6   80.2   (f) 3.9   3.09   3.91   3.019

2. Rewrite in ascending order.

   (a) 0.04   1.04   0.14   1.14

   (b) 20   19.09   20.01   19.9

   (c) 14.19   19.14   14.9   19.4

   (d) 6.23   6.32   6.4   6

   (e) 9.09   0.99   1.1   6

   (f) 7.162   7.23   7.02   7.2

challenge

Use these digits with a decimal point.

| 7 | 8 | 2 |

- Build the biggest number less than one.
- Build the smallest number less than one.
- The biggest number between 7 and 8.

Problem Solving

(a) In a quiz competition Team A secured 84.5 points and Team B secured 85 points. Which team won the quiz?

(b) Shanay can swim the 100 m race in 68.1 seconds. Swapneel can swim the same distance in 68.02 seconds. Who is faster?

(c) Smriti, Saroj, and Shamin were comparing their test marks. They got 15.05, 15.25 and 15.5 marks respectively. Who did the best?

(d) The table below gives the names of the top runners of a 100 metres race. Who came first? Who came last? List the names in order, beginning with the person who came first.

Names	100 m race timings
Rohan	20.52 seconds
Ananth	20.5 seconds
Suraj	20.25 seconds
Prashant	20.05 seconds

Remember, the person who has the lowest timing is the winner!

Addition of Decimals

These pictures will help you understand how to add decimals.

(a) $0.3 + 0.5 = ?$ (b) $0.6 + 0.4 = ?$ (c) $0.8 + 0.5 = ?$

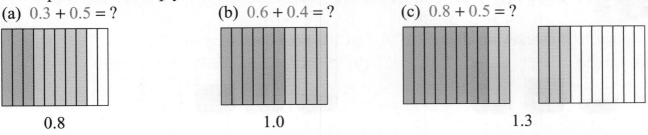

0.8   1.0   1.3

Adding decimal numbers is just like adding whole numbers but remember to place the decimals points one below the other and regroup if required.

ones	tenths
0	3
+ 0	5
0	8

ones	tenths
0	6
+ 0	4
1	0

ones	tenths
0	8
+ 0	5
1	3

(a) Alka is practising for her school sports day. She runs 2.37 km in the morning and 3.8 km in the evening. How far does she run in all?
2.37 + 3.8 = ?

Step 1: Write the digits according to the place value, that is one below the other, making sure that the decimals are also exactly one below the other—ones below ones, tenths below tenths, and so on.

Decimal points should be one below the other.

$$\begin{array}{r} 2.37 \\ + 3.8 \\ \hline \end{array}$$

Step 2: Change the decimals to like decimals.

$$\left.\begin{array}{r} 2.37 \\ + 3.80 \end{array}\right\} \text{Like decimals}$$

Step 3: Add as usual. Start from the hundredths. Carry over if needed.
Place the decimal point in the answer in the same place as the numbers above it.

$$\begin{array}{r} 2.37 \\ + 3.80 \\ \hline 6.17 \end{array}$$

Do not forget the decimal point in the answer.

Answer: Alka runs 6.17 km in all.

Common Mistake

$$\begin{array}{r} 5.4 \\ + 6.7 \\ \hline 121 \end{array} \times$$

$$\begin{array}{r} 5.4 \\ + 6.7 \\ \hline 12.1 \end{array} \checkmark$$

$$\begin{array}{r} 14 \\ + 0.59 \end{array} \times$$

$$\begin{array}{r} 14.00 \\ + 0.59 \end{array} \checkmark$$

Exercise 7.4

1. Colour to show how much juice in all. One has been done for you.

(a)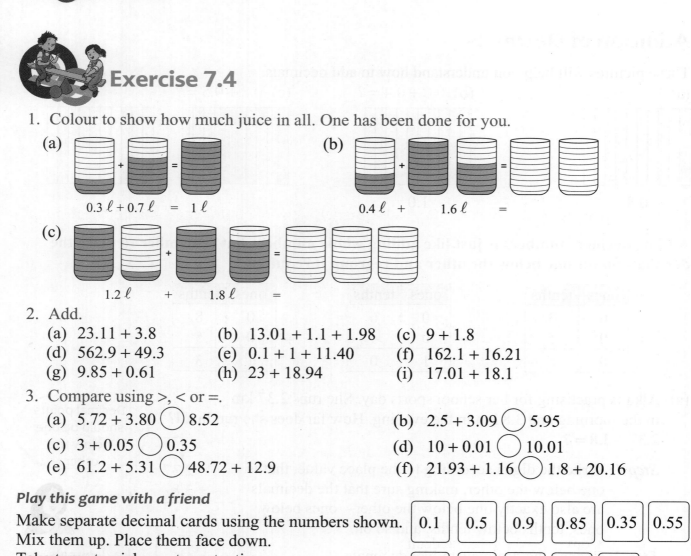

$0.3\,\ell + 0.7\,\ell = 1\,\ell$

(b) $0.4\,\ell + 1.6\,\ell =$

(c) $1.2\,\ell + 1.8\,\ell =$

2. Add.

(a) $23.11 + 3.8$ (b) $13.01 + 1.1 + 1.98$ (c) $9 + 1.8$

(d) $562.9 + 49.3$ (e) $0.1 + 1 + 11.40$ (f) $162.1 + 16.21$

(g) $9.85 + 0.61$ (h) $23 + 18.94$ (i) $17.01 + 18.1$

3. Compare using >, < or =.

(a) $5.72 + 3.80 \bigcirc 8.52$ (b) $2.5 + 3.09 \bigcirc 5.95$

(c) $3 + 0.05 \bigcirc 0.35$ (d) $10 + 0.01 \bigcirc 10.01$

(e) $61.2 + 5.31 \bigcirc 48.72 + 12.9$ (f) $21.93 + 1.16 \bigcirc 1.8 + 20.16$

Play this game with a friend

Make separate decimal cards using the numbers shown.
Mix them up. Place them face down.
Take turns to pick any two at a time.
If they add up to 1 keep them.
If they don't, put them back.
Continue till you have found all the pairs. The person
who has more cards wins the game.

0.1	0.5	0.9	0.85	0.35	0.55
0.2	0.6	0.25	0.45	0.65	
0.4	0.8	0.15	0.75	0.50	

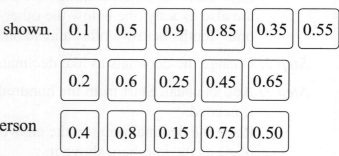

Mental Maths

$5 - 1.9 = ?$

$2 - 0.1$
$5 - 2 = 3$
$3 + 0.1 = 3.1$
$5 - 1.9 = 3.1$

$8 - 3.9$

$4 - 0.1$
$8 - 4 = 4$
$4 + 0.1 = 4.1$
$8 - 3.9 = 4.1$

Solve the following.

(a) $6 - 1.9$
(b) $8 - 2.9$
(c) $5 - 3.9$
(d) $9 - 4.9$
(e) $12 - 1.9$

Subtraction of Decimals

These pictures will help you understand how to subtract decimals.

(a) 0.9 − 0.4

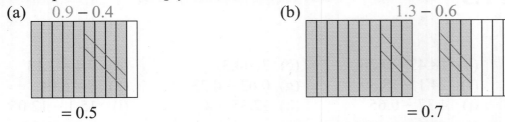

= 0.5

(b) 1.3 − 0.6

= 0.7

Subtracting decimal numbers is just like subtracting whole numbers. Line up the decimal points one below the other and regroup if necessary.

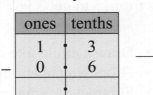

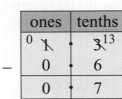

ones	tenths
0	9
− 0	4
0	5

ones	tenths
1	3
− 0	6

→

ones	tenths
0 $\cancel{1}$	$\cancel{3}^{13}$
− 0	6
0	7

(a) Rajeev was measuring how far he could throw a ball. On the first try, it went 17.5 m. On the second try, it went 16.75 m. How much farther did it go on the first try?

17.5 − 16.75 = ?

Step 1: Put the greater number on top and the lesser one below, taking care to match place value and keeping the decimals one below the other.

$$\begin{array}{r} 17.5 \\ -\ 16.75 \end{array}$$

Step 2: Convert them into like decimals.

$$\left.\begin{array}{r} 17.50 \\ -\ 16.75 \end{array}\right\} \text{Like decimals}$$

Step 3: Subtract as usual. Regroup if necessary.

$$\begin{array}{r} 17.50 \\ -\ 16.75 \\ \hline 0.75 \end{array}$$

Do not forget the decimal point in the answer.

The decimal point in the answer must be in the same place as in the numbers above it.

Answer: Rajiv's first throw was 0.75 m farther than his second throw.

(b) **6 − 4.5 = ?**

$$\begin{array}{r} 6 \\ -\ 4.5 \end{array} \rightarrow \begin{array}{r} 6.0 \\ -\ 4.5 \end{array} \rightarrow \begin{array}{r} \overset{5\ \ 10}{\cancel{6}.\cancel{0}} \\ -\ 4.5 \\ \hline 1.5 \end{array}$$

Answer: 6 − 4.5 = 1.5

Common Mistake

$$\begin{array}{r} 18.2 \\ -\ 7.25 \end{array} \times \qquad \begin{array}{r} 18.20 \\ -\ 7.25 \end{array} \checkmark$$

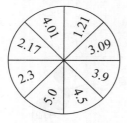

Exercise 7.5

1. Subtract.

   (a) 9.32 – 4.16   (b) 18.43 – 9.26   (c) 7 – 4.32   (d) 9.4 – 3.13
   (e) 11.01 – 10.11   (f) 24.1 – 18.39   (g) 0.62 – 0.23   (h) 8 – 6.04
   (i) 14.1 – 9.25   (j) 4.37 – 0.65   (k) 12.35 – 4   (l) 15.1 – 12.05

2. What should be added to 2.1 to get 10?

3. What should be taken away from 15 to get 3.96?

4. Play a game.

   • Draw a circle like this in your notebook.
   • Drop two paper clips or *rajma* seeds on the circle.
   • Subtract the smaller number from the greater one.
   • Ask a friend to do the same.
   • Whose difference is smaller?
   • Record all your work.

   Circle sections: 4.01, 1.21, 3.09, 3.9, 4.5, 5.0, 2.3, 2.17

5. The table below gives the scores of the participants of a quiz competition. Study the table and answer the questions below.

Names	Points
Arpita	99.52 points
Jagriti	80.2 points
Edmond	80.5 points
Akeel	99.25 points

   (a) Arrange the names in order. Starting from the winner.
   (b) How many more points did the winner get than the person who was last?
   (c) How many points less did Edmond get than Akeel?

6. Application in real life. Use addition or subtraction to solve.

   (a) Akshit's father drove 158.3 km on Monday and 79.8 km on Tuesday. How many kilometres less did he drive on Tuesday?

   (b) A bean plant measured 8.5 cm on Friday. It grew another 0.75 cm on Saturday. What was its height on Saturday?

   (c) The thickness of one book is 3.8 cm. The thickness of another is 2.03 cm. What is the thickness of the two books together when placed one on top of the other?

   (d) Shanay can swim the 100 m lap in 68.1 seconds. Swapneel can swim the same distance in 68.02 seconds. Who is faster? How much faster?

Chapter Check-Up

1. Express as a decimal.

   (a) $\dfrac{73}{1000}$ = _____   (b) $\dfrac{9}{1000}$ = _____   (c) $\dfrac{462}{10000}$ = _____

2. Express as a decimal.

   (a) Three thousandths: _____
   (b) One and fourteen hundredths: _____
   (c) Two hundred thirty-eight thousandths: _____

3. Express in words.

   (a) 0.095: _____   (b) 0.101: _____   (c) 1.43: _____

4. Compare using >, < or =

   (a) 40.9 ◯ 4.09

   (b) 3.84 ◯ 3.08

   (c) 0.78 ◯ 0.718

   (d) 0.6 ◯ 0.600

5. Solve.

   (a) 5.2 + 3.67   (b) 16.95 + 12   (c) 0.95 + 1.6   (d) 18.99 + 3.1
   (e) 3 − 1.1   (f) 28.1 − 16.25   (g) 40 − 13.25   (h) 18.93 − 9.64

6. (a) Smriti, Saroj and Shamim were comparing their test marks. They got 15.05, 15.25 and 15.5 marks respectively. Who did the best?
   (b) Pranay has travelled 62.5 km so far. How much farther does he have to ride to reach 100 km?

   (c) Ananth and Gurpreet were on the school quiz team. Ananth scored 32.5 points and Gurpreet scored 36.75 points. How much did the team make?

Keeping in Touch

Solve:

(a) $3\dfrac{2}{3} + 1\dfrac{5}{7}$ (b) $3\dfrac{2}{3} - 1\dfrac{5}{7}$ (c) $9 - 1\dfrac{1}{9}$

More About Decimals

Multiplication of Decimals

Multiplication of Whole Number by Decimal

These pictures will help you understand how to multiply decimals.

(a) **4 × 0.2 = ?**

4 groups of 2 tenths = ?

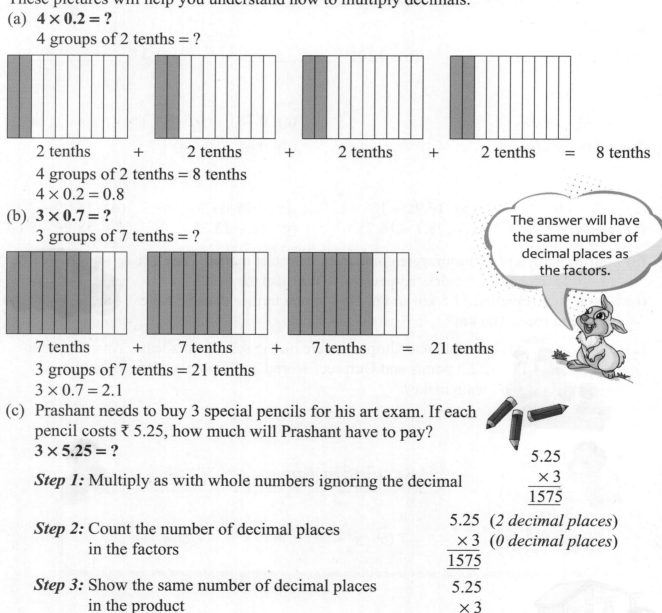

2 tenths + 2 tenths + 2 tenths + 2 tenths = 8 tenths

4 groups of 2 tenths = 8 tenths

4 × 0.2 = 0.8

(b) **3 × 0.7 = ?**

3 groups of 7 tenths = ?

7 tenths + 7 tenths + 7 tenths = 21 tenths

3 groups of 7 tenths = 21 tenths

3 × 0.7 = 2.1

> The answer will have the same number of decimal places as the factors.

(c) Prashant needs to buy 3 special pencils for his art exam. If each pencil costs ₹ 5.25, how much will Prashant have to pay?

3 × 5.25 = ?

Step 1: Multiply as with whole numbers ignoring the decimal

$$\begin{array}{r} 5.25 \\ \times\, 3 \\ \hline 1575 \end{array}$$

Step 2: Count the number of decimal places in the factors

$$\begin{array}{r} 5.25 \ \textit{(2 decimal places)} \\ \times\, 3 \ \textit{(0 decimal places)} \\ \hline 1575 \end{array}$$

Step 3: Show the same number of decimal places in the product

$$\begin{array}{r} 5.25 \\ \times\, 3 \\ \hline 15.75 \ \textit{(2 + 0 = 2 decimal places)} \end{array}$$

Answer: Prashant has to pay ₹ 15.75.

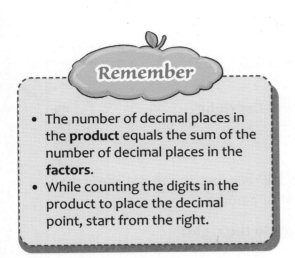
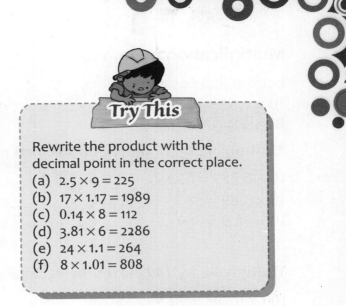
Zeros in the Product

(a) **$0.02 \times 3 = ?$**

Step 1: Multiply as you would with whole numbers

$$\begin{array}{r} 0.0\,2 \\ \times\ 3 \\ \hline 6 \end{array}$$

Answer: $0.02 \times 3 = 0.06$

Step 2: Write the decimal point

$$\begin{array}{r} 0.0\,2 \\ \times\ 3 \\ \hline 0.0\,6 \end{array}$$

This zero shows that the product is less than 1

Write this zero to show the correct number of decimal places

(b) **$0.05 \times 6 = ?$**

$$\begin{array}{r} 0.0\,5 \\ \times\ 6 \\ \hline 3\,0 \end{array} \longrightarrow \begin{array}{r} 0.0\,5 \\ \times\ 6 \\ \hline 0.3\,0 \end{array}$$ or 0.3 as zero at the end of a decimal has no value

Answer: $0.05 \times 6 = 0.30$

30 hundredths is the same as 3 tenths.

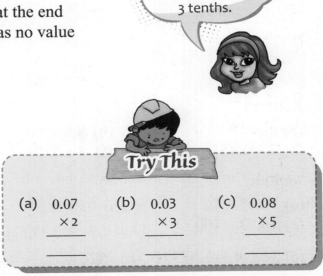

Common Mistake

$$\begin{array}{r} 0.02 \\ \times\ 4 \\ \hline 0.80 \end{array} \ ✗ \qquad \begin{array}{r} 0.02 \\ \times\ 4 \\ \hline 0.08 \end{array} \ ✓$$

Try This

(a) $\begin{array}{r} 0.07 \\ \times\ 2 \\ \hline \ \end{array}$ (b) $\begin{array}{r} 0.03 \\ \times\ 3 \\ \hline \ \end{array}$ (c) $\begin{array}{r} 0.08 \\ \times\ 5 \\ \hline \ \end{array}$

Multiplication by 10, 100, 1000

Look at these examples.

$10 \times 5.623 = 56.23$ $100 \times 5.623 = 562.3$ $1000 \times 5.623 = 5623$

What do you observe?

> Look for a pattern. Watch the decimal points.

Multiplying by *10* moves the decimal point *one* place to the right:

$10 \times 0.389 = 03.89$ 0.389

$10 \times 3.89 = 38.9$ 3.89

$10 \times 38.9 = 389$ $38.9 \longrightarrow$ 389. is written as 389 because we do not show the decimal at the end of a number

Multiplying by *100* moves the decimal point *two* places to the right:

$100 \times 0.795 = 79.5$ 0.795

$100 \times 7.95 = 795$ 7.95

$100 \times 79.5 = 7950$ $79.50 \longleftarrow$ extra zero

Multiplying by *1000* moves the decimal point *three* places to the right:

$1000 \times 1.987 = 1987$ 1.987

$1000 \times 19.87 = 19870$ $19.870 \longleftarrow$ extra zero

$1000 \times 1.9 = 1900$ $1.900 \longleftarrow$ two extra zeros

Exercise 8.1

1. Multiply only the first in the series. Then use the rules of decimals to fill in the rest.

   (a) 127×8 12.7×8 1.27×8

   (b) 312×5 312×0.5 312×0.05

2. Multiply.
   (a) 5.3×9 (b) 8.4×11 (c) 24×0.9 (d) 1.9×68
   (e) 2×3.45 (f) 7×8.39 (g) 0.04×5 (h) 0.03×2

3. Multiply.
   (a) 28.25×10 (b) 0.81×10 (c) 1.23×10 (d) 1.1×100
   (e) 16.73×100 (f) 3.19×100 (g) 0.14×1000 (h) 0.8×1000

4. (a) $32.1 \times \underline{\quad} = 321$ (b) $15.26 \times \underline{\quad} = 152.6$ (c) $0.03 \times \underline{\quad} = 3$ (d) $2.834 \times \underline{\quad} = 2834$
   (e) $1.86 \times \underline{\quad} = 18.6$ (f) $1.75 \times \underline{\quad} = 175$ (g) $0.18 \times \underline{\quad} = 18$ (h) $15.26 \times \underline{\quad} = 15260$

Division in Decimal Numbers

Dividing by Whole Numbers

VB(a) When paper is needed in large quantities, it can be bought in kilograms. Three friends bought 4.35 kg of paper to make paper bags which they wanted to use instead of plastic bags. How did they share it among themselves?

4.35 ÷ 3 = ? *(divisor smaller than dividend)*

Dividing by decimals is just like dividing whole numbers, except for placing the decimal point.

> Place decimal point directly above the decimal in the dividend.

$$3 \overline{\smash{)}\, 4\overset{\cdot}{.}35}$$

Step 1: Place the **decimal point in the quotient** directly above the decimal point.

Step 2: Then **divide** as if you were dividing whole numbers.

Divide the ones	Divide the tenths	Divide the hundredths

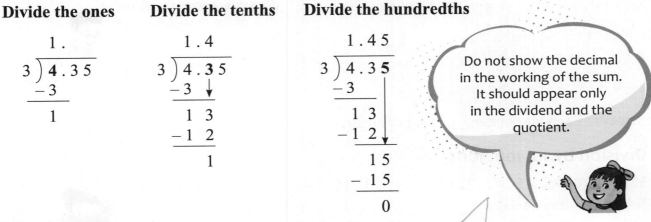

> Do not show the decimal in the working of the sum. It should appear only in the dividend and the quotient.

4.35 ÷ 3 = 1.45
Answer: Each friend gets 1.45 kg of paper to make paper bags.

(b) 1.33 ÷ 7 = ? *(divisor greater than dividend)*

$$7\overline{\smash{)}\,1\overset{\cdot}{.}33} \longrightarrow 7\overline{\smash{)}\,\overset{0.}{1.33}} \longrightarrow 7\overline{\smash{)}\,\overset{0.19}{1.33}}$$

$$\begin{array}{r} -7\downarrow \\ \hline 63 \\ -63 \\ \hline 0 \end{array}$$

Check:
$$\begin{array}{r} 0.19 \\ \times 7 \\ \hline 1.33 \end{array}$$

(Divisor × Quotient = Dividend)

Answer: 0.19

Try This

(a) $5\overline{)6.15}$

(b) $4\overline{)2.36}$

(c) $3\overline{)0.36}$

(d) $2\overline{)4.18}$

(e) $6\overline{)2.40}$

115

Remainders while Dividing Decimals

(a) Mrs Khandelwal had bought 3.5 kg of sugar. She puts the sugar equally into 2 jars. How much sugar did she put in each jar?

3.5 ÷ 2 = ?

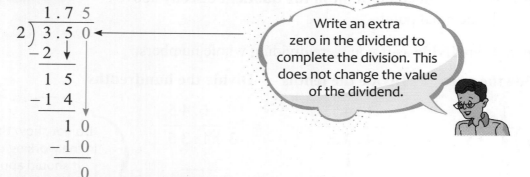

```
        1 . 7
  2 ) 3 . 5
     − 2 ↓
       1 5
       1 4
         1  ←——— Remainder
```

When you divide decimals, you **do not show remainders**. You have to **write extra zeros to complete the division.**

```
        1 . 7 5
  2 ) 3 . 5 0  ←
     − 2 ↓
       1 5 ↓
     − 1 4 ↓
         1 0
       − 1 0
           0
```

Write an extra zero in the dividend to complete the division. This does not change the value of the dividend.

Answer: Each jar contains 1.75 kg of sugar.

Division by 10, 100, 1000

321.5 ÷ 10 = 32.15   321.5 ÷ 100 = 3.215   321.5 ÷ 1000 = 0.3215

What do you observe?

The decimal point moves to the **left** as many places as there are zeros.

When dividing by	the decimal point moves to the left by
10	1 decimal place
100	2 decimal places
1000	3 decimal places

(a) 4 ÷ 10 is the same as 4.0 ÷ 10.
So 4 ÷ 10 = 0.4
(b) 2.35 ÷ 100 = 0.0235
extra zero
(c) 8 ÷ 1000 = 0.008
two extra zeros

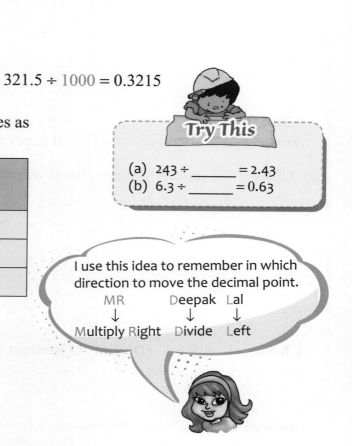

Try This

(a) 243 ÷ _____ = 2.43
(b) 6.3 ÷ _____ = 0.63

I use this idea to remember in which direction to move the decimal point.

MR	Deepak	Lal
↓	↓	↓
Multiply Right	Divide	Left

Exercise 8.2

1. Place the decimal points correctly in these quotients.

   (a)
   $$\begin{array}{r} 0\ \ 0\ 6 \\ 8\overline{)0\,.\,4\,8} \end{array}$$

   (b)
   $$\begin{array}{r} 1\ 2\ 4 \\ 4\overline{)4\,9\,.\,6} \end{array}$$

   (c)
   $$\begin{array}{r} 0\ \ 0\ 5 \\ 7\overline{)0\,.\,3\,5} \end{array}$$

   (d)
   $$\begin{array}{r} 0\ 3\ 4 \\ 8\overline{)2\,7\,.\,2} \end{array}$$

2. Divide. Check your answer with multiplication.

   (a) $82.17 \div 9$ (b) $0.65 \div 5$ (c) $272.22 \div 6$ (d) $168.6 \div 3$
   (e) $17.73 \div 3$ (f) $1.80 \div 5$ (g) $27.54 \div 9$ (h) $4.8 \div 12$

3. Divide until the remainder is zero.

   (a) $90.3 \div 6$ (b) $17.2 \div 8$ (c) $3.1 \div 4$ (d) $9.15 \div 2$
   (e) $7.4 \div 4$ (f) $5.2 \div 8$ (g) $2.67 \div 5$ (h) $18.9 \div 2$

4. Divide.

   (a) $42.8 \div 10$ (b) $725 \div 10$ (c) $0.9 \div 10$ (d) $2.56 \div 1000$
       $42.8 \div 100$ $725 \div 100$ $9 \div 100$ $25.6 \div 1000$

5. Fill in the blanks.

   (a) $0.6 \div \underline{\hspace{1cm}} = 0.06$ (b) $68.14 \div \underline{\hspace{1cm}} = 0.6814$ (c) $31.6 \div \underline{\hspace{1cm}} = 3.16$
   (d) $0.91 \div \underline{\hspace{1cm}} = 0.091$ (e) $7 \div \underline{\hspace{1cm}} = 0.007$ (f) $1.1 \div \underline{\hspace{1cm}} = .011$

6. Application in real life. Solve using multiplication or division.

   (a) On a hiking trip, the hikers needed 1.75 litres of water each day. If the trip lasted 10 days how many litres of water did they carry?

   (b) The Koshy family was visiting Delhi. They rode 11.5 km a day for 3 days in the city. How many kilometres did they travel?

   (c) Mr Shah bought 1.76 m of wire and cut it into 8 equal pieces. What was the length of each piece of wire?

   (d) The total weight of 9 identical gold rings is 40.5g. What is the weight of each ring?

Project

Students from the class who live in different areas should find the price of a kilogram of potatoes, onions and tomatoes in their area. They should also find out whether it is cheaper to buy a larger quantity. How much would it cost then? Pairs of students compare the prices per kilogram. What is the saving per kilogram?

Decimals and Money

1 rupee = 100 paise

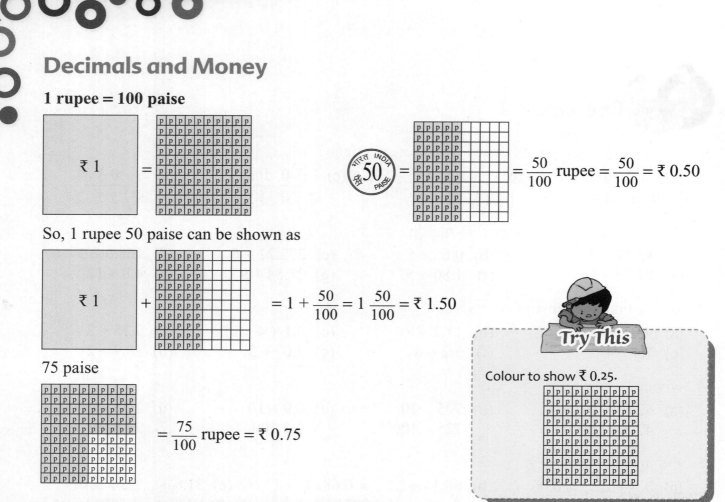

So, 1 rupee 50 paise can be shown as

$$= 1 + \frac{50}{100} = 1\frac{50}{100} = ₹\,1.50$$

75 paise

$$= \frac{75}{100} \text{ rupee} = ₹\,0.75$$

Try This

Colour to show ₹ 0.25.

Multiplying and Dividing with Money

Unitary Method

(a)

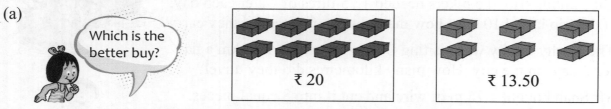

Which is the better buy?

₹ 20   ₹ 13.50

To find out compare the price of one blue eraser to the price of one pink eraser.

Price of one blue eraser: ₹ 20 ÷ 8 = ?

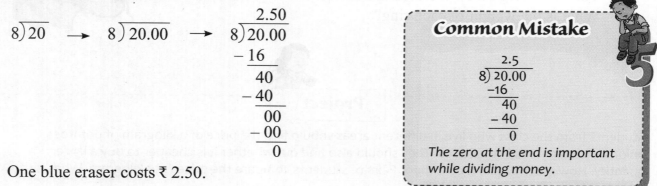

$$8)\overline{20} \rightarrow 8)\overline{20.00} \rightarrow \begin{array}{r} 2.50 \\ 8)\overline{20.00} \\ -16 \\ \hline 40 \\ -40 \\ \hline 00 \\ -00 \\ \hline 0 \end{array}$$

One blue eraser costs ₹ 2.50.

Common Mistake

$$\begin{array}{r} 2.5 \\ 8)\overline{20.00} \\ -16 \\ \hline 40 \\ -40 \\ \hline 0 \end{array}$$

The zero at the end is important while dividing money.

Price of one pink eraser: ₹ 13.50 ÷ 6 = ?

```
         2.25
    6 ) 13.50
      − 12
       ─────
         15
       − 12
       ─────
         30
         30
       ─────
          0
```

→ One pink eraser costs ₹ 2.25

Answer: The box of pink erasers is the better buy because one pink eraser is cheaper than one blue eraser.

Finding the 'price of one' is called finding the unit price for which we use the unitary method.

(b)

How much will I have to pay for 10 pencils?

₹ 2.25

To find out how much 10 pencils will cost, you have to first find out the price of one pencil.

```
        0.75
   3 ) 2.25
     − 2 1
      ─────
        15
      − 15
      ─────
        00
```

One pencil costs ₹ 0.75.

Multiply like you normally multiply decimals.

Now find out the cost of 10 pencils by multiplying.
₹ 0.75 × 10 = ₹ 7.50
Answer: 10 pencils will cost ₹ 7.50.

Project

You know that like we have rupees in India, other countries have other currencies.
Find the currencies of these countries and fill in the Indian rupee equivalent.

Country	Currency	Indian rupees	Country	Currency	Indian Rupees
China	1 Yuan	₹	Russia	1	
France	1 Euro		U.K.	1	
Pakistan	1		U.S.A	1	

Exercise 8.3

1. Here are some things needed to make a model air plane and their prices.

| 3 for ₹ 16.50 | 2 for ₹ 23 | 3 for ₹ 25.50 | 1 for ₹ 12 | 5 for ₹ 76.25 |

The pictures below show how many of each item Ranbir needs. How much will it cost him?

2. This is Mrs Viswanathan's grocery bill. First find the cost of one of each item then use the information to fill up the other two bills.

Item	Quantity	Price in rupees
Toothpaste	3	85.50
Soap	4	60.00
Rice	8 kg	202.00
Wheat flour	10 kg	185.00
Washing powder	2 kg	86.00
Biscuits	6 packets	70.50
Buns	10 pieces	42.00
	Total	731.00

Item	Quantity	Price
Toothpaste	2	
Rice	5 kg	
Wheat flour	5 kg	
Biscuits	3 packets	
	Total	

Item	Quantity	Price
Soap	2	
Rice	10 kg	
Washing powder	1 kg	
Biscuits	5 packets	
Buns	6 pieces	
	Total	

Chapter Check-Up

1. Multiply.

    (a) $\begin{array}{r} 2.3 \\ \times\ 7 \\ \hline \end{array}$ (b) $\begin{array}{r} 7.92 \\ \times\ 8 \\ \hline \end{array}$ (c) $\begin{array}{r} 0.05 \\ \times\ 4 \\ \hline \end{array}$ (d) $\begin{array}{r} 0.04 \\ \times\ 2 \\ \hline \end{array}$

2. Divide.

    (a) $9.25 \div 5$ (b) $8.79 \div 3$ (c) $39.96 \div 6$ (d) $40.5 \div 9$

3. Multiply or divide.

    (a) 5.76×10 (b) $8.3 \div 10$ (c) 0.9×10 (d) $3.6 \div 1000$

    (e) 53.1×100 (f) $62 \div 100$ (g) 2.8×100 (h) $114 \div 1000$

4. Solve using addition, subtraction, multiplication or division.

    (a) 9 ice creams cost ₹ 67.50. What will 10 ice creams cost?

    (b) 6 kg of grapes cost ₹ 195. How much will 17 kg cost?

    (c) 3 kg of peanuts cost ₹ 76.50. How much will 1 kg cost?

    (d) Mrs Swaroop bought 6.25 m of dress material for her older daughter and 5.75 m for the younger one. How many metres of dress material did Mrs Swaroop buy?

    (e) An adult's toothbrush is 15.5 cm long and a child's toothbrush is 13.7 cm long. How much longer is an adult's toothbrush?

Keeping in Touch

Solve:

(a) $3 \times \frac{7}{9}$ (b) $7 \times \frac{2}{3}$ (c) $\frac{4}{5} \times 3$

(d) $8 \div \frac{1}{3}$ (e) $\frac{9}{11} \div \frac{6}{7}$ (f) $\frac{6}{11} \div 3$

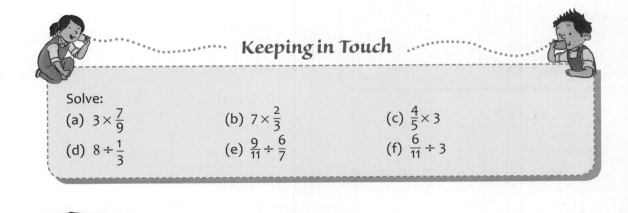

Mental Maths

Learn

To find 5.2×3

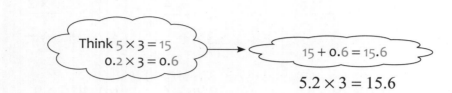

Think $5 \times 3 = 15$
$0.2 \times 3 = 0.6$

$15 + 0.6 = 15.6$

$5.2 \times 3 = 15.6$

Practice

(a) 4.3×2 (b) 9.2×2 (c) 5.2×4 (d) 3.3×3 (e) 4.2×3 (f) 8.1×3

Use

1. $52 \div 1000 = $ _____

2. $6 - \dfrac{1}{3} = $ _____

3. $17.31 \times $ _____ $= 173.1$

4. $8\dfrac{1}{4} + \dfrac{3}{4} = $ _____

5. $13.5 + 1.5 = $ _____

6. $789 + 211 = $ _____

7. $60.06 \;\boxed{}\; 60.6$ (Use >, < or =)

8. $5000 \times 50 = $ _____

9. $10 - 2.9 = $ _____

10. _____ $\times 50 = 2500$

11. $4 - 0.9 = $ _____

12. $1.1 \times 4 \;\bigcirc\; 4.4 \times 1$ (Use >, < or =)

13. $6 - 1.9 = $ _____

14. $\dfrac{2}{5}$ of $45 = $ _____

15. $0.5 \div $ _____ $= 0.05$

16. $699 + 51 = $ _____

17. $8.4 + 1.6 = $ _____

18. $\dfrac{4}{7} = \dfrac{28}{\boxed{}}$

19. $9 \div $ _____ $= 0.09$

20. $1.2 \times 100 = $ _____

Test Your Skills

(For Chapters 5, 6, 7, 8)

1. Solve.

   (a) $2\frac{3}{7}+1\frac{2}{5}$ (b) $\frac{6}{11}\times2$ (c) $\frac{8}{9}\times\frac{3}{5}$ (d) $18\div\frac{3}{4}$ (e) $\frac{4}{5}\div\frac{1}{2}$

2. Solve.

   (a) $9.05+3.8$ (b) $10-6.38$ (c) 5.3×6 (d) $8.25\div3$ (e) $3\div100$

3. (a) Anisha jogged $1\frac{3}{4}$ km and walked $2\frac{2}{3}$ km. How far did she go?

   (b) It takes Pradeep $\frac{1}{4}$ of an hour to wash one car. How long will it take him to wash 8 cars?

   (c) Half a dozen friendship bands cost ₹ 79.50. How much will 10 bands cost?

4. Fill in the blanks:

   (a) $2.2\div$ _____ $= 0.22$

   (b) $0.14\times100=$ _____

   (c) Decimals having different number of decimal places are called _____ decimals.

   (d) $\frac{18}{63}$ in its lowest term is _____.

   (e) Two numbers whose product is 1 are called _____.

5. (✓) the correct answer.

(a) The LCM of 3, 7, 14 is	(b) Equivalent fraction of $\frac{3}{5}$ is	(c) Write the next three in the sequence 1.6, 1.7, 1.8
(i) 28	(i) $\frac{5}{7}$	(i) 1.9, 1.10, 1.11
(ii) 42	(ii) $\frac{9}{25}$	(ii) 1.9, 2.0, 2.1
(iii) 14	(iii) $\frac{12}{20}$	(iii) 1.9, 1.01, 1.02
(iv) 294	(iv) $\frac{5}{3}$	(iv) 1.9, 1.19, 1.119

Shapes, Patterns and Nets

Looking Back

1. Ring the shapes that do not have symmetry.

2. Draw the line of symmetry for these shapes.

3. Complete the pattern in each of the following.

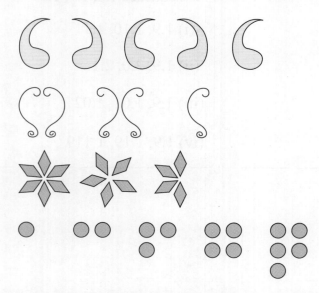

Symmetry

Line of Symmetry

The Charminar in Hyderabad is a symmetrical monument because one half is a **reflection** of the other half.

This image has one line of symmetry.

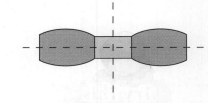

This image has two lines of symmetry.

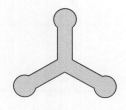

How many lines of symmetry can you find in this image?

The dotted lines here are not lines of symmetry.

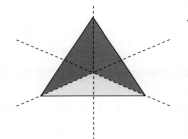

The shape alone does not give symmetry. The details within the shape also decide whether the shape is symmetrical or not.

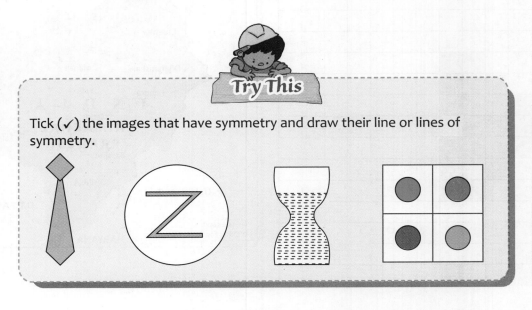

Try This

Tick (✓) the images that have symmetry and draw their line or lines of symmetry.

The line of symmetry shows where the shape has been reflected.
You can take any shape drawn on a piece of paper and make it a symmetrical shape with the help of a mirror.

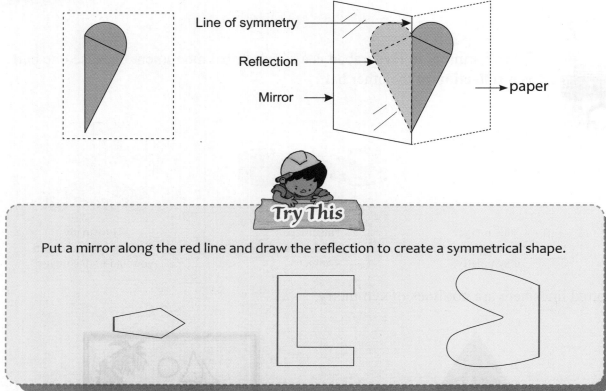

Line of symmetry

Reflection

Mirror

paper

Try This

Put a mirror along the red line and draw the reflection to create a symmetrical shape.

Kullu Valley in Himachal Pradesh is famous for its woollen shawls with traditional border designs. Colour the other half of this square by reflecting the design to make a basic Kullu shawl border pattern.

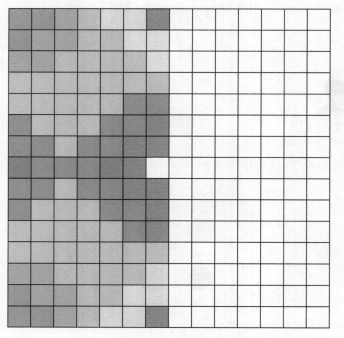

126

Exercise 9.1

1. Draw the lines of symmetry for these shapes.

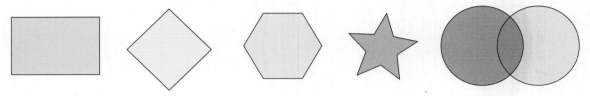

2. Look at these flags and say whether they have 0, 1 or 2 lines of symmetry.

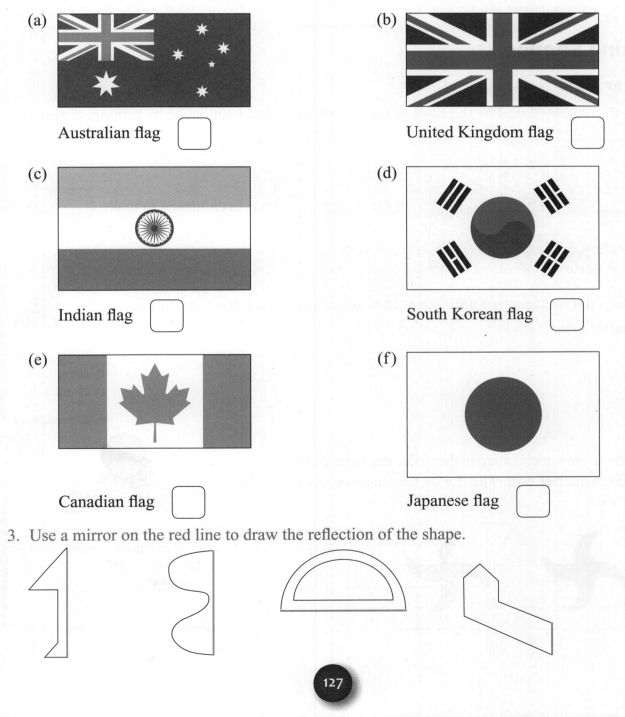

(a) Australian flag ☐

(b) United Kingdom flag ☐

(c) Indian flag ☐

(d) South Korean flag ☐

(e) Canadian flag ☐

(f) Japanese flag ☐

3. Use a mirror on the red line to draw the reflection of the shape.

4. Traditionally, people decorate eggs for the festival of Easter. Draw a design on one side of the egg and use a mirror on the line of symmetry to copy the reflection on the other side. One has been partly done for you.

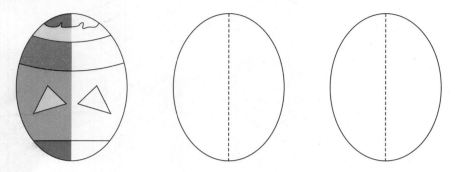

Turning Shapes

Quarter Turn

This design can be found on the floor of the Taj Mahal. It has been made by turning shapes.

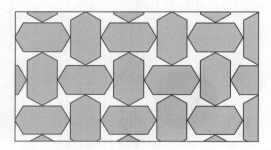

In the design,  has been turned to make .

If we put a dot on the shape and then turn it, we can see that it has been turned $\frac{1}{4}$ or quarter turn.

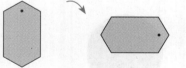

Quarter turn
or $\frac{1}{4}$ turn

There are some special shapes that look the same even if we give them a quarter turn. The dot on the shape below will help you see that.

Try This

Tick the shape that will look the same after a quarter turn.

(a)   (b)

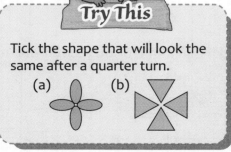

128

Complete this pattern using quarter turns.
The first quarter turn has been outlined for you.

Create a simple pattern of your own using the same idea.

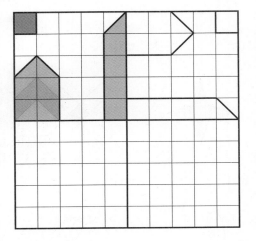

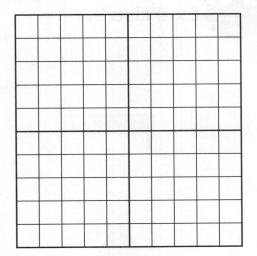

Half Turn

Some shapes look the same after a half turn.
Look at this design.

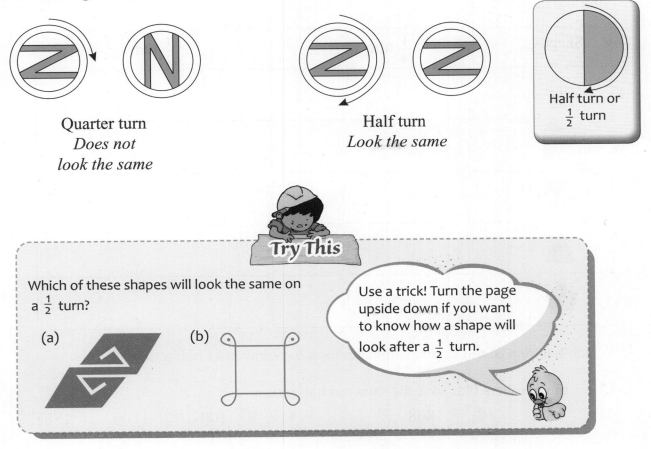

Quarter turn
*Does not
look the same*

Half turn
Look the same

Half turn or
$\frac{1}{2}$ turn

Try This

Which of these shapes will look the same on a $\frac{1}{2}$ turn?

(a)

(b)

Use a trick! Turn the page upside down if you want to know how a shape will look after a $\frac{1}{2}$ turn.

Exercise 9.2

1. Which of these shapes will look the same after $\frac{1}{4}$ turn? Put a tick mark (✓) next to it.

2. Which of these shapes will look the same after $\frac{1}{2}$ turn? Put a tick mark (✓) next to it.

3. Draw how these shapes will look after these turns. Tick (✓) those which look the same after the turn.

Shapes	$\frac{1}{4}$ turn	$\frac{1}{2}$ turn
▯		
▪		
●		
▲		
⬠		

4. Which 6 letters of the English alphabet look the same after half a turn?

5. Circle the numbers that look the same on half a turn.

11,   88,   18,   808,   118,   818,   1001,   1100,   1881

6. Which is the largest 4-digit number you can make that will look the same on a $\frac{1}{2}$ turn? Which is the smallest?

7. Change the shape so that the new shape looks the same on a $\frac{1}{2}$ turn. The first one has been done for you.

(a)

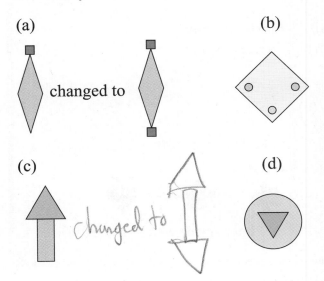

changed to

(b)

(c)

changed to

(d)

Project

Many crosswords have the same shape when turned. Go through newspapers to find such crosswords and paste them in your notebook in columns. Show how many turns they need to come back to their original position. Ignore those that need a full turn.

Creating Patterns

This pattern has been created by repeating the same design over and over again without any change.

If we take the basic design and rotate it by $\frac{1}{2}$ turn,

we can create a new pattern by repeating the two designs.

What happens when we repeat a basic design with a $\frac{1}{4}$ turn every time?

I. Use this basic design
- Create a pattern by repeating the design
- Create a new pattern by rotating the design by $\frac{1}{2}$ turn every time.
- Create another pattern by turning the design by $\frac{1}{2}$ turn every time.

II. Spot the pattern and continue.

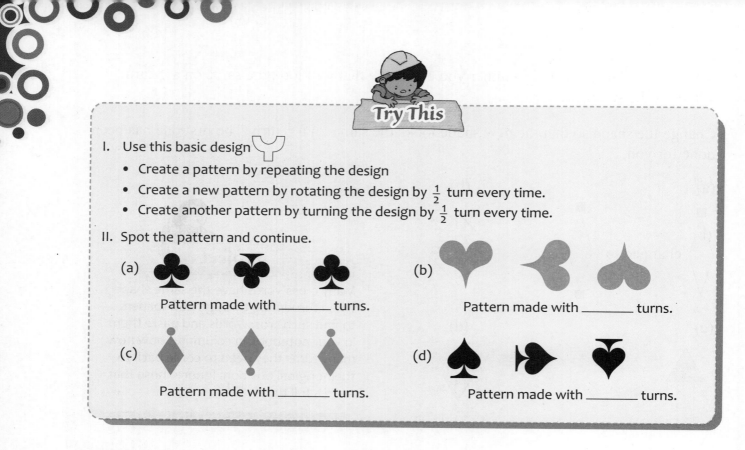

(a)

Pattern made with _____ turns.

(b)

Pattern made with _____ turns.

(c)

Pattern made with _____ turns.

(d)

Pattern made with _____ turns.

Exercise 9.3

1. Use the designs shown below and create three sets of patterns for each as mentioned with the help of tracing paper in your notebooks.

(a)   (b)   (c)

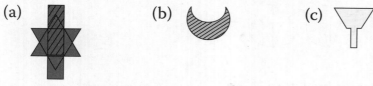

(i) Repeat the design.

(ii) Repeat by giving a $\frac{1}{2}$ turn every time.

(iii) Repeat by giving a $\frac{1}{4}$ turn every time.

2. These patterns have been made by moving the designs anti-clockwise. What will come next?

(a)

(b)

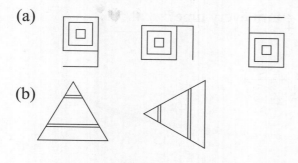

(c)

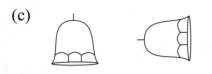

3. Circle the design that breaks the pattern and then set it right.

(a)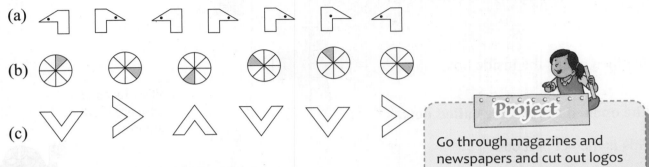

(b)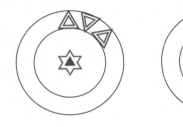

(c)

4. Complete the designs on the plates.

Challenge

This set has 4 playing cards kept in a row.

One card has been rotated at $\frac{1}{2}$ turn in this set.

Which card has been turned?

Nets

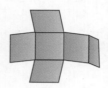

Ashima has an empty box.

She opens the outer cover carefully.

She then opens the inside box.

The opened shapes are called nets.

This is the net of a cube.

This net has _____ squares.

This net can also be folded back to make a cube.

All six faces of a cube are identical squares.

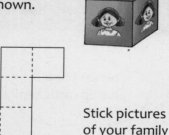

Project

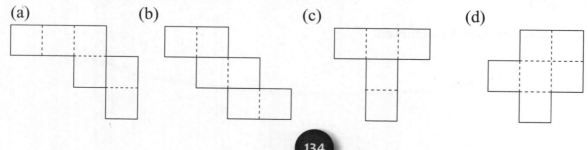

Cut out a square piece of card paper with sides of 10 cm. Copy the net below by outlining the square six times as shown. The sides should touch. Cut out the whole shape.

Fold along the dotted lines. Seal the cube with the help of a cello tape.

Stick pictures of your family and friends on each side.

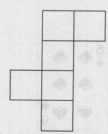

Exercise 9.4

1. Which of these nets can be folded to make cubes?

(a)   (b)   (c)   (d)

2. Match the shape to its net.

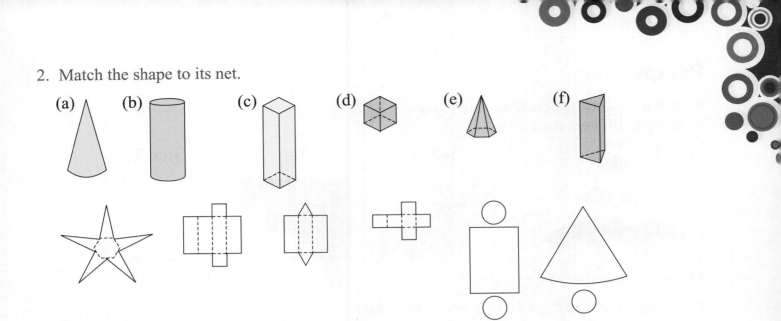

Drawing Cubes and Cuboids

You can use special dotted paper called isometric dot paper to help you draw solid shapes like cubes and cuboids.

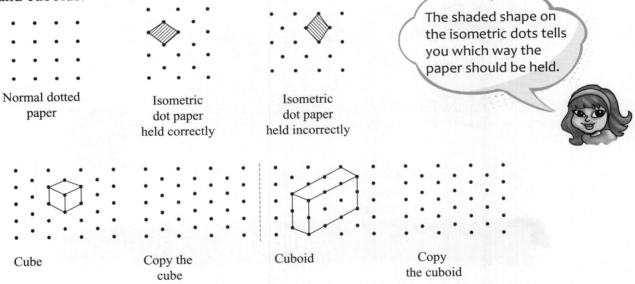

Normal dotted paper

Isometric dot paper held correctly

Isometric dot paper held incorrectly

The shaded shape on the isometric dots tells you which way the paper should be held.

Cube

Copy the cube

Cuboid

Copy the cuboid

Complete the following figures to make cuboids.

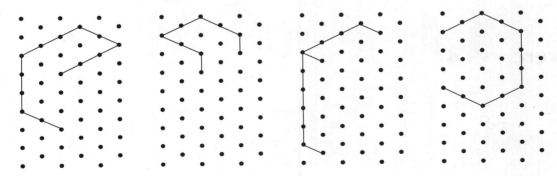

Perspective

Shapes often look different when you view them from different directions.

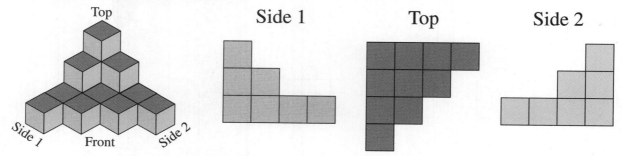

Top   Side 1   Top   Side 2

Side 1   Front   Side 2

The picture on the left gives the front view of the shape.
The adjacent pictures show the other views.

Colour to match the view of each shape.

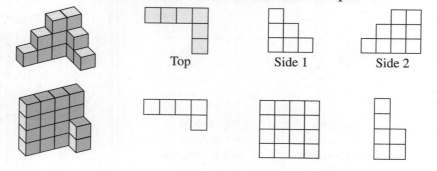

Top   Side 1   Side 2

Challenge

Match the houses to their floor plans by colouring them the same colour.

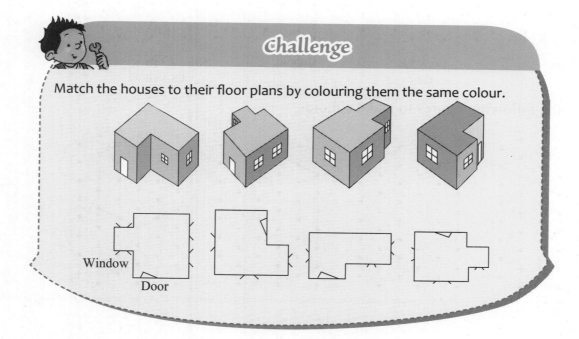

Window

Door

Chapter Check-Up

1. Which of these are lines of symmetry?

   (a)   (b)   (c)   (d)   (e)   (f)

2. Decide which need $\frac{1}{2}$ turn and $\frac{1}{4}$ turn to come back to their original shape.

   (a)   (b)   (c)   (d)   (e)   (f)

3. Complete the pattern till it comes back to its original position.

   (a)   (b)

4. Complete the cuboids.

5. Which of these nets can be made into cubes?

   (a)   (b)   (c)   (d)

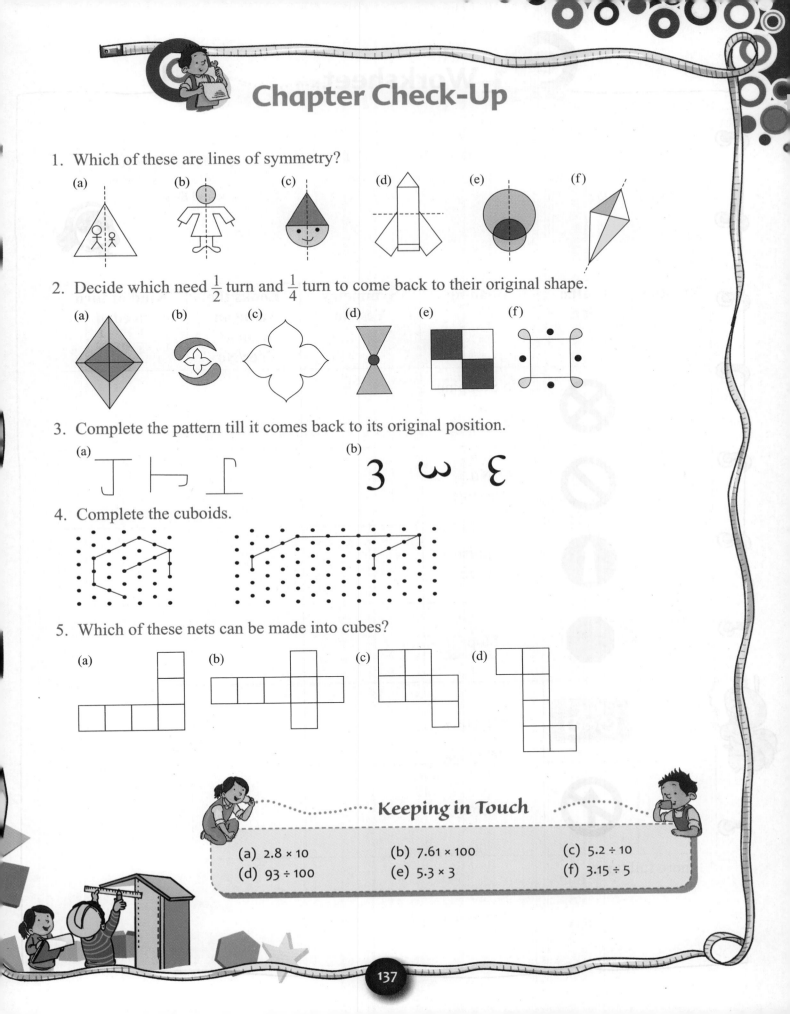

······· **Keeping in Touch** ·······

(a) 2.8 × 10   (b) 7.61 × 100   (c) 5.2 ÷ 10

(d) 93 ÷ 100   (e) 5.3 × 3   (f) 3.15 ÷ 5

This worksheet integrates Maths and EVS.

Number	Traffic sign	Meaning	Symmetry Yes/No	Looks the same on a turn* Yes/No	Kind of turn needed $\frac{1}{4}$ or $\frac{1}{2}$
(a)		No Stopping or Standing			
(b)		No Parking			
(c)		Compulsory Ahead			
(d)		Stop			
(e)		Cycle Track			
(f)		No Entry			

* Ignore full turns.

Maths Lab Activity

Objective: To reinforce the concept of rotation.

Materials Required: Map of India, tracing paper, dark pencil, plain paper

Preparation: Students work independently or in pairs.

This activity integrates Maths and Geography.

Steps:

1. The students use the map of India to trace out the shape of any state they want.

2. The student then carefully turns the tracing paper through a half or a quarter turn and creates a **rotated shape** of the state.

3. Both the students now stick the rotated shapes on a fresh sheet of paper. Then they go around asking their classmates to guess the state on their sheet. In turn they too try to name the states that the others have traced.

Try this out:

These outlines of states have been rotated. Identify them.

Geometry Basics

Recognising Angles

Put these closed shapes into two groups. Colour the shapes with straight lines in yellow and the shapes with curved lines in blue.

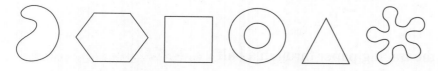

Angles

All the shapes you have coloured above in yellow are called polygons and their sides meet at corners.

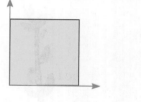 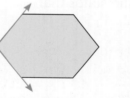

The two sides that meet at a corner form an angle.

We see angles around us all the time.

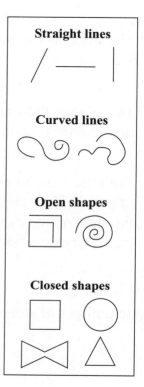

| Straight lines |
| Curved lines |
| Open shapes |
| Closed shapes |

Mark the angles that you can see in these dance forms.

Lavani   Kathak   Dandiya Rass   Bharatnatyam

Understanding Angles in Geometric Terms

To understand angles in geometric terms, we must first understand some of the following basic concepts that are also called the building blocks of geometry.

Point

A point is the basic unit of geometry. It shows an exact location.

We represent a point with the help of a dot and name it with a capital letter.

- A   This is point A.

> The tip of a pin can be taken as a physical model of a point. In reality, a point in geometry is even smaller than the tip of a pin.

Line

A line is a collection of points going endlessly in both directions along a straight path.

A line has no beginning and no end, so it has no end points. It is named by using two points on it. The symbol for a line is ⟷. The arrow heads show that the line goes on and on.

> When you stand at a seashore the horizon gives you the idea of a never-ending line.

A ———— B   Point A and Point B are two points on the line. We call it line AB and write it as $\overleftrightarrow{AB}$ or $\overleftrightarrow{BA}$.

Line segment

A line segment is part of a line. It has two endpoints. We name it by its endpoints. The symbol for a line segment is ———.

Points M and N are the two endpoints of the line segment MN. We write it as $\overline{MN}$ or $\overline{NM}$.

Ray

A ray is part of a line. It has one endpoint and goes on endlessly in one direction.

The symbol for a ray is →.

Ray PQ is written as $\overrightarrow{PQ}$.

The edge of your blackboard in class can be taken as a physical representation of a line segment. It has a definite starting point and ending point.

A beam of light from a torch in a dark room can be compared to a ray. It has a definite endpoint and goes on continuously in one direction.

Try This

Which geometrical concept does each of these remind you of?

Imagine a never ending clothes line

The tip of a needle

The rays of the sun

The edge of this book

Parts of an Angle

When two rays have a common endpoint they form an angle.

$\overrightarrow{SR}$ and $\overrightarrow{ST}$ together form an angle.
The common endpoint (S) is called the **vertex** of the angle.
SR and ST are called the **arms** of the angle.
The angle alongside is called **angle RST** or **angle TSR**.
The symbol for angle is $\angle$.
We write $\angle$**RST** or $\angle$**TSR** to name the angle.

The middle letter is always the vertex of the angle.

The plural of vertex is vertices.

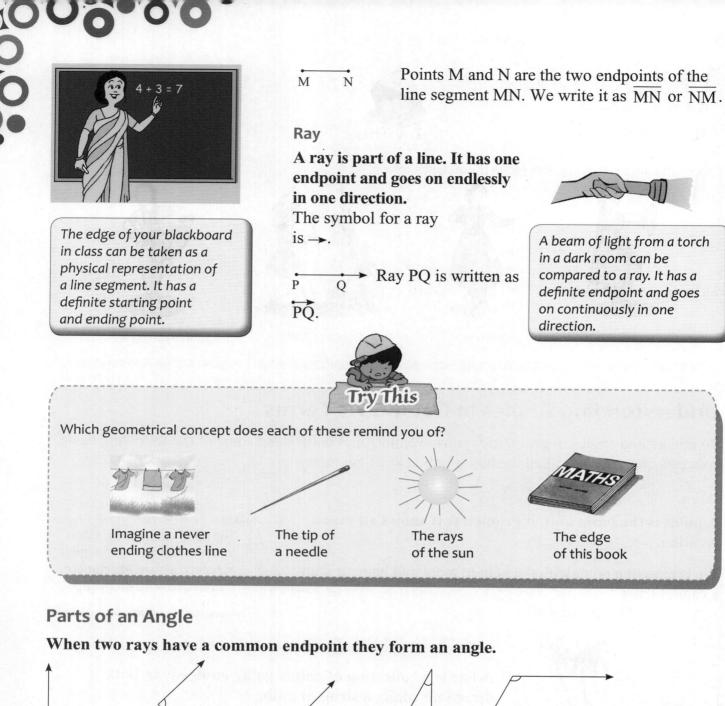

Types of Angles

Right angles

Angles that look like the corners of this page are called **right angles**.

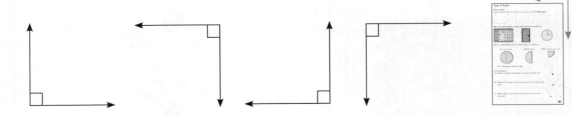

Here are some examples of right angles that we see around us.

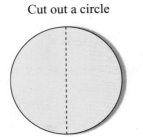

March 2014					
Monday	31	3	10	17	24
Tuesday		4	11	18	25
Wednesday		5	12	19	26
Thursday		6	13	20	27
Friday		7	14	21	28
Saturday	1	8	15	22	29
Sunday	2	9	16	23	30

Make a 'right angle tester' to find right angles around you.

Cut out a circle   Fold it in half   Fold it in half once more

Your 'right angle tester' is ready!

Use the tester to:

(a) Make a list of the right angles you can find around you.

(b) Make a list of angles that you found that are less than a right angle.

(c) Make a list of angles that you found that are more than a right angle.

How many right angles can you find in this diagram of a tennis court?

(*Hint:* The number is more than 30 but less than 50.)

Acute angles

Angles that are less than a right angle are called **acute** angles.

Here are some examples of acute angles that we see around us.

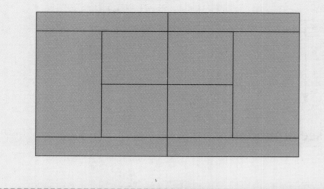

Obtuse angles

Angles that are more than a right angle are called **obtuse** angles.

Here are some examples of obtuse angles that we see around us.

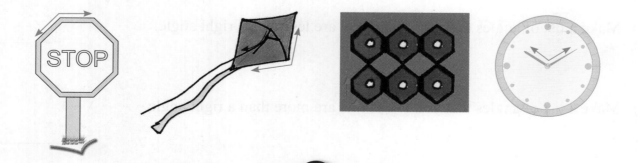

Mark the acute angles in blue and the obtuse angles in green on these pictures of yoga postures.

Straight angles

If you have two right angles next to one another, they form a **straight angle**.

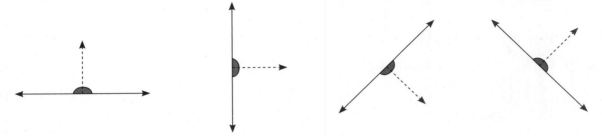

Here are some examples of straight angles that we see around us.

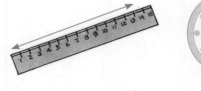

Exercise 10.1

1. In the following figures colour the right angles in red, the acute angles in blue, and the obtuse angles in green. Some are done for you.

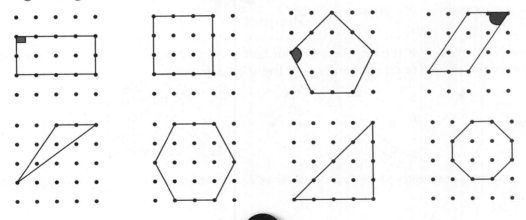

2. The pictures you see below form part of a signalling system called 'semaphore' which was used by the navy long ago. Name the angle that each signal forms.

3. Draw three examples (objects) each of acute, obtuse and right angles that you see around you.

4. Name and identify the following angles. One has been done for you.

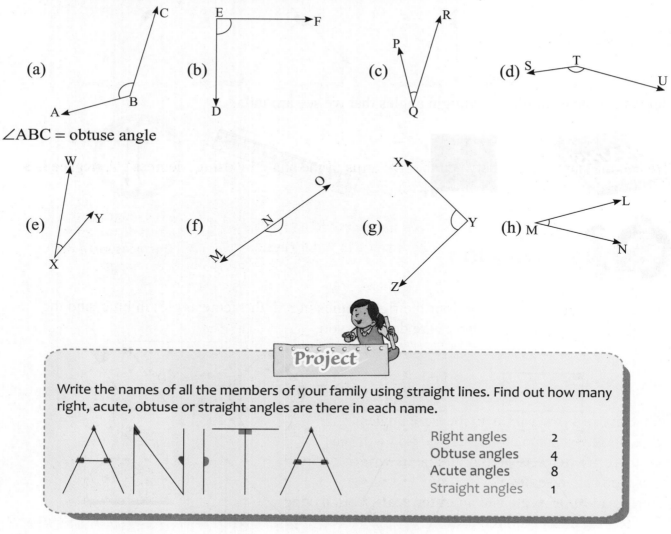

(a)

∠ABC = obtuse angle

(b)

(c)

(d)

(e)

(f)

(g)

(h)

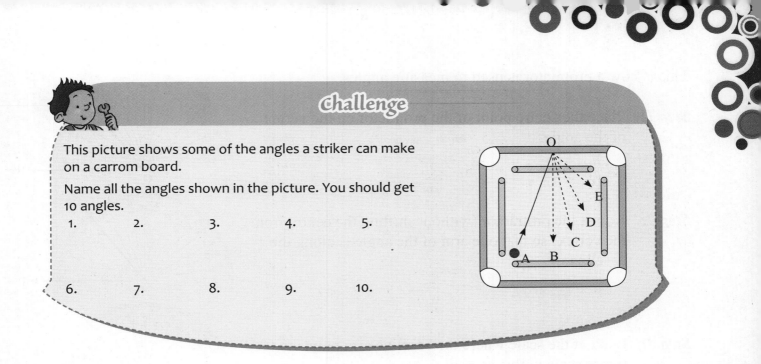

This picture shows some of the angles a striker can make on a carrom board.

Name all the angles shown in the picture. You should get 10 angles.

1.   2.   3.   4.   5.

6.   7.   8.   9.   10.

Measuring Angles

Use two pencils to represent the arms of an angle. Slowly move one pencil as shown. See how the gap between the two pencils slowly increases.

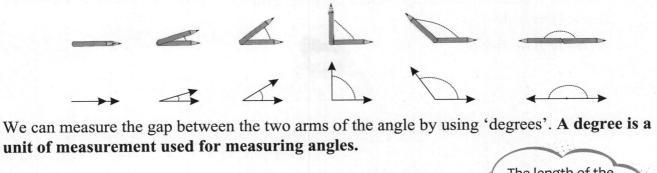

We can measure the gap between the two arms of the angle by using 'degrees'. **A degree is a unit of measurement used for measuring angles.**

B $\overset{2°}{\longrightarrow}$ A, C

We say that ∠ABC is 2°.
2° is read as 2 degrees.

The length of the arms do not affect the measure of the angle.

∠XYZ = 10°   ∠PQR = 25°   ∠LMN = 90°

You can use a **protractor** to measure angles.
If you look at a protractor carefully, you will see that there are two sets of measurements written on it. These are called **scales**.
There is an **inner scale** and an **outer scale**, both having 0° to 180° in different directions.

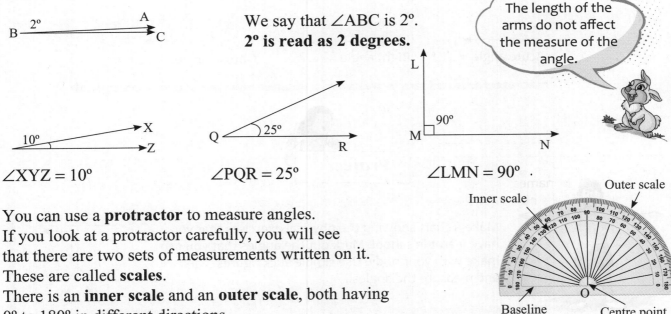

This is how a protractor is used to measure angles.

Step 1: Place the centre point of the protractor on the vertex of the angle.

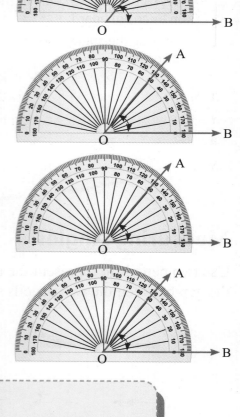

Step 2: Adjust the protractor (without shifting the centre from the vertex) so that one arm of the angle is along the baseline.

Step 3: Look at the scale where the baseline arm points to 0° (inner scale in this example).

Step 4: Read the measure of this angle where the other arm crosses the scale.

Answer: $\angle AOB = 50°$.

Try This

Use a protractor to measure these angles.

Acute angle = ____°   Right angle = ____°   Obtuse angle = ____°

Project

Make a chart showing the physical exercises that you have learnt in school. Mark out the angles that you can make with your body. Use simple stick figures and measure the angles.

Right angle

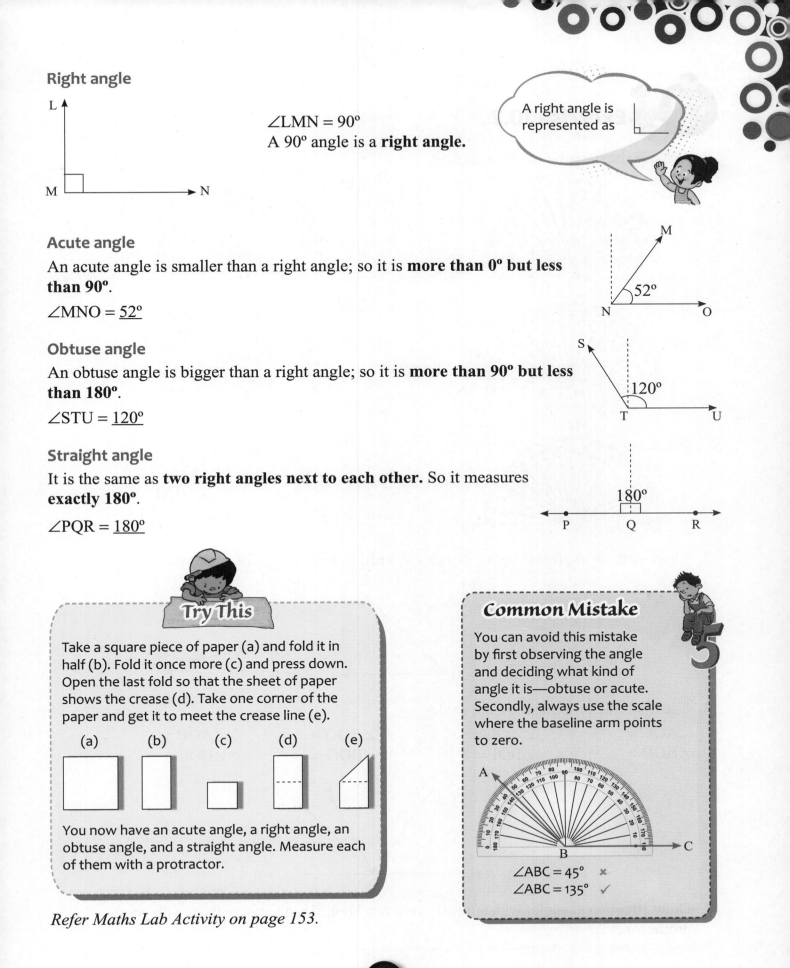

$\angle LMN = 90°$
A 90° angle is a **right angle**.

A right angle is represented as

Acute angle

An acute angle is smaller than a right angle; so it is **more than 0° but less than 90°**.

$\angle MNO = \underline{52°}$

Obtuse angle

An obtuse angle is bigger than a right angle; so it is **more than 90° but less than 180°**.

$\angle STU = \underline{120°}$

Straight angle

It is the same as **two right angles next to each other.** So it measures **exactly 180°**.

$\angle PQR = \underline{180°}$

Try This

Take a square piece of paper (a) and fold it in half (b). Fold it once more (c) and press down. Open the last fold so that the sheet of paper shows the crease (d). Take one corner of the paper and get it to meet the crease line (e).

(a)   (b)   (c)   (d)   (e)

You now have an acute angle, a right angle, an obtuse angle, and a straight angle. Measure each of them with a protractor.

Refer Maths Lab Activity on page 153.

Common Mistake

You can avoid this mistake by first observing the angle and deciding what kind of angle it is—obtuse or acute. Secondly, always use the scale where the baseline arm points to zero.

$\angle ABC = 45°$ ✗
$\angle ABC = 135°$ ✓

Exercise 10.2

1. What is the measure of these angles?

(a)

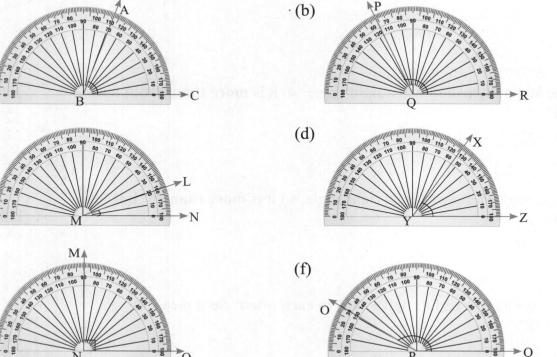

(b)

(c)

(d)

(e)

(f)

2. Measure these angles with your protractor. Then state what type of angles they are.

(a)   (b)   (c)

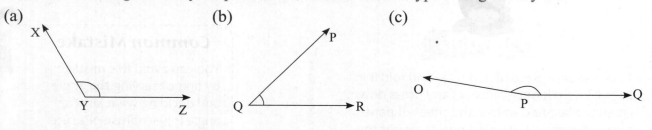

3. Use a protractor to measure the angles.

∠AOC =   ∠AOE =   ∠AOG =   ∠AOB =
∠BOD =   ∠BOF =   ∠BOG =   ∠BOC =

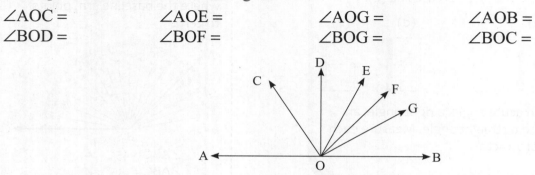

4. Draw 10 different angles with a ruler in your notebook. Then measure them with your protractor.

Chapter Check-Up

1. Fill in the blanks.

   (a) A ray extends endlessly in _____ direction.
   (b) You cannot measure a ray and a _____ .
   (c) A part of a line that has two endpoints is a _____.
   (d) An angle that looks like the corner of a cupboard is a _____ .
   (e) An angle is formed by two _____ having a common endpoint.
   (f) An obtuse angle is more than _____° and less than _____°.
   (g) An angle that measures 1° is an _____ angle.

2. Mark the right angles in red, acute angles in blue, and obtuse angles in green.

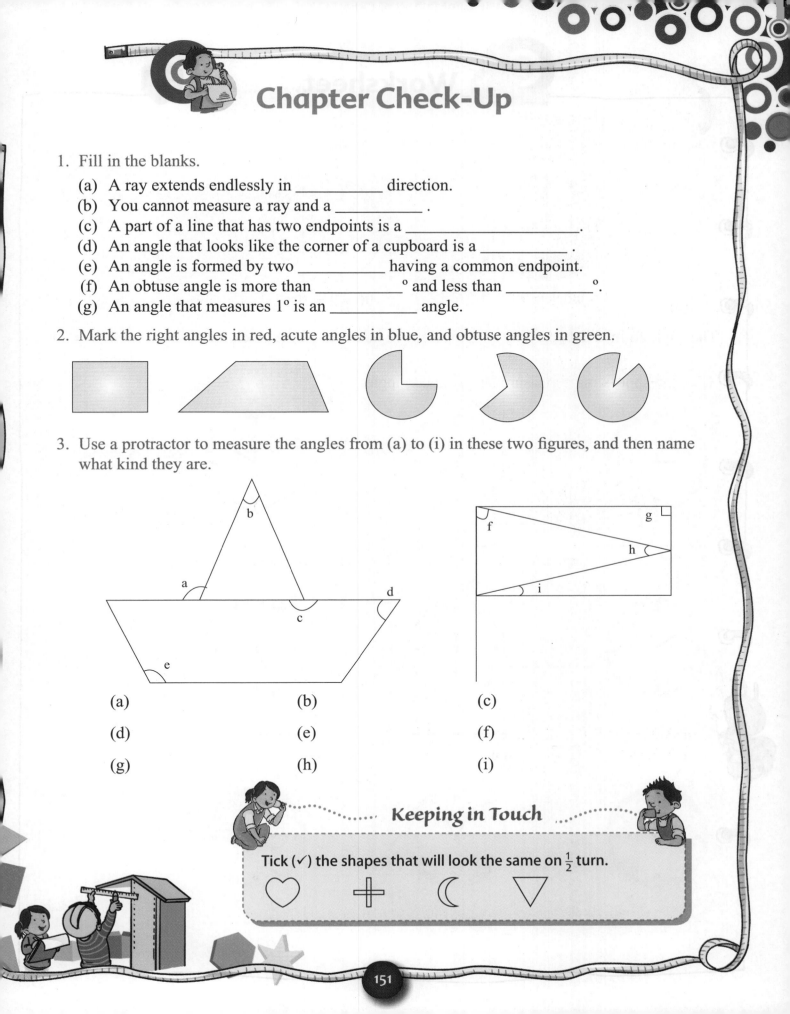

3. Use a protractor to measure the angles from (a) to (i) in these two figures, and then name what kind they are.

   (a)   (b)   (c)

   (d)   (e)   (f)

   (g)   (h)   (i)

Keeping in Touch

Tick (✓) the shapes that will look the same on $\frac{1}{2}$ turn.

Use this guide to help you find the approximate measurement of clock angles.

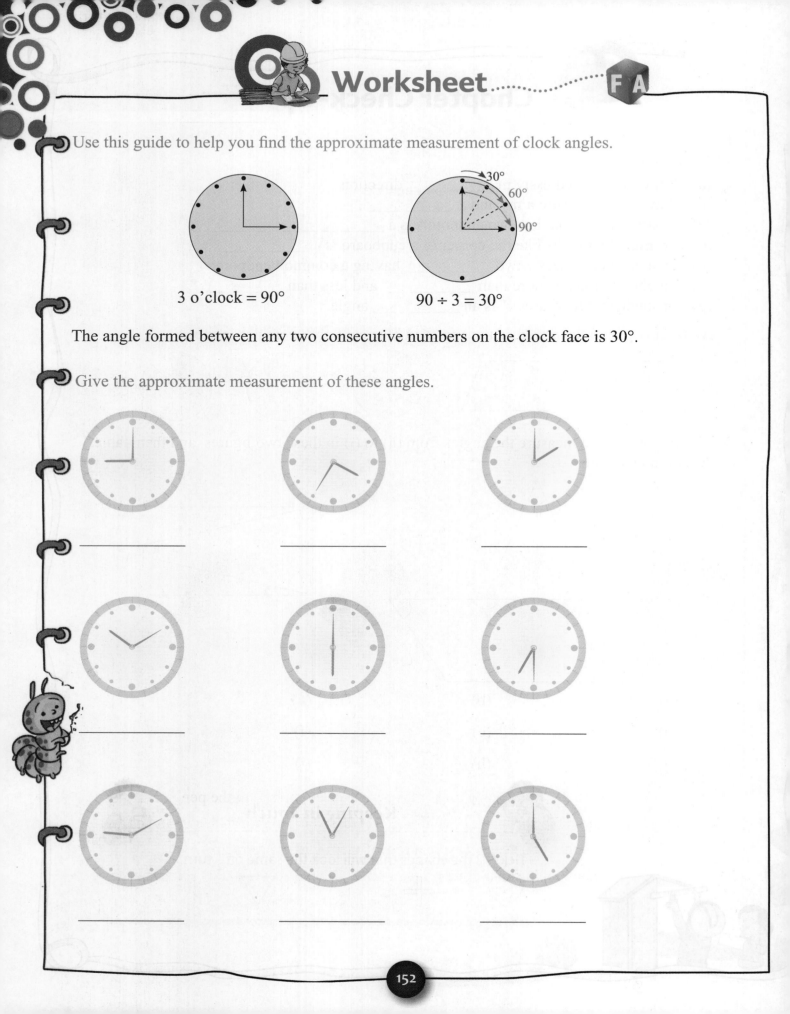

3 o'clock = 90°

90 ÷ 3 = 30°

The angle formed between any two consecutive numbers on the clock face is 30°.

Give the approximate measurement of these angles.

_____   _____   _____

_____   _____   _____

_____   _____   _____

Objective: To create and recognise angles through paper folding.

Materials Required: Square sheet of origami paper (about 12 cm × 12 cm) with one side white and one side black.

Preparation: None

Method: To make an origami penguin

Steps:

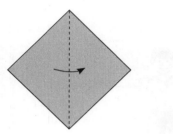

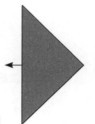

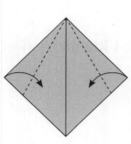

1. Fold the square sheet into a triangle.
2. Open the triangle.
3. Fold the sides as shown. Corners should not touch the centre crease.
4. Fold the top as shown.

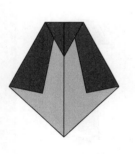

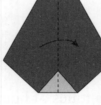

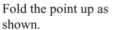

5. Turn over the paper.
6. Fold the point up as shown.
7. Fold the paper in half.
8. Lift the head up as shown.

Your penguin is ready.

Record the activity:

1. How many right, acute and obtuse angles can you see in the penguin?
2. Open up the sheet and note all the creases. Mark the right, acute, and obtuse angles that you see. Measure a few of them with a protractor.
3. Research to do some more origami paper folding on your own. Record each one.

Measurement

Looking Back

Length

It takes Paresh 10 minutes to walk **1 kilometre (km)**.

1 km = 1000 metres (m)
1 m = 100 centimetres (cm)

About 1 m

Breadth of a finger is about 1 cm

Mass

We use **kilograms (kg)** to weigh heavier objects and **grams (g)** to weigh lighter ones.

1 kg = 1000 g

About 1 g   About 1 kg

Capacity

Litre (ℓ) is used to measure larger quantities of liquid and **millilitres (mℓ)** is used to measure smaller quantities of liquid.

1ℓ = 1000 mℓ

Holds about 5 mℓ of water

Holds about 1 ℓ of water

Convert the following.

(a) 300 cm = _____ m

(b) 5 m = _____ cm

(c) 8000 g = _____ kg

(d) 4 kg = _____ g

(e) 2000 mℓ = _____ ℓ

(f) 9ℓ = _____ mℓ

(g) 7500 g = _____ kg

(h) $3\frac{1}{2}$ ℓ = _____ mℓ

(i) 2520 m = ___ km ___ m

Measurement of Length

If you were asked to measure the lead tip of your pencil, what would you use?

A centimetre is too big to measure my pencil point!

So you need a smaller unit of measurement.

If a centimetre is further put into 10 equal parts, each part is called a millimetre (mm).

10 mm

0   1   2 cm

1 cm = 10 mm

1 mm

0   1   2 cm

1 mm = $\frac{1}{10}$ cm

The breadth of the hour hand of your watch is about 1 mm.

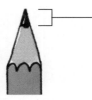 → 5 mm

We use millimetres to measure very small lengths or when we want to measure longer lengths with greater accuracy.

 The diameter of this 5-rupee coin is about 2 cm 3 mm.

Try This

(a) Take a grain of rice and measure its length to the nearest mm.

(b) Find a bangle and measure its thickness to the nearest mm.

Exercise 11.1

1. Measure. Give your answer in (a) cm and mm, (b) cm, (c) mm.

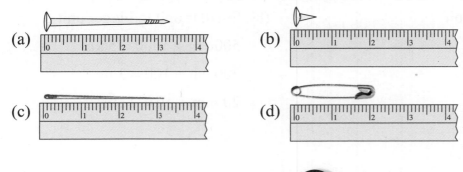

(a)

(b)

(c)

(d)

2. Use your ruler to measure the wing span of the butterfly at the marked lines.

Top = _____ cm _____ mm or _____ cm

Middle = _____ cm _____ mm or _____ cm

Bottom = _____ cm _____ mm or _____ cm

Relating Different Units of Length

You have now learnt four units of measurement of length. They are given below in order from big to small.

KILOMETRE (km)	→	More than a metre
METRE (m)	→	BASIC UNIT OF LENGTH
CENTIMETRE (cm)	}	Less than a metre
MILLIMETRE (mm)		

Let us see how they are connected to each other in the place value system.

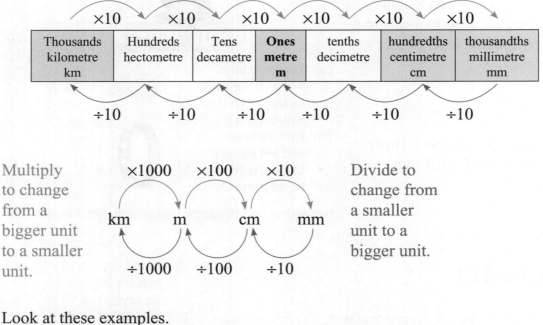

×10   ×10   ×10   ×10   ×10   ×10

Thousands kilometre km	Hundreds hectometre	Tens decametre	**Ones metre m**	tenths decimetre	hundredths centimetre cm	thousandths millimetre mm

÷10   ÷10   ÷10   ÷10   ÷10   ÷10

Multiply to change from a bigger unit to a smaller unit.

×1000   ×100   ×10

km   m   cm   mm

÷1000   ÷100   ÷10

Divide to change from a smaller unit to a bigger unit.

Look at these examples.

(a) Bigger unit to smaller unit

2 km × 1000 = 2000 m

5 m × 100 = 500 cm

3 cm × 10 = 30 mm

(b) Smaller unit to bigger unit

5000 m ÷ 1000 = 5 km

300 cm ÷ 100 = 3 m

20 mm ÷ 10 = 2 cm

Using Decimals to Express Measurements

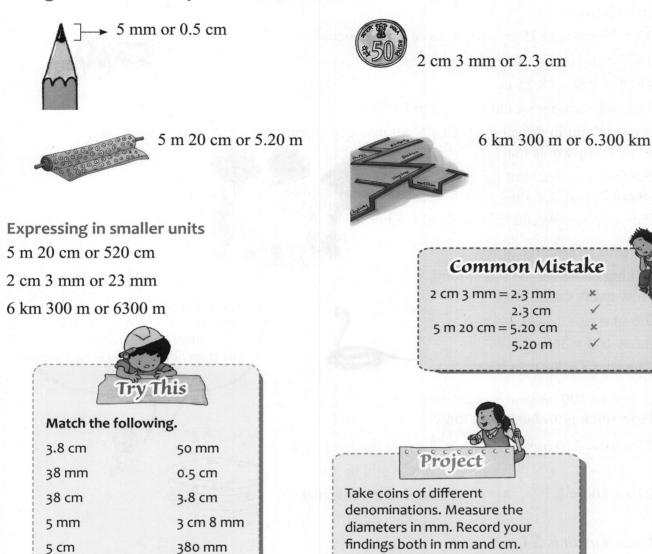

5 mm or 0.5 cm

2 cm 3 mm or 2.3 cm

5 m 20 cm or 5.20 m

6 km 300 m or 6.300 km

Expressing in smaller units

5 m 20 cm or 520 cm

2 cm 3 mm or 23 mm

6 km 300 m or 6300 m

Common Mistake

2 cm 3 mm =	2.3 mm	✗
	2.3 cm	✓
5 m 20 cm =	5.20 cm	✗
	5.20 m	✓

Try This

Match the following.

3.8 cm	50 mm
38 mm	0.5 cm
38 cm	3.8 cm
5 mm	3 cm 8 mm
5 cm	380 mm

Project

Take coins of different denominations. Measure the diameters in mm. Record your findings both in mm and cm.

Converting One Unit into Another

Smaller unit to bigger unit

mm is the smaller unit and cm is the bigger unit. The rule says Small to Big Divide (SBD). The chart on page 156 will help you.

(a) If each ant is 8 mm in length, how long is the line in cm?

$11 \times 8 = 88$ mm is the length of the line in mm.

88 mm = ____?____ cm

$88 \div 10 = 8.8$ cm

The line is 8.8 cm long.

(b) A grasshopper which can go 25 cm with one hop would have gone how many metres in 75 hops?

75 × 25 cm = 1875 cm would have been covered.

1875 cm = ___?___ m

1875 ÷ 100 = 18.75 m

The grasshopper would have gone 18.75 m.

(c) An elephant in the jungle walks 5500 m every morning to drink water at the lake. How many km is that?

5500 m = _____ km

5500 ÷ 1000 = 5.5 km

The elephant would have walked 5.5 km.

Bigger unit to smaller unit

(a) A king cobra can be 3.6 m long. How many cm is that?

3.6 m = _____ cm

3.6 × 100 = 360 cm

The snake is 360 cm long.

> m is the bigger unit and cm is the smaller unit. The rule says Big to Small Multiply (BSM). The chart on page 156 will help you.

(b) A pile of 100 *chapattis* is 21 cm. How thick is 1 *chapatti* in mm?

21 × 10 = 210 mm ⟶ To find the thickness of the pile in mm

210 ÷ 100 = 2.1 ⟶ To find the thickness of one *chapatti*

One *chapatti* is 2.1 mm.

Exercise 11.2

1. Fill in the blanks.

   (a) Height of a glass = 0.12 m = _____ cm

   (b) Height of a tree = 960 cm = _____ m

   (c) Height of a building = 0.1 km = _____ m

   (d) Distance from floor to ceiling = 3.8 m = _____ cm

   (e) Length of a cricket bat = 0.87 m = _____ cm

   (f) Length of a tennis racket = 72 cm = _____ mm

   (g) Height of a table = 70 cm = _____ m

   (h) Thickness of a pencil = 0.8 cm = _____ mm

(i) Length of a mobile phone = 9.2 cm = _____ mm

(j) Thickness of an encyclopaedia = 42 mm = _____ cm

2. Fill in the blanks.

(a) 6.2 km = _____ m
(b) 0.12 km = _____ m
(c) 9.1 km = _____ m
(d) 6300 m = _____ km
(e) 1100 m = _____ km
(f) 2800 m = _____ km

3. Complete the table.

	Full form	In bigger units	In smaller units
(a)	36 m 14 cm	36.14 m	3614 cm
(b)		98.98 m	9898 cm
(c)	16 m 24 cm		1624 cm
(d)	11 cm 2 mm		112 mm
(e)		2.87 cm	287 mm
(f)	49 cm 8 mm	49.8 cm	

Challenge

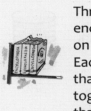

Three volumes of an encyclopaedia are kept on a shelf as shown. Each volume has pages that are 2 cm thick together and covers that are each 2 mm thick.

If a worm starts eating from page 1 of volume 1 to the last page of volume 3, how far would it travel? (**Hint:** Keep three books as shown and see where the page numbers start before giving your answer.)

Project

Find out your height and the height of the members of your family. Express it in cm and then in m. Who is the tallest? Who is the shortest?

Problem Solving

(a) Mrs Kapoor has two clotheslines in her backyard. One is 5 m long and the other is 4.05 m long. How much longer is the first clothesline than the second?

(b)  A rabbit's hop is about 2 m long. How many hops does a rabbit take to travel 1 km? [Hint: convert km to m first]

(c) Varsha runs 3.2 km a day. How far does Varsha run in a week?

(d) Karan has placed a stool on a table to reach the top of his cupboard. If the height of the table is 98 cm, and the stool is 65 cm, at what height in metres is Karan standing?

(e) A bookshelf is 45 cm wide. How many books of width 9 mm can fit in the shelf? [Hint: Convert cm to mm first]

(f)  Avinash is 1.8 m tall. Arun is 191 cm tall. How much taller is Arun than Avinash? [Hint: Convert m to cm first]

(g) Monika's shoe is 20.8 cm long. Kabir's shoe is 6 mm longer than Monika's shoe. How long is Kabir's shoe in cm?

Fill in the blanks.

(a) A pile of 100 ₹ 5 coins is 150 mm high. One coin is _____ mm thick.

(b) A pile of 100 biscuits is 580 mm high. One biscuit is _____ mm thick.

(c) A pile of 10 erasers is 9.8 cm high. One eraser is _____ mm thick.

(d) A pile of 100 comic books is 6.2 cm high. One comic book is _____ mm thick.

(e) A pile of 10 mobile phones is 8 cm high. One phone is _____ mm thick.

(f) A pile of 100 sheets of cardboard is 30 cm high. One sheet is _____ mm thick.

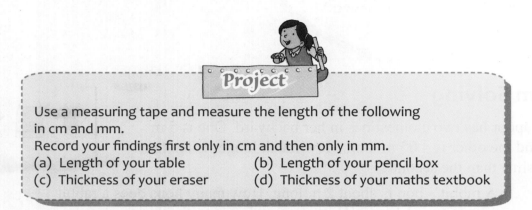

Project

Use a measuring tape and measure the length of the following in cm and mm.
Record your findings first only in cm and then only in mm.
(a) Length of your table
(b) Length of your pencil box
(c) Thickness of your eraser
(d) Thickness of your maths textbook

Measurement of Mass

You know that **1 kg = 1000 g**.

Let us see how these units are related to each other using the place value system.

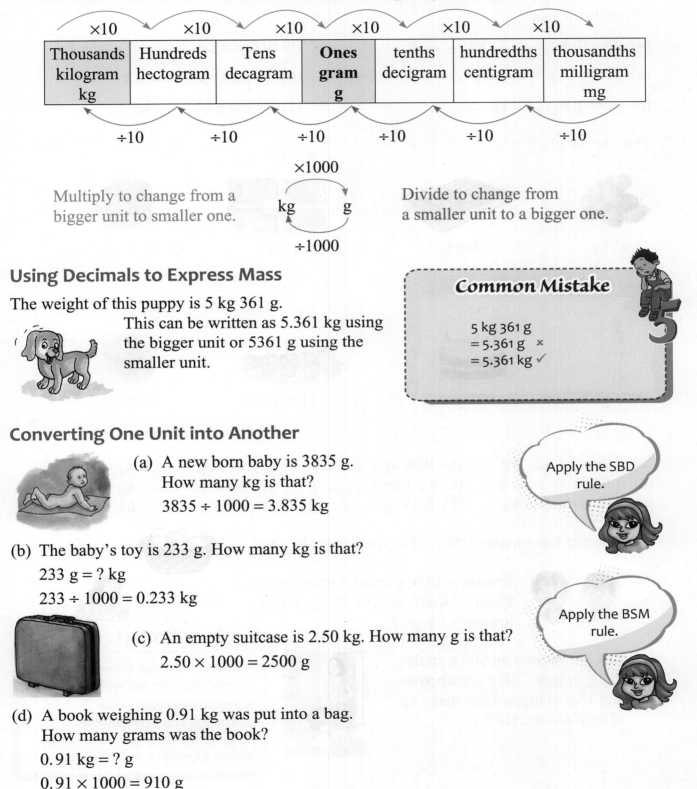

Thousands kilogram kg	Hundreds hectogram	Tens decagram	**Ones gram g**	tenths decigram	hundredths centigram	thousandths milligram mg

×1000

Multiply to change from a bigger unit to smaller one.

kg   g

Divide to change from a smaller unit to a bigger one.

÷1000

Using Decimals to Express Mass

The weight of this puppy is 5 kg 361 g.

This can be written as 5.361 kg using the bigger unit or 5361 g using the smaller unit.

Common Mistake

5 kg 361 g
= 5.361 g ✗
= 5.361 kg ✓

Converting One Unit into Another

(a) A new born baby is 3835 g. How many kg is that?

$3835 \div 1000 = 3.835$ kg

Apply the SBD rule.

(b) The baby's toy is 233 g. How many kg is that?

233 g = ? kg

$233 \div 1000 = 0.233$ kg

(c) An empty suitcase is 2.50 kg. How many g is that?

$2.50 \times 1000 = 2500$ g

Apply the BSM rule.

(d) A book weighing 0.91 kg was put into a bag. How many grams was the book?

0.91 kg = ? g

$0.91 \times 1000 = 910$ g

Exercise 11.3

1. Fill in the blanks.

   (a) 19.386 kg = _____ kg _____ g

   (b) 0.832 kg = _____ kg _____ g

   (c) 26 kg 14 g = _____ g

   (d) 86 kg 10 g = _____ g

   (e) 3246 g = _____ kg _____ g

   (f) 11296 g = _____ kg

2. Find the weight in g.

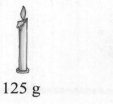

0.42 kg

0.9 kg

1.6 kg

5.19 kg

3. Find the weight in kg.

125 g

900 g

1120 g

9500 g

4. Convert.

   (a) 715 g = _____ kg

   (b) 0.06 kg = _____ g

   (c) 2375 g = _____ kg

   (d) 1.04 kg = _____ g

   (e) 12.1 kg = _____ g

   (f) 8008 g = _____ kg

   (g) 932 g = _____ kg

   (h) 0.35 kg = _____ g

   (i) 6125 g = _____ kg

5. (a) One egg has a mass of 50 g. How many eggs in 1 kg?

   (b)  Srinath is 1750 g heavier than his friend Kabir. If Kabir weighs 32 kg, what is Srinath's weight?

   (c) Mrs Anwar bought 500 g apples, 750 g grapes, 250 g strawberries, and 1 kg oranges. How many kg of fruit did she buy?

Project

A tonne is 1000 kg. How many people together will weigh a tonne?

Record the weight of your classmates and perhaps other students also to find out how many people together weigh a tonne.

Measurement of Capacity

You know that **1 ℓ = 1000 mℓ**.

Let us see how these units are related to each other using the place value system.

×10	×10	×10	×10	×10	×10

Thousands kilolitre	Hundreds hectolitre	Tens decalitre	**Ones litre** ℓ	tenths decilitre	hundredths centilitre	thousandths millilitre mℓ

÷10	÷10	÷10	÷10	÷10	÷10

×1000

Multiply to change from a bigger unit to smaller one.

ℓ mℓ

Divide to change from a smaller unit to a bigger one.

÷1000

Using Decimals to Express Capacity

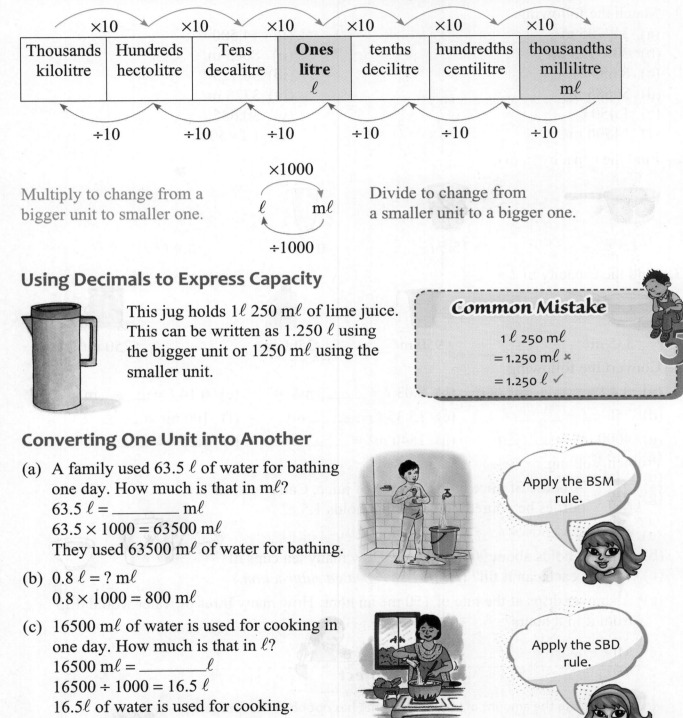

This jug holds 1ℓ 250 mℓ of lime juice. This can be written as 1.250 ℓ using the bigger unit or 1250 mℓ using the smaller unit.

Common Mistake

1 ℓ 250 mℓ
= 1.250 mℓ ✗
= 1.250 ℓ ✓

Converting One Unit into Another

(a) A family used 63.5 ℓ of water for bathing one day. How much is that in mℓ?
63.5 ℓ = _____ mℓ
63.5 × 1000 = 63500 mℓ
They used 63500 mℓ of water for bathing.

Apply the BSM rule.

(b) 0.8 ℓ = ? mℓ
0.8 × 1000 = 800 mℓ

(c) 16500 mℓ of water is used for cooking in one day. How much is that in ℓ?
16500 mℓ = _____ ℓ
16500 ÷ 1000 = 16.5 ℓ
16.5ℓ of water is used for cooking.

Apply the SBD rule.

(d) 550 mℓ = ? ℓ
550 ÷ 1000 = 0.550 ℓ

163

Exercise 11.4

1. Match the following:
   - (a) 3 ℓ 725 mℓ
   - (b) 30 ℓ 725 mℓ
   - (c) 8.685 ℓ
   - (d) 80685 mℓ
   - (e) 1.450 ℓ
   - (f) 14500 mℓ

   - (i) 14.500 ℓ
   - (ii) 8685 mℓ
   - (iii) 30.725 ℓ
   - (iv) 3725 mℓ
   - (v) 80.685 ℓ
   - (vi) 1 ℓ 450 mℓ

2. Find the capacity in mℓ.

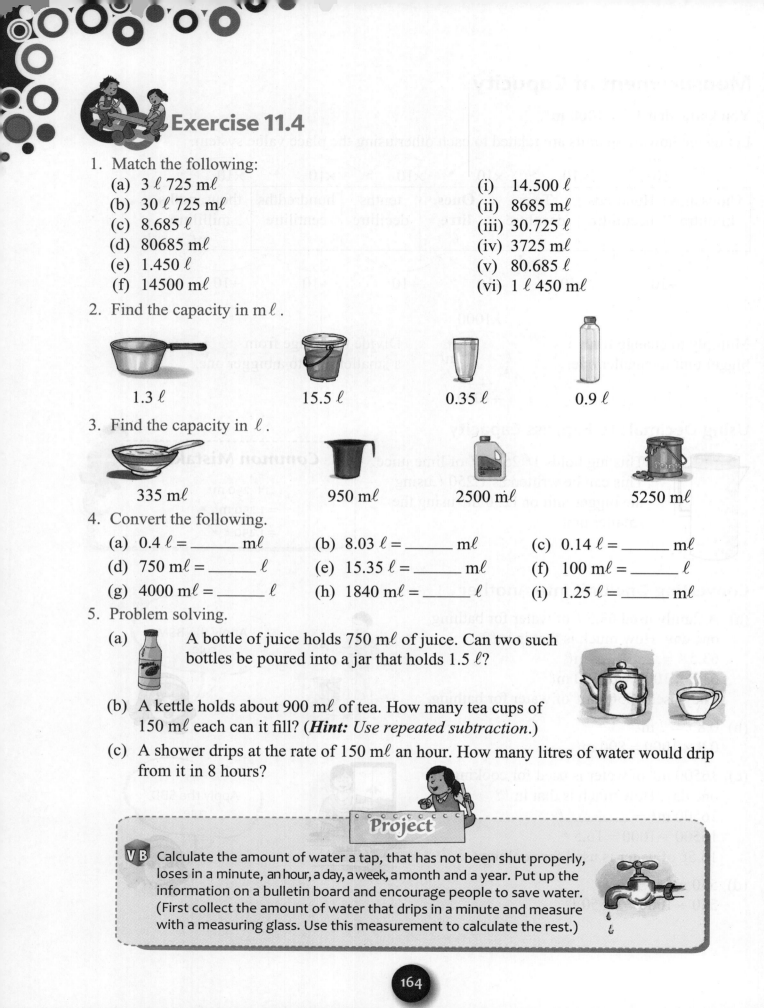

   1.3 ℓ   15.5 ℓ   0.35 ℓ   0.9 ℓ

3. Find the capacity in ℓ.

   335 mℓ   950 mℓ   2500 mℓ   5250 mℓ

4. Convert the following.
   - (a) 0.4 ℓ = _____ mℓ
   - (b) 8.03 ℓ = _____ mℓ
   - (c) 0.14 ℓ = _____ mℓ
   - (d) 750 mℓ = _____ ℓ
   - (e) 15.35 ℓ = _____ mℓ
   - (f) 100 mℓ = _____ ℓ
   - (g) 4000 mℓ = _____ ℓ
   - (h) 1840 mℓ = _____ ℓ
   - (i) 1.25 ℓ = _____ mℓ

5. Problem solving.
   - (a) A bottle of juice holds 750 mℓ of juice. Can two such bottles be poured into a jar that holds 1.5 ℓ?

   - (b) A kettle holds about 900 mℓ of tea. How many tea cups of 150 mℓ each can it fill? (**Hint:** *Use repeated subtraction.*)

   - (c) A shower drips at the rate of 150 mℓ an hour. How many litres of water would drip from it in 8 hours?

Project

V B Calculate the amount of water a tap, that has not been shut properly, loses in a minute, an hour, a day, a week, a month and a year. Put up the information on a bulletin board and encourage people to save water. (First collect the amount of water that drips in a minute and measure with a measuring glass. Use this measurement to calculate the rest.)

Theme: A School Play!

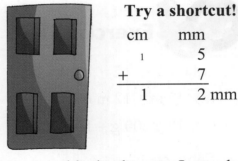

(a) A cardboard door was made for the school play by sticking 2 sheets of cardboard, one 5 mm thick and the other 7 mm thick. How thick was the door?

5 mm + 7 mm = _____ mm

12 mm = _____ cm _____ mm

The door was _____ cm _____ mm thick.

Try a shortcut!

cm	mm
¹1	5
+	7
1	2 mm

(b) The teacher draws a line 3 m 75 cm long on the floor of stage to guide the dancers. Later she increased the length by another 2 m 50 cm.
How long is the line now?

   3 m 75 cm + 2 m 50 cm = ?

   3 m + 2 m = _____ m

   75 cm + 50 cm = _____ cm

   125 cm = _____ m _____ cm

   5 m + 1 m 25 cm = _____ m _____ cm

The line is _____ m _____ cm long now.

m	cm
¹3	75
+ 2	50
6	25

(c) There were two earthenware pots kept on the stage. One weighed 980 g and the other weighed 1 kg 200 g. How heavy were both the pots together?

   1 kg 200 g + 980 g = ?

   1 kg 200 g + 980 g = 1 kg 1180 g

But 1180 g = 1 kg 180 g

So 1 kg + 1 kg 180 g = 2 kg 180 g

Both pots together weigh 2 kg 180 g.

kg	g
¹1	200
+	980
2	180

(d) For one scene 13 ℓ 500 mℓ water was poured into a bucket of 24 ℓ capacity. How much more water could the bucket hold?

   24 ℓ – 13 ℓ 500 mℓ = ?

   24 ℓ is the same as 23 ℓ 1000 mℓ

   23 ℓ – 13 ℓ = 10 ℓ

   1000 mℓ – 500 mℓ = 500 mℓ

There was space enough for 10 ℓ 500 mℓ more water in the bucket.

ℓ	mℓ
2$\overset{3}{\cancel{4}}$	$\overset{1000}{\cancel{000}}$
– 13	500
10	500

(e) Out of 2 kg of sweets that was kept for distribution to all the actors after the play, 250 g was still remaining. How much was eaten?

   2 kg – 250 g = ?

   2 kg is the same as 1 kg 1000 g.

   1 kg 1000 g – 250 g = 1 kg 750 g

   1 kg 750 g was eaten.

kg	g
¹$\cancel{2}$	$\overset{1000}{\cancel{000}}$
–	250
1	750

Exercise 11.5

1. Add.

   (a) 17 m + 12 m 6 cm

   (b) 6 cm 5 mm + 1 cm 9 mm

   (c) 5 kg 200 g + 6 kg 800 g

   (d) 1 kg 500 g + 1 kg 750 g

   (e) 2 ℓ 250 mℓ + 900 mℓ

   (f) 5 ℓ 600 mℓ + 2 ℓ 500 mℓ

2. Subtract.

   (a) 10 m – 6 m 50 cm

   (b) 7 cm 8 mm – 1 cm 9 mm

   (c) 2 kg 200 g – 1 kg 100 g

   (d) 5 kg – 1 kg 250 g

   (e) 2 ℓ 800 m ℓ – 1 ℓ 100 mℓ

   (f) 10 ℓ 250 mℓ – 1 ℓ 750 mℓ

3. Application in real life.

   (a) A snail travelled 2 m 32 cm on one day and 1 m 93 cm on the second day. How far had the snail travelled in all?

   (b) A worm climbing up a high wall went 12 m on one day but slipped back by 2 m 35 cm in the evening. How far up had the worm reached on that day?

   (c) A jug that contained 1 ℓ of lime juice was poured out into 3 glasses of 200 mℓ, 150 mℓ, and 300 mℓ. How much juice was left in the jug?

   (d) A gold brick weighing 4 kg was melted. It lost 150 g of weight during melting. How much gold was left in the brick?

   (e) A porter was carrying two bags—one weighing 16 kg 800 g and the other weighing 10 kg 950 g. How much weight was the porter carrying?

   (f) Akhilesh is 150 cm tall. When he raises his arms up he touches 215 cm. How long is Akhilesh's arm?

Project

Take the help of a teacher to use the science laboratory in your school. Find the weight of these.

5-rupee coin = _____ g

2-rupee coin = _____ g

1-rupee coin = _____ g

Calculate to find these answers.

(a) Find the weight of 100 ₹ 2 coins.

(b) What will be the weight of 1000 ₹ 1 coins?

(c) How many ₹ 5 coins in 900 g?

Estimating Measures

Arun is having a birthday party. He has invited 15 friends over. He thinks 3 litres of juice should be enough to serve 15 people. He decorates the room with streamers. He buys ten 5-metre strips for decoration.

Arun has used **estimation**. He mentally measures the juice and streamers to decide whether they will be enough.

In real life, we often estimate measures. But before we estimate we need to have experience of real measures.

The following illustrations may help you.

Comparison helps in estimation. My finger is about 1 cm wide. The pencil is about 12 finger widths, so the pencil is about 12 cm.

About 1 mg

About 1 g

About 1 kg

About 1 mℓ

About 1ℓ

Thickness of a finger nail
About 1 mm

Width of an index finger
About 1 cm

Breadth of a door
About 1 m

Try This

Fill in the blanks.
(a) A slice of bread weighs about 24 _____.
(b) A dropper for medicine holds 2 _____.
(c) A bench is about 2 _____ long.

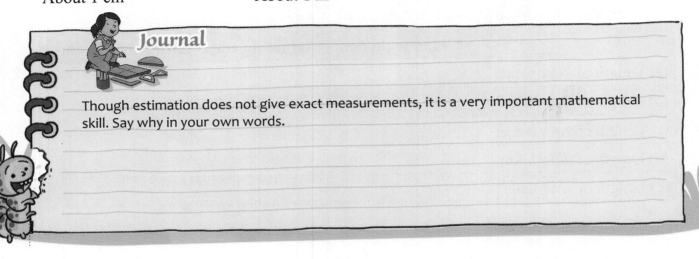

Journal

Though estimation does not give exact measurements, it is a very important mathematical skill. Say why in your own words.

Exercise 11.6

1. Circle the correct answer.

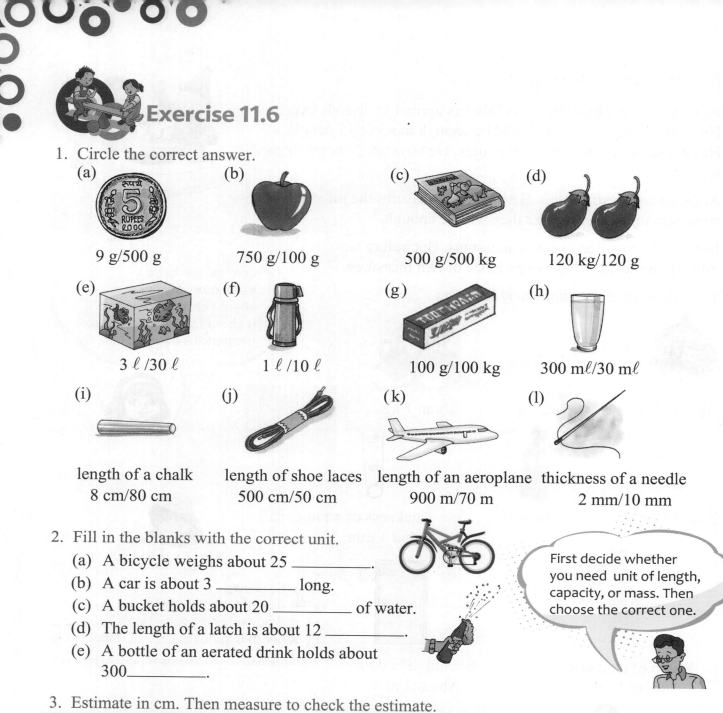

(a) 9 g/500 g

(b) 750 g/100 g

(c) 500 g/500 kg

(d) 120 kg/120 g

(e) 3 ℓ /30 ℓ

(f) 1 ℓ /10 ℓ

(g) 100 g/100 kg

(h) 300 mℓ/30 mℓ

(i) length of a chalk
8 cm/80 cm

(j) length of shoe laces
500 cm/50 cm

(k) length of an aeroplane
900 m/70 m

(l) thickness of a needle
2 mm/10 mm

2. Fill in the blanks with the correct unit.

(a) A bicycle weighs about 25 _____.

(b) A car is about 3 _____ long.

(c) A bucket holds about 20 _____ of water.

(d) The length of a latch is about 12 _____.

(e) A bottle of an aerated drink holds about 300_____.

First decide whether you need unit of length, capacity, or mass. Then choose the correct one.

3. Estimate in cm. Then measure to check the estimate.

	Estimate (in cm)	Actual (in cm)	Difference (in cm)
(a) Length of your pencil			
(b) Length of your thumb			
(c) Length of your eraser			
(d) Length of your book			
(e) Length of your table			

Chapter Check-Up

1. Convert.
   (a) 0.8 km = _____ m
   (b) 1500 m = _____ km
   (c) 8.4 km = _____ m
   (d) 0.18 m = _____ cm
   (e) 720 cm = _____ m
   (f) 3.5 m = _____ cm
   (g) 1.2 cm = _____ mm
   (h) 220 mm = _____ cm
   (i) 0.3 cm = _____ mm

2. (a) 850 g = _____ kg
   (b) 0.09 kg = _____ g
   (c) 1380 g = _____ kg
   (d) 0.90 kg = _____ g
   (e) 1.15 kg = _____ g
   (f) 2200 g = _____ kg

3. (a) 0.5 ℓ = _____ mℓ
   (b) 0.17 ℓ = _____ mℓ
   (c) 1880 mℓ = _____ ℓ
   (d) 7.25 ℓ = _____ mℓ
   (e) 200 mℓ = _____ ℓ
   (f) 950 mℓ = _____ ℓ

4. Cross out the wrong one.
   (a) A book weighs about 20 g/200 g.
   (b) A bottle of medicine has 50 mℓ /5000 mℓ of liquid.
   (c) A pencil is about 15 cm/150 cm long.

5. Measure the stamps. Give the length in two ways —cm and mm.

   (a)   (b)

6. (a) Mrs Arora buys 1 m 40 cm of cloth for her younger son and 1 m 80 cm of cloth for her older son. How much cloth does she buy in all?

   (b) A full suitcase weighs 9 kg 100g. A book weighing 750 g was removed from it. What is the weight of the suitcase now?

   (c) 1 ℓ 200 mℓ oil was used up from an oil can of 5 ℓ. How much is left in the can now?

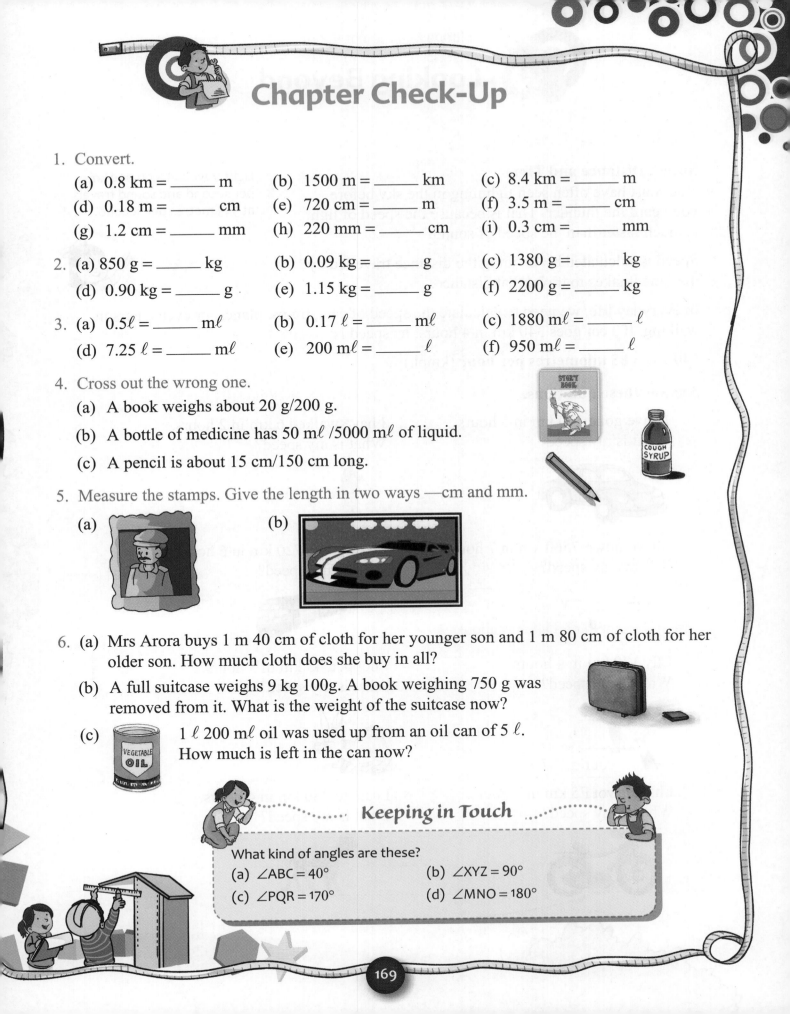

Keeping in Touch

What kind of angles are these?
(a) ∠ABC = 40°
(b) ∠XYZ = 90°
(c) ∠PQR = 170°
(d) ∠MNO = 180°

Looking Beyond

Enrichment Time

Speed, Distance and Time

You must have often seen lightning in the sky before you heard the thunder. That is because the speed of light is much faster than the speed of sound.

> Light travels at 3,00,000 km per second and sound travels at 343 metres per second.

Speed is calculated by dividing the distance travelled by the time it takes to travel that distance.

In everyday life, we need to calculate the speed of cars, trains, planes, or even a person walking. If a car goes 340 km in 4 hours, its speed is:

$340 \div 4 = $ **85 kilometres per hour** (kmph)

Answer these questions.

1. I have gone 350 km in 5 hours. What is my speed?

2. I have walked 6 km in 2 hours. What is my speed?

3. I have flown 7560 km in 7 hours. What is my speed?

4. I have gone 720 km in 6 hours. What is my speed?

5. I fly 120 km in 4 hours. What is my speed?

6. I hopped 45 km in 3 hours. What is my speed?

7. I have gone 75 km in 5 hours. What is my speed?

8. I can go 480 km in 4 hours. What is my speed?

Perimeter, Area and Volume

Looking Back

Perimeter is the distance around the edge of a figure.

The perimeter of this stamp is
3 cm + 4 cm + 3 cm + 4 cm = 14 cm.

Area is the amount of surface a figure covers.

The stamp covers 12 squares of 1 cm sides. The area of this stamp is 12 square centimetres or 12 sq. cm.

Here is a clue to remember the terms:

```
    p   e   r
r  ┌─────────┐  i
   │         │
e  │         │
   └─────────┘  m
    t   e
```

area

1. Find the perimeter of these posters.

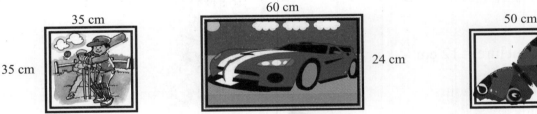

35 cm, 35 cm

60 cm, 24 cm

50 cm, 50 cm

2. Find the area of these stickers. Give your answers in sq. units.

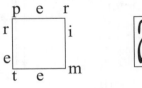

SAY NO TO PLASTICS

Reduce Reuse Recycle

SAVE PLANET EARTH

3. Use a cm squared sheet of paper. Draw the outline of your hand on it. Find the perimeter and the area of your hand.

Perimeter of a Rectangle

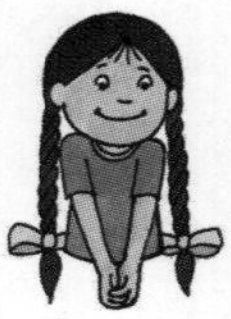

Asmi has made a table mat for her mother.

20 cm
30 cm

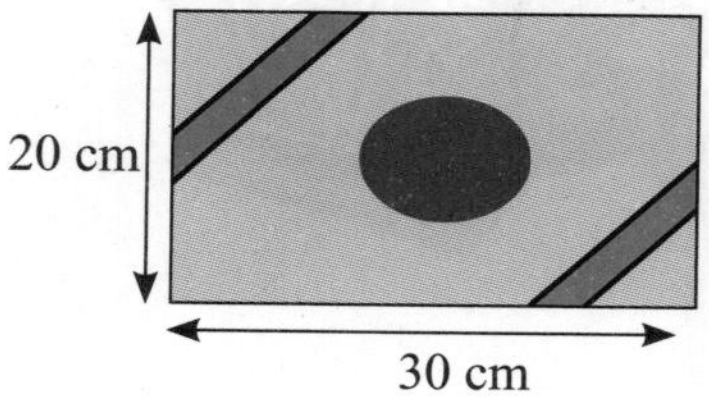

The perimeter of Asmi's mat is:
30 cm + 20 cm + 30 cm + 20 cm = 100 cm

Since we are adding 2 lengths and 2 breadths of equal size, we can also find the perimeter by using a shortcut.

Perimeter of a rectangle = 2 × (length + breadth)

l (30 cm)
b
b (20 cm)
l

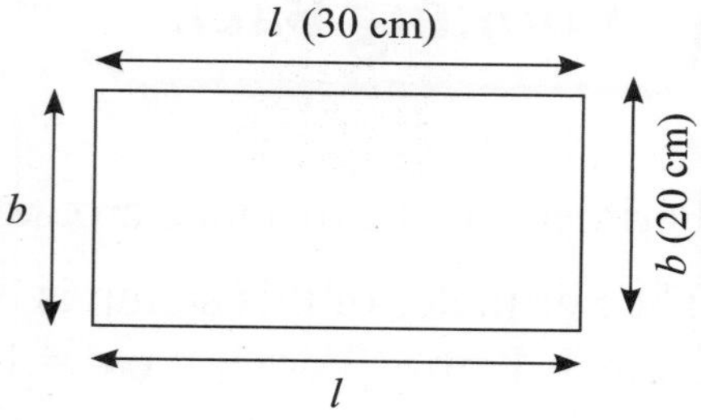

$P = 2\,(l + b)$
Here $l = 30$ cm; $b = 20$ cm
$P = 2\,(30 + 20)$
$= 2 \times 50 = 100$ cm
Perimeter of the table mat = 100 cm

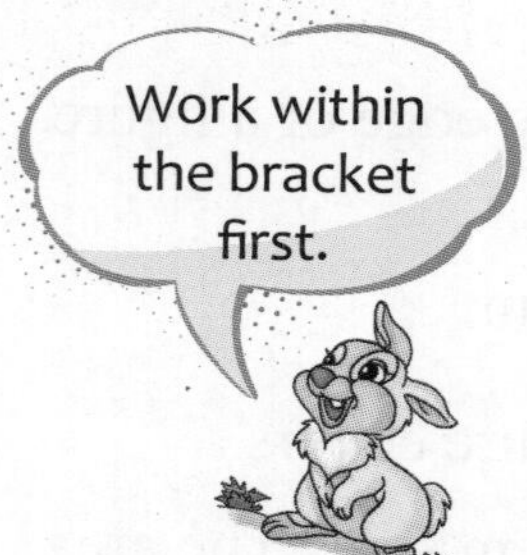

Work within the bracket first.

Perimeter of a Square

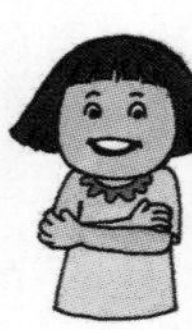

Asmi's sister has drawn this picture of her favourite cartoon character. Find its perimeter.

3 cm
3 cm
3 cm
3 cm

The perimeter of this picture is:
3 cm + 3 cm + 3 cm + 3 cm = 12 cm
All the sides of a square are equal.
So perimeter of a square = side + side + side + side

Perimeter of a square = 4 × length of side
$P = 4 \times 3$
$P = 12$ cm
Perimeter of the picture = 12 cm

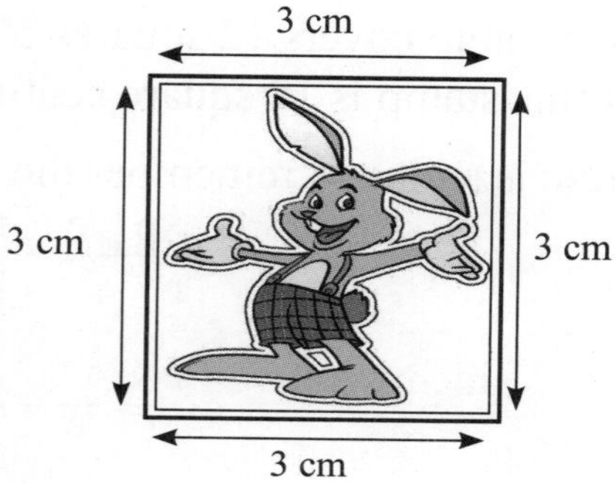

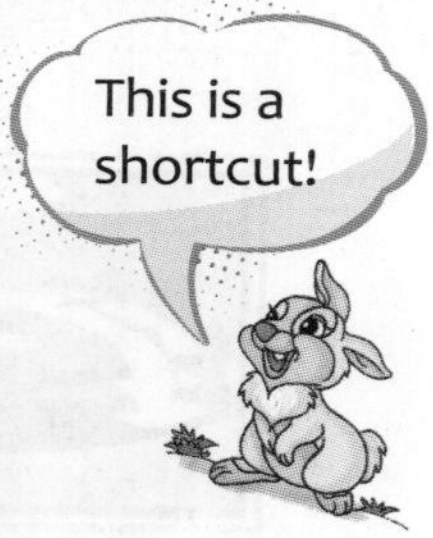

This is a shortcut!

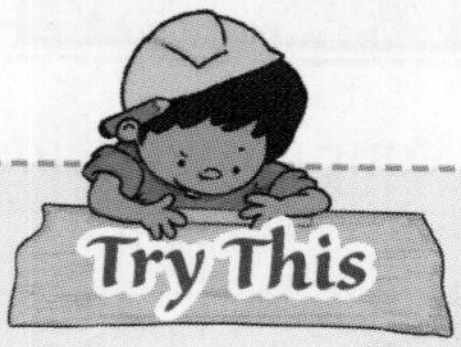

Try This

Find the perimeter of the following.

(a)

14 cm
14 cm
TOP
SONGS

(b)

3 cm
7 cm
PEN-DRIVE

Always remember to mention the units in your answer.

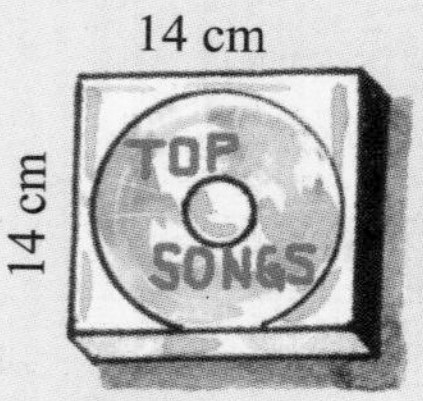

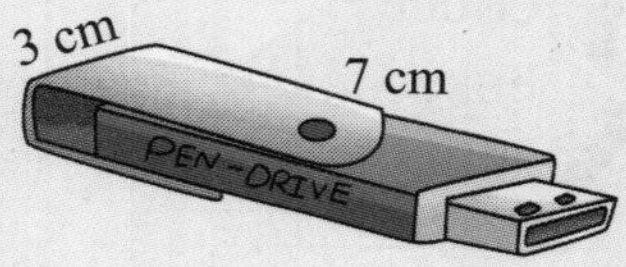

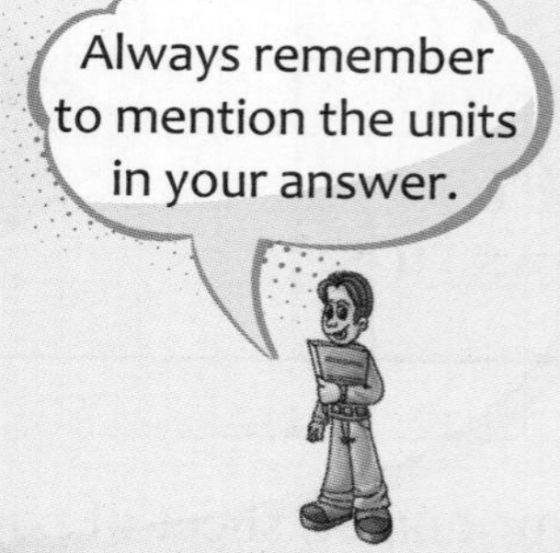

Exercise 12.1

1. Find the perimeter of these objects by using the shortcut.

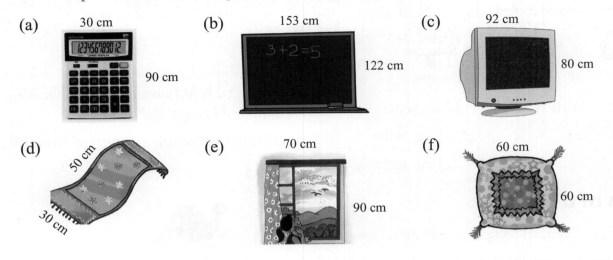

(a)   30 cm   90 cm

(b)   153 cm   122 cm

(c)   92 cm   80 cm

(d)   50 cm   30 cm

(e)   70 cm   90 cm

(f)   60 cm   60 cm

2. Find the perimeter of these squares.

	(a)	(b)	(c)	(d)	(e)	(f)	(g)	(h)	(i)	(j)
Side of square in cm	3	5	11	18	25	30	41	55	63	92
Perimeter in cm	12									

(**Hint:** $4 \times 3 = 12$)

3. Find the perimeter of these rectangles.

	(a)	(b)	(c)	(d)	(e)	(f)	(g)	(h)	(i)	(j)
l in cm	2	2	3	5	5	3	4	5	8	7
b in cm	3	4	4	4	2	6	6	6	6	9
P in cm	10									

(**Hint:** $2 + 3 = 5; 2 \times 5 = 10$)

4. The perimeter is given. Find the side of these squares.

	(a)	(b)	(c)	(d)	(e)	(f)	(g)	(h)	(i)	(j)
P in cm	28	40	64	96	120	172	232	300	384	556
Side of square in cm	7									

(**Hint:** $28 \div 4 = 7$)

Area of a Rectangle

The wall in front of each washbasin has been tiled.

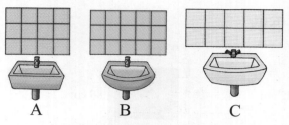

A   B   C

So area of Wall A = 3 × 4 = 12 sq. units

Wall B = _____ × _____ = _____ sq. units

Wall C = _____ × _____ = _____ sq. units

Area of a Square

A square is a special rectangle with equal length and breadth.

Fill in the columns for these squares as you did for the rectangles.

Figure	Length	Breadth	Area
A	3 units	3 units	9 sq. units
B			
C			

Do you see a relationship between the length, breadth and area of a square?

Area of a square = Side × Side

$A = S \times S$

So $A = 3 \times 3 = 9$ sq. units

B = _____ × _____ = _____ sq. units

C = _____ × _____ = _____ sq. units

Find the area of each tiled wall by counting the tiles.

Wall	Length	Breadth	Area
A	4 units	3 units	12 sq. units
B			
C			

Do you see a relationship between the length, breadth and area of the rectangle?

Area of the rectangle = length × breadth

$A = l \times b$

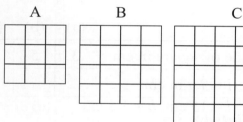

This is a shortcut!

A   B   C

Project

Take a newspaper sheet and measure and record its length and breadth in cm. Calculate its perimeter and area. Then fold it in half and measure the length and breadth and calculate the new area and perimeter. Record your findings.

Keep doing this till you cannot fold the paper anymore. Compare your findings with a friend's. Is it the same?

Exercise 12.2

1. Use the shortcut to find the area of these figures. Give your answer in square units.

(a)

$l =$ _____ ; $b =$ _____

$A =$ _____

(b)

$l =$ _____ ; $b =$ _____

$A =$ _____

(c)

$l =$ _____ ; $b =$ _____

$A =$ _____

2. Find the area of these shapes using the shortcut. Give your answer in square units.

(a) 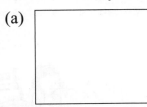   (b) 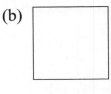   (c)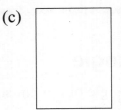

3. Use a cm ruler to find the length and breadth of these shapes. Then find their area using the shortcut. Give your answer in sq. cm.

(a) (b) (c)

4. Find the area of these shapes.

(a) $l = 9$ cm $b = 5$ cm   (b) $l = 12$ cm $b = 10$ cm   (c) $l = 13$ cm $b = 5$ cm

(d) $l = 15$ cm $b = 1.5$ cm   (e) $l = 9$ cm $b = 2.1$ cm   (f) $l = 10$ cm $b = 5.2$ cm

5. Fill in the columns.

	(a)	(b)	(c)	(d)	(e)	(f)	(g)	(h)	(i)	(j)
Length in cm	7	4	2	9			13	11		
Breadth in cm	3				7	4			20	8
Area in sq. cm	21	48	16	36	42	112	130	187	220	136

Journal

Explain using examples of everyday life, the difference between area and perimeter in your own words.

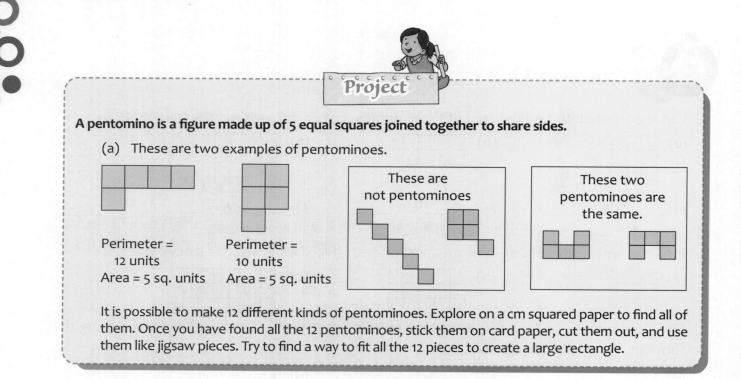

Project

A pentomino is a figure made up of 5 equal squares joined together to share sides.

(a) These are two examples of pentominoes.

Perimeter = 12 units
Area = 5 sq. units

Perimeter = 10 units
Area = 5 sq. units

These are not pentominoes

These two pentominoes are the same.

It is possible to make 12 different kinds of pentominoes. Explore on a cm squared paper to find all of them. Once you have found all the 12 pentominoes, stick them on card paper, cut them out, and use them like jigsaw pieces. Try to find a way to fit all the 12 pieces to create a large rectangle.

Area of a Triangle

Ragini has cut a rectangle out of cm squared paper like this.

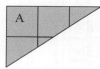

What is the area of the rectangle? _____ sq. cm.

She then cuts the rectangle into two equal triangles like this. What is the area of each triangle?

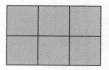

Since triangle A is half the rectangle, its area will be half the area of the rectangle.

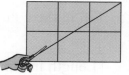

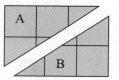

So, the area of triangle A = 3 sq. cm.

Next Ragini cut another rectangle like this. Its area is 20 sq. units.

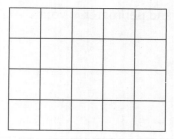

If she cuts a triangle out of it like this, what will its area be?

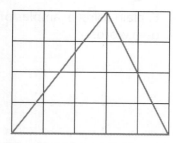

176

To find the area of the triangle, we can look at the big rectangle as two smaller rectangles like this. Then let us look at each small rectangle separately.

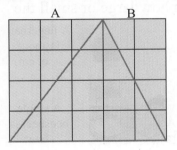

A   B

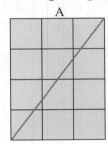

A

Rectangle A = 12 sq. units
Triangle A = 6 sq. units

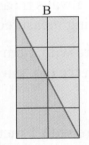

B

Rectangle B = 8 sq. units
Triangle B = 4 sq. units

A   B

Looking at it together

Rectangle A + B = 20 sq. units
Triangle A + B = 10 sq. units

Try This

First find the area of the rectangle. Then break it up into smaller rectangles to find the area of the triangles.

Exercise 12.3

1. Give the area of the shaded triangle in each figure.

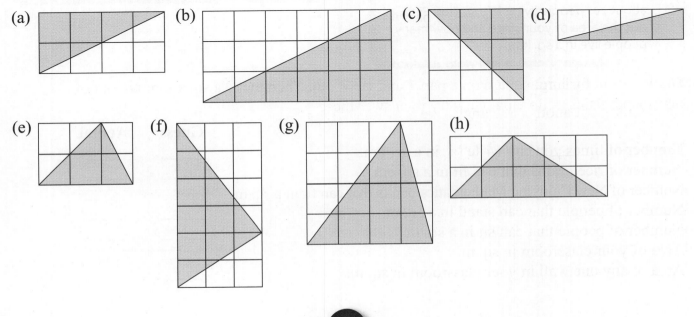

(a)   (b)   (c)   (d)

(e)   (f)   (g)   (h)

Different Units of Area

Area is always measured in square units. The unit we choose depends on how large or small the area being measured is.

A square with 1 cm sides is **a square centimetre (sq. cm).**

1 cm
1 cm | 1 cm
1 cm

A fingernail is about 1 sq. cm.

A square with 1 metre sides is **a square metre (sq. m).**

1 m
1 m | 1 m
1 m

A single bedsheet is about 2 sq. m.

A square with 1 kilometre sides is **a square kilometre (sq. km).**

1 km
1 km | 1 km
1 km

TRIPURA

The state of Tripura has an area of about 10,500 sq. km.

Smaller areas are measured in sq. cm and large areas in sq. km.

A sq. km. is a very large unit of area. Your school playground is perhaps smaller than 1 sq. km.

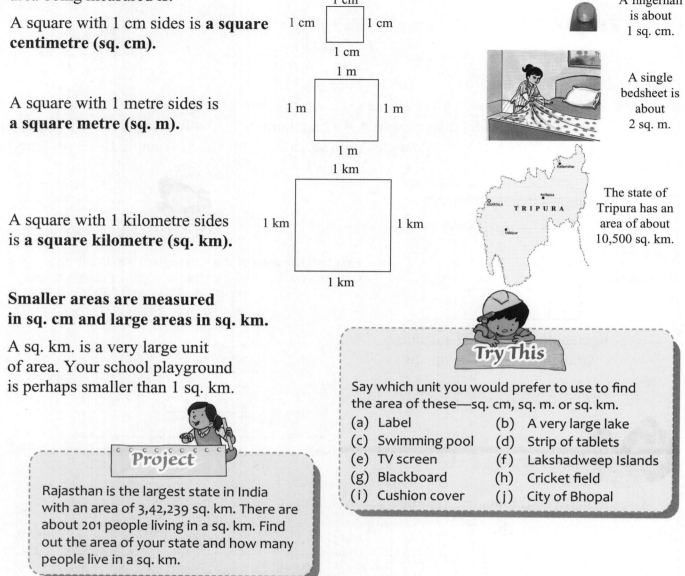

Try This

Say which unit you would prefer to use to find the area of these—sq. cm, sq. m. or sq. km.
(a) Label   (b) A very large lake
(c) Swimming pool   (d) Strip of tablets
(e) TV screen   (f) Lakshadweep Islands
(g) Blackboard   (h) Cricket field
(i) Cushion cover   (j) City of Bhopal

Project

Rajasthan is the largest state in India with an area of 3,42,239 sq. km. There are about 201 people living in a sq. km. Find out the area of your state and how many people live in a sq. km.

Draw a 1 cm by 1 cm square on a paper and cut it out. Then make a square metre out of newspaper using cello tape. Now try to answer these.

	Guess	Actual
Number of times you can write 'a' in a sq. cm.	_____	_____
Number of rice grains that can fit in a sq. cm.	_____	_____
Number of New Enjoying Mathematics books that can fit in a sq. m.	_____	_____
Number of people that can stand in a sq. m.	_____	_____
Number of people that can sit in a sq. m.	_____	_____
Area of your classroom in sq. m.	_____	_____
Area of any one wall in your classroom in sq. m.	_____	_____

Area of Irregular Shapes

You remember that we found the area of an irregular shape in Class IV using this method.

There are 4 whole squares.

There are 6 squares which are half or more than half.

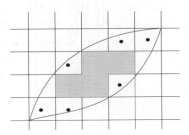

Approximate area = about 10 square units

You can also estimate the area of an irregular figure using a shortcut.

- Find the **under estimate** by counting only the whole squares. There are 4 whole squares.

- Find the **over estimate** by counting all the squares (whole and part). There are such 14 squares.

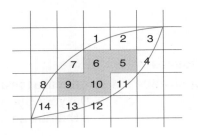

- **Add** the two figures and divide by 2 (ignore the remainder if any). $14 + 4 = 18 \div 2 = 9$

Approximate area = 9 square units

The answers in both the methods are close but not the same because both are only approximated or estimated answers.

 **Exercise 12.4**

1. Estimate the area of each of these figures in square units.

   (a)
   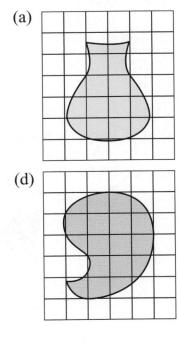

   (b)

   (c)

   (d)

   (e)
   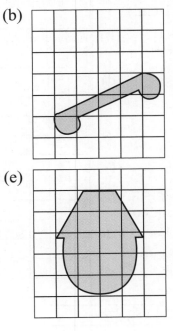

   (f)
   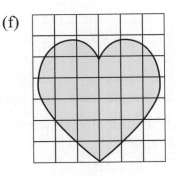

2. Find the approximate area of these islands. Take each square centimetre in the drawing to be the same as one sq. km. Give your answers in sq. km.

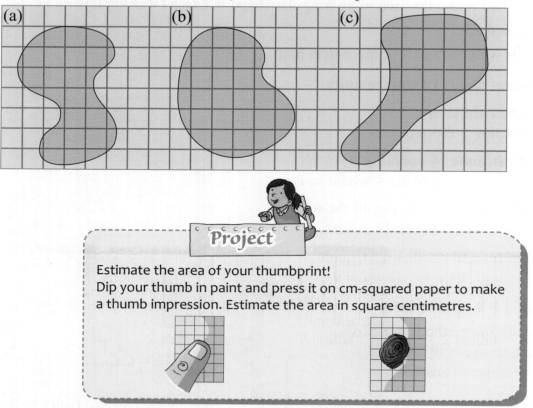

Project

Estimate the area of your thumbprint!
Dip your thumb in paint and press it on cm-squared paper to make a thumb impression. Estimate the area in square centimetres.

Relationship between Area and Perimeter

Rectangles of the Same Perimeter

How many different kinds of rectangles can you make with a perimeter of 24 cm?
(Take the squares below to be 1 cm × 1 cm.)

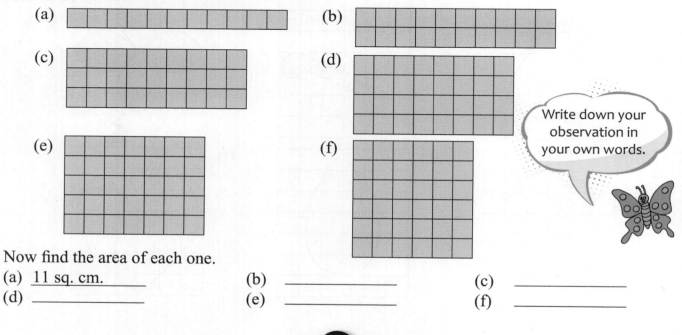

Write down your observation in your own words.

Now find the area of each one.
(a) 11 sq. cm.

(b) _____

(c) _____

(d) _____

(e) _____

(f) _____

180

Rectangles of the Same Area

How many different rectangles can you make with an area of 24 sq. cm.? Find the perimeter of each one. One is done for you. (Take the squares below to be 1 cm × 1 cm.)

(a)

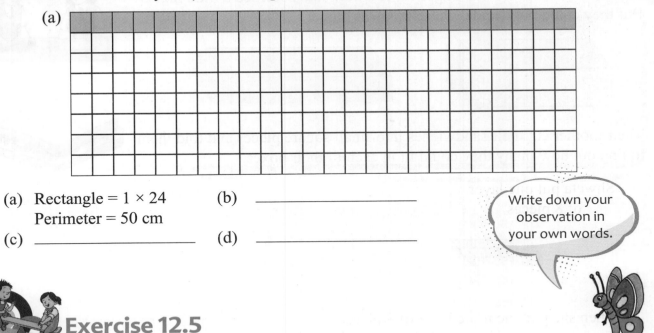

(a) Rectangle = 1 × 24
    Perimeter = 50 cm

(b) _____

(c) _____

(d) _____

Write down your observation in your own words.

 **Exercise 12.5**

1. Use a 15-cm-long string and join its ends. Place it on a centimetre squared paper to make a square, a circle, a triangle and a rectangle. Find the area of each shape. Which shape has the largest area? Which shape has the smallest area?

2. Use a centimetre squared paper to create as many different rectangles as you can with a perimeter of 18 cm. Find the area of each rectangle.

3. Use centimetre squared paper to create as many different rectangles as you can with an area of 36 sq. cm. Find the perimeter of each rectangle.

4. Application in real life.

   (a) The breadth of a garden is 9.3 m and its length is 17.7 m. What is the perimeter of the garden?

   (b) Prabhu has a rectangular backyard that is 32 m wide and 46 m long. How much fencing will he need to enclose the yard? If fencing costs ₹ 98 per metre, how much will he have to pay?

   (c) Sapna walks around a square park whose side is 70 m. One day she walked around the park 5 times. How much did she walk in all?

   (d) A square picture has a frame of 100 cm. What is the length of each side? What is its area?

Volume

The twins Shweta and Swati were comparing the size of their snack boxes. Shweta's box was a little longer while Swati's box seemed a little higher. But they could not decide whose box was bigger.

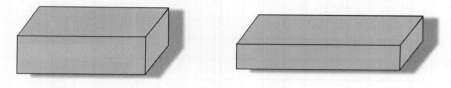

Their mother cut their sandwiches into small square pieces and told them to find out how many they could fit in each of their boxes.

Shweta put one layer
of 8 pieces.

1 layer

Swati could fit only 6 pieces
in one layer in her box.

1 layer

Then she put one more layer of 8 pieces.
There was no more space left in her snack box.

2 layers

She could fit two more such layers
in the box. Then the box was full.

3 layers

Shweta's box could hold
(8 × 2) = 16 sandwich pieces.

Swati's box could hold
(6 × 3) = 18 sandwich pieces.

So, we can say that Swati's snack box is bigger because it could hold more pieces.

We can say that Swati's snack box has a greater **'volume'** than Shweta's snack box.

The volume of an object is the amount of space it occupies.

In order to find the volume of objects we fill them up with cubes. We can choose one of the three kinds:

1 mm
1 mm

A millimetre cube (mm cube) is about the size of a grain of sugar.

1 cm
1 cm
1 cm

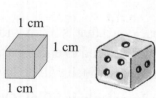

A centimetre cube (cm cube) is about the size of a die.

1 m
1 m
1 m

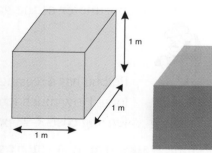

A metre cube (m cube) is about the size of a very large TV box.

A mm cube is used to measure the volume of very small objects.
A m cube is used to measure the volume of large objects.

Let us find the volume of this shoe box by filling it with cm cubes.

Put in 1 cm cubes to fit one layer and count them. There are 10 rows with 4 cubes in each row. So there are 40 cubes in one layer. There are four layers of 40 cubes each. There are 160 one-cm cubes filling the box.

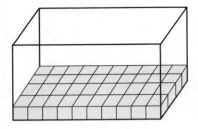

Whether a box is full or empty it takes up the same amount of space on your shelf. So both have the same volume.

Since the box can hold 160 one-cm cubes, the **volume of the box is said to be 160 cubic centimetres**.

The unit of measurement of volume is cubic centimetres and is written as cu. cm.
Volume of the shoe box = 160 cu. cm.

1 mm cubes give the volume in cubic millimetres and is written as cu. mm.

1 m cubes give the volume in cubic metres and is written as cu. m.

Find the volume of these solids. Each cube is of 1 cm sides.

(a)

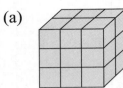

One layer = 3 × 2 = 6 cubes
  3 layers = 6 × 3 = 18 cubes
Answer: Volume = 18 cu. cm.

Common Mistake

Volume = 18 cm ✗
       = 18 cu.cm. ✓

(b)

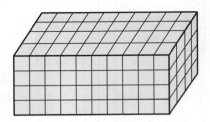

Layer 3
Layer 2
Layer 1

Add the different layers.

Layer 1	5
Layer 2	4
Layer 3	3
	12

Answer: Volume = 12 cu. cm.

Exercise 12.6

1. Find the volume of each of these. Give your answer in cu. cm.

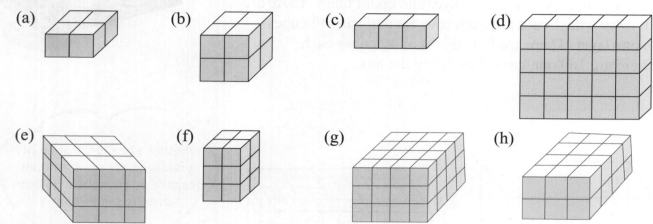

(a) (b) (c) (d)

(e) (f) (g) (h)

2. Find the volume of each of these solid shapes. Give your answer in cu. cm.

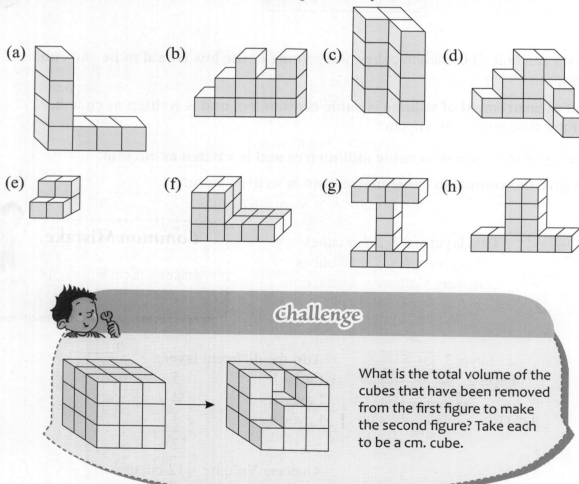

(a) (b) (c) (d)

(e) (f) (g) (h)

Challenge

What is the total volume of the cubes that have been removed from the first figure to make the second figure? Take each to be a cm. cube.

Calculating Volume

We can use a shortcut to calculate the volume of a cube or a cuboid.

While finding the volume of a cube or a cuboid, you have been first counting the number of cubes in a layer and then finding the number of layers.

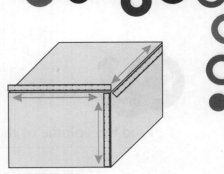

Cuboid

Cubes per layer × Number of layers = Volume

Length × Breadth × Height = Volume

This can be used as a shortcut to calculate the volume.

Volume = length × breadth × height

$$V = \ell \times b \times h$$

(a) Find the volume of this cuboid.

Volume of the cuboid $= \ell \times b \times h$

$V = 7 \text{ cm} \times 4 \text{ cm} \times 4 \text{ cm}$

$V = 112$ cu. cm

Answer: Volume of the cuboid is 112 cu. cm.

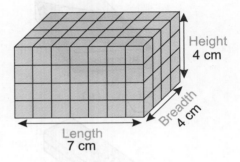

Height 4 cm

Breadth 4 cm

Length 7 cm

(b) Find the volume of this cube.

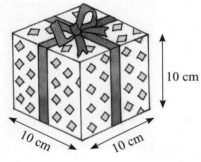

10 cm

10 cm 10 cm

Volume of a cube $= \ell \times b \times h$

$V = 10 \text{ cm} \times 10 \text{ cm} \times 10 \text{ cm}$

$V = 10 \times 10 \times 10$ cu. cm.

$V = 1000$ cu. cm.

Answer: Volume of the cube is 1000 cu. cm.

Another word for breadth is width.

Try This

Use a ruler to measure the length, breadth and height of these objects to the nearest cm. Then calculate their volume.

Your Maths textbook

ℓ _____ cm   b _____ cm   h _____ cm

Volume = _____ cu. cm.

Your eraser

ℓ _____ cm   b _____ cm   h _____ cm

Volume = _____ cu. cm.

Your pencil box

ℓ _____ cm   b _____ cm   h _____ cm

Volume = _____ cu. cm.

Exercise 12.7

1. Find the volume of these solids.

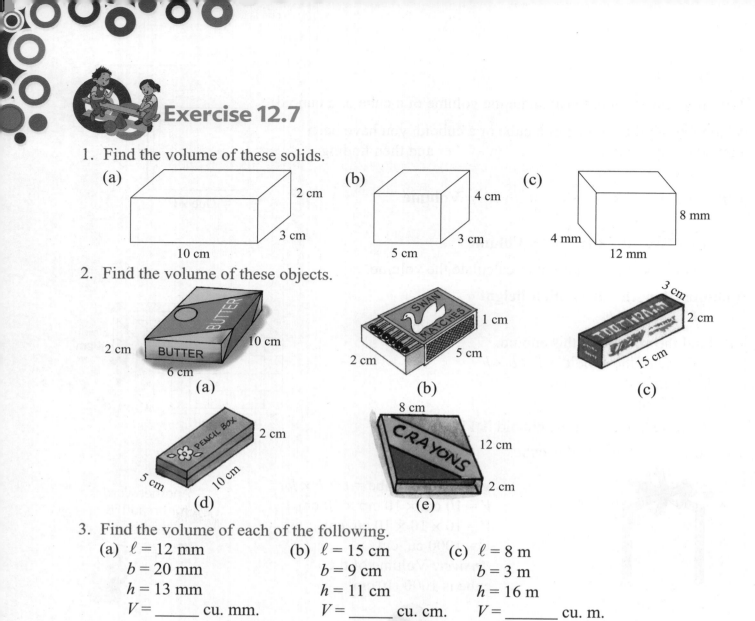

(a)

2 cm
3 cm
10 cm

(b)

4 cm
3 cm
5 cm

(c)

8 mm
4 mm
12 mm

2. Find the volume of these objects.

BUTTER
2 cm
10 cm
BUTTER
6 cm
(a)

SWAN MATCHES
1 cm
2 cm
5 cm
(b)

3 cm
TOOTHPASTE
2 cm
15 cm
(c)

PENCIL BOX
2 cm
5 cm
10 cm
(d)

8 cm
CRAYONS
12 cm
2 cm
(e)

3. Find the volume of each of the following.

(a) ℓ = 12 mm
    b = 20 mm
    h = 13 mm
    V = _____ cu. mm.

(b) ℓ = 15 cm
    b = 9 cm
    h = 11 cm
    V = _____ cu. cm.

(c) ℓ = 8 m
    b = 3 m
    h = 16 m
    V = _____ cu. m.

4. Complete the table.

	Length	Breadth	Height	Volume
(a)	3 m	8 m	7 m	
(b)	6 cm	4 cm		120 cu. cm.
(c)	14 cm		8 cm	448 cu. cm.
(d)		11 mm	10 mm	1210 cu. mm.

Hint: Divide 120 by the product of 6 and 4 to get the height.

5. Application in real life.

(a) A book is 24 cm long, 14 cm wide and 2 cm high.
    What is the volume of 2 such books piled one on top of the other?

(b) The drawer in Kalpana's cupboard is 30 cm long, 10 cm high and 45 cm wide.
    What is the volume of the drawer?

(c) A brick has a length of 18 cm, breadth of 6 cm and height of 5 cm.
    What will be the volume of 10 such bricks?

Finding the Volume of Other Shapes

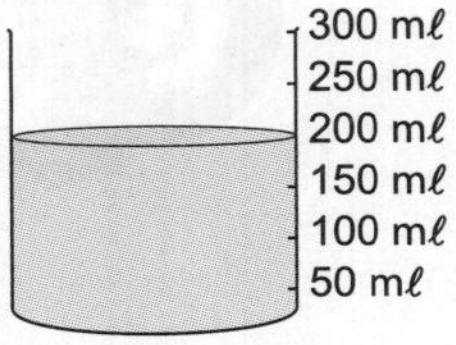

Here is another way to find the volume of shape.
Take a measuring glass and fill it with water up to the 200 mℓ mark.

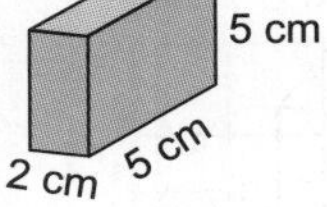

Use fifty interlocking 1-centimetre cubes and fix them to make a cuboid
with length 2 cm, breadth 5 cm, and height 5 cm.
What is the volume of the cuboid? _____ cu. cm.

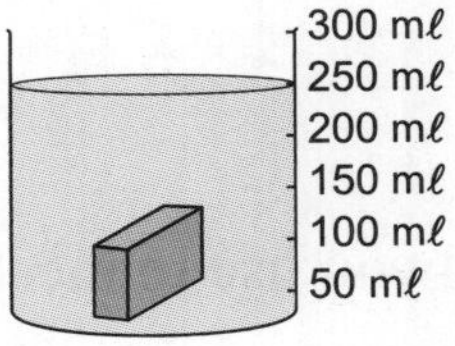

Put the cuboid into the water in the measuring glass.

By how much has the level of water risen? _____ mℓ.

That means a cuboid of 50 cu. cm. occupies
the same space as 50 mℓ of water!

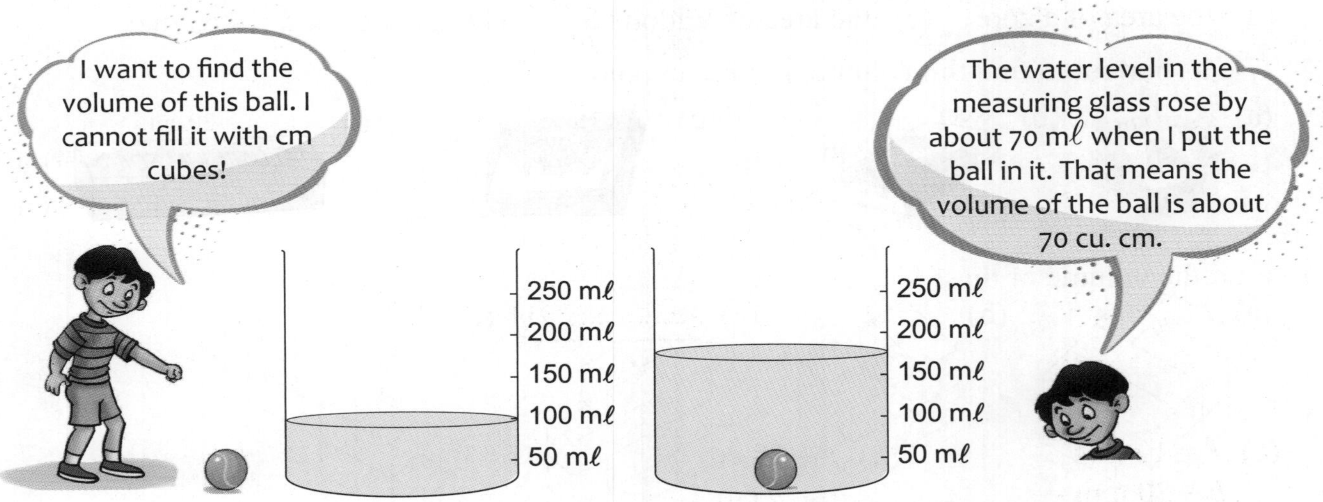

> I want to find the volume of this ball. I cannot fill it with cm cubes!

> The water level in the measuring glass rose by about 70 mℓ when I put the ball in it. That means the volume of the ball is about 70 cu. cm.

Exercise 12.8

1. Find the volume of Stone A and Stone B.

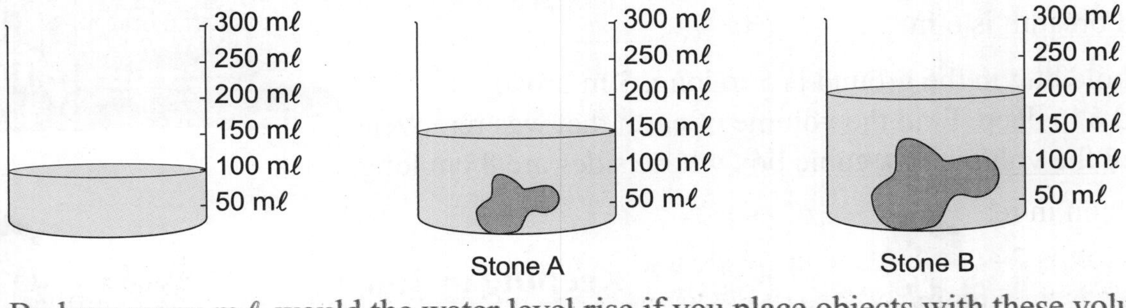

Stone A

Stone B

2. By how many mℓ would the water level rise if you place objects with these volumes in the measuring glass?

   (a) 20 cu. cm.   (b) 60 cu. cm.   (c) 75 cu. cm.

3. What is the volume of objects that make the level of water rise by:

   (a) 9 mℓ   (b) 30 mℓ   (c) 96 mℓ

Chapter Check-Up

1. Find the perimeter and area of:
   (a) a square with sides 7 cm.
   (b) a rectangle of sides 5 m and 11 m.

2. Find the area of these shapes in square units.
   (a)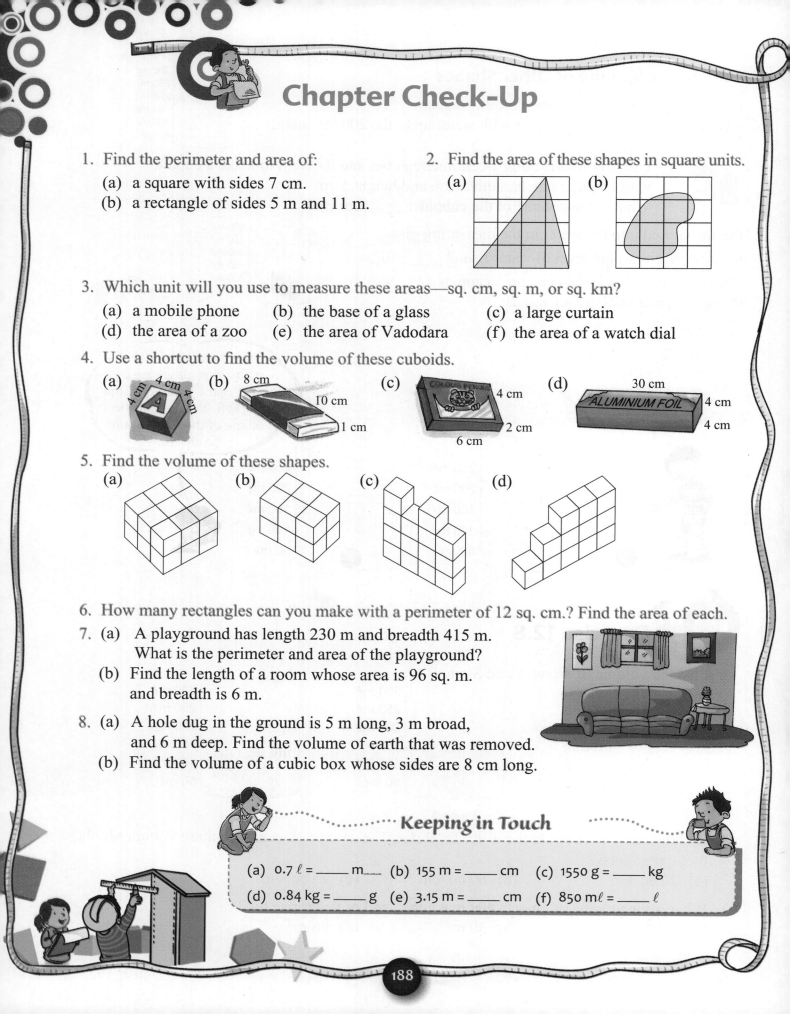
   (b)

3. Which unit will you use to measure these areas—sq. cm, sq. m, or sq. km?
   (a) a mobile phone
   (b) the base of a glass
   (c) a large curtain
   (d) the area of a zoo
   (e) the area of Vadodara
   (f) the area of a watch dial

4. Use a shortcut to find the volume of these cuboids.
   (a) 4 cm 4 cm 4 cm
   (b) 8 cm 10 cm 1 cm
   (c) 4 cm 2 cm 6 cm
   (d) 30 cm 4 cm 4 cm

5. Find the volume of these shapes.
   (a)   (b)   (c)   (d)

6. How many rectangles can you make with a perimeter of 12 sq. cm.? Find the area of each.

7. (a) A playground has length 230 m and breadth 415 m.
       What is the perimeter and area of the playground?
   (b) Find the length of a room whose area is 96 sq. m.
       and breadth is 6 m.

8. (a) A hole dug in the ground is 5 m long, 3 m broad,
       and 6 m deep. Find the volume of earth that was removed.
   (b) Find the volume of a cubic box whose sides are 8 cm long.

Keeping in Touch

(a) 0.7 ℓ = _____ m____
(b) 155 m = _____ cm
(c) 1550 g = _____ kg
(d) 0.84 kg = _____ g
(e) 3.15 m = _____ cm
(f) 850 mℓ = _____ ℓ

Maths Lab Activity

Objective: To create a tessellating pattern.

Materials Required: Plain paper, a pair of scissors, card paper, cello tape, pencil, crayons.

Preparation: Card paper may be cut into a 6 cm × 6 cm square.

Steps:

1. Take the square card paper.

2. Mark out a portion as shown.

3. Cut it and attach it to the opposite side without overlapping and by using cello tape.

4. Now mark out another portion as shown.

5. Cut and attach to the opposite side.

6. Your basic stencil is ready. Use it to draw repeated shapes like this. Then fill in details to make an interesting design.

M. C. Escher was a well-known Dutch artist who used tessellation to create beautiful designs.

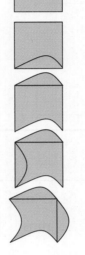

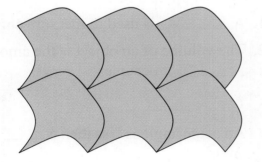

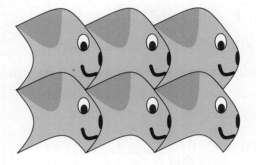

Experiment with different cut out portions to create other interesting designs.

Try one:

1. l = 5 m, b = 20 m, Area = _____

2. Volume of a cube of sides 5 m = _____

3. When two rays have a common endpoint they form a _____.

4. 20 cm × 5 = _____ m

5. A straight angle = 90° + _____ °

6. Factors of 31 = _____

7. A cube that is opened makes a _____.

8. LCM of 3 and 12 is _____.

9. 23.15 m in smaller units is _____.

10. 102 cm in bigger units is _____.

11. 1kg = _____ g + 900 g

12. 8.1 km in smaller units is _____.

13. 8.3 cm = _____ mm

14. 5 kg – 600 g = _____ kg _____ g

15. l = 2 cm, b = 2 cm, h = 2 cm, Volume = _____

16. A _____ shows exact location.

17. 350 ml + 650 ml = _____ l

18. Area of a square room of sides 10 m is _____.

19. 9 l 800 ml + 600 ml = ___ l ___ ml

20. 6 cm – 5 mm = _____ cm ___ mm

21. 95 mm = _____ cm

22. HCF of 13 and 23 is _____ .

23. 1 km = 800 m + _____ m

24. Sides of a square with area 49 sq. cm. is _____

25. 8 – 1.9 = _____

26. 200 m × 10 = _____ km

27. 9500 m = _____ km

28. 79 in Roman numerals is _____.

29. Perimeter of a square of sides 200 m is _____.

30. The number in the thousandths place of 184.095 is _____.

31. A _____ is used to measure angles.

32. The volume of an object is the amount of _____ it occupies.

33. $6 - \dfrac{3}{5}$ = _____

34. An acute angle is less than a _____ angle.

35. 300 g × 30 = _____ kg

36. 2.25 m = _____ cm

Test Your Skills

(For Chapters 9, 10, 11, 12)

1. Find the volume of these shapes.

2. Name all the line segments here. There are six.

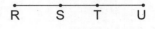

3. Which of these are the lines of symmetry?

4. Find the area of the shape in square units.

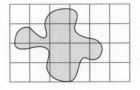

5. Say whether these shapes need $\frac{1}{2}$ or $\frac{1}{4}$ turn to come back to its original shape.

6. Use a protractor to measure these angles and say what kind each is.

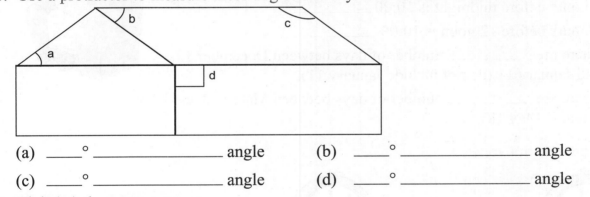

(a) _____° _____ angle   (b) _____° _____ angle

(c) _____° _____ angle   (d) _____° _____ angle

7. Tick (✓) the correct answer.

(a) Express 0.9 km in m.	(b) A book is 30 cm long and 20 cm wide. What is its area and perimeter?	(c) A full suitcase weighs 19 kg 200 g. An empty suitcase weighs 2 kg 500 g. What is the weight of the contents?
(i) 9 m	(i) A = 100 sq cm P = 60 cm	(i) 16 kg 700 g
(ii) 90 m	(ii) A = 60 sq cm P = 100 cm	(ii) 21 kg 700 g
(iii) 900 m	(iii) A = 600 cm P = 100 sq cm	(iii) 16 kg 300 g
(iv) 9000 m	(iv) A = 600 sq cm P = 100 cm	(iv) 21 kg

Time and Temperature

Looking Back

1. Write how many minutes past the hour?

     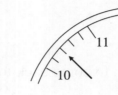

_____   _____

2. Fill in the blanks.

   (a) 3:30 p.m. is written as _____ in the 24-hour clock.

   (b) 00:25 hours is written as _____ in the 12-hour clock.

   (c) 2 hours before midnight is 10:00 _____.

   (d) 2 hours before 12 noon is 10:00 _____.

   (e) There are _____ number of days between December 12 and January 11 (do not include January 11).

   (f) There are _____ number of days between March 23 and May 18 (include May 18).

3. Give the time in two ways:

 _____    _____

_____   _____

4. (a) A play that started at 5:45 p.m. was 2 hours 30 minutes long. When did it get over?

   (b) Another play that started at 6:30 p.m. got over at 8:55 p.m. How long was the play?

Time

Converting from One Unit into Another

Just like we convert units of measurement, we can also convert different units of time.

Multiply to change from a bigger unit to a smaller unit.

$$\times 60 \qquad \times 60$$

Hours ⟶ Minutes ⟶ Seconds

$$\div 60 \qquad \div 60$$

Divide to change from a smaller unit to a bigger unit.

Converting a bigger unit into a smaller unit

(a) 4 hours = ___?___ minutes

$4 \times 60 = 240$

4 hours = 240 minutes

(b) $2\frac{1}{2}$ minutes = ___?___ seconds

$2 \times 60 = 120$ seconds

$\frac{1}{2}$ minute = 30 seconds

$120 + 30 = 150$ seconds

$2\frac{1}{2}$ minutes = 150 seconds

Converting a smaller unit into a bigger unit

(a) 920 minutes = ? hours

```
        1 5  ← hours
  60 ) 9 2 0
      − 6 0
        3 2 0
      − 3 0 0
          2 0  ← minutes
```

920 minutes = 15 hours 20 minutes

(b) 150 seconds = ? minutes

```
          2  ← minutes
  60 ) 1 5 0
     − 1 2 0
         3 0  ← seconds
```

150 seconds = 2 minutes 30 seconds

Try This

(a) 3 minutes = _____ seconds

(b) $3\frac{1}{2}$ hours = _____ minutes

(c) 720 seconds = _____ minutes

(d) 400 minutes = _____ hours _____ minutes

Exercise 13.1

1. Change to minutes.

   (a) 8 hours   (b) 11 hours

   (c) 7 hours   (d) 9 hours 20 minutes

   (e) 3 hours 12 minutes   (f) 4 hours 42 minutes

2. Change to hours and minutes.

   (a) 720 minutes   (b) 132 minutes

   (c) 130 minutes   (d) 360 minutes

   (e) 410 minutes   (f) 500 minutes

3. Change to seconds.

   (a) 13 minutes   (b) 5 minutes

   (c) 26 minutes   (d) $10\frac{1}{2}$ minutes

   (e) 15 minutes   (f) 45 minutes

4. Change to minutes and seconds.

   (a) 840 seconds   (b) 480 seconds

   (c) 280 seconds   (d) 600 seconds

   (e) 93 seconds   (f) 950 seconds

5. Application in real life.

   (a) A television programme had 11 minutes of advertisements in it. How many seconds were the advertisements for?

   (b) It takes Manisha 38 seconds to climb up the steps of her house. In one week if she spends 504 seconds doing this, how many minutes has she spent climbing up the steps? (Use only the information you need)

   (c)  An advertisement on radio lasted for 30 seconds. If the same advertisement is played daily for 10 days, for how many minutes will it be played?

   (d) Smriti jogged for $1\frac{1}{2}$ hours on Monday and 90 minutes on Tuesday. On which day did she jog longer?

Adding and subtracting Measures of Time

Theme: It is a Holiday!

(a) Ruchi and her family went for a weekend holiday to Mussorie. The train journey from Delhi to Dehradun was 5 hours 50 minutes. After that a taxi took 1 hour 45 minutes to Mussorie. How long did they spend travelling?

5 h 50 min + 1 h 45 min = ?

5 + 1 = _____ h

50 + 45 = _____ min

Project

Many world and olympic sports records are made with differences of even less than a second. For example, Usain Bolt of Jamaica won the 100 m race at the Beijing Olympics in 2008 with 9.69 seconds. That is less than 10 seconds! Find other similar sports records and list them in your notebook.

95 minutes is the same as _____ hour _____ minutes.

6 h + 1 h 35 min = _____ hours _____ minutes

They spent _____ hours _____ minutes travelling.

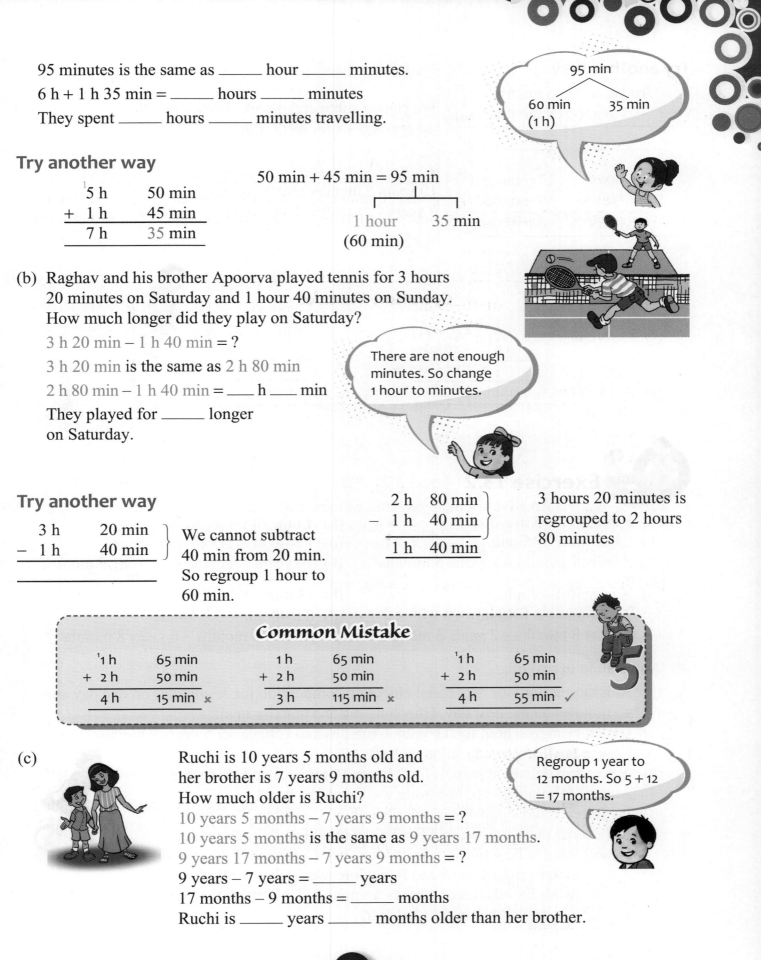

95 min

60 min   35 min
(1 h)

Try another way

¹5 h   50 min
+ 1 h   45 min
_____
7 h   35 min

50 min + 45 min = 95 min

1 hour   35 min
(60 min)

(b) Raghav and his brother Apoorva played tennis for 3 hours
20 minutes on Saturday and 1 hour 40 minutes on Sunday.
How much longer did they play on Saturday?

3 h 20 min − 1 h 40 min = ?

3 h 20 min is the same as 2 h 80 min

2 h 80 min − 1 h 40 min = ___ h ___ min

They played for _____ longer
on Saturday.

There are not enough
minutes. So change
1 hour to minutes.

Try another way

3 h   20 min
− 1 h   40 min
_____

We cannot subtract
40 min from 20 min.
So regroup 1 hour to
60 min.

2 h   80 min
− 1 h   40 min
_____
1 h   40 min

3 hours 20 minutes is
regrouped to 2 hours
80 minutes

Common Mistake

¹1 h   65 min
+ 2 h   50 min
_____
4 h   15 min ✗

1 h   65 min
+ 2 h   50 min
_____
3 h   115 min ✗

¹1 h   65 min
+ 2 h   50 min
_____
4 h   55 min ✓

(c) Ruchi is 10 years 5 months old and
her brother is 7 years 9 months old.
How much older is Ruchi?

10 years 5 months − 7 years 9 months = ?

10 years 5 months is the same as 9 years 17 months.

9 years 17 months − 7 years 9 months = ?

9 years − 7 years = _____ years

17 months − 9 months = _____ months

Ruchi is _____ years _____ months older than her brother.

Regroup 1 year to
12 months. So 5 + 12
= 17 months.

195

Try another way

$$
\begin{array}{rl}
10 \text{ years} & 5 \text{ months} \\
-7 \text{ years} & 9 \text{ months} \\
\hline
\end{array}
\Big\}
$$
We cannot subtract 5 months from 9 months, so regroup 1 year to 12 months

$$
\begin{array}{rl}
9 \text{ years} & 17 \text{ months} \\
-7 \text{ years} & 9 \text{ months} \\
\hline
2 \text{ years} & 8 \text{ months} \\
\hline
\end{array}
\Big\}
$$
10 years 5 months regrouped to 9 years 17 months (5 months + 12 months)

Common Mistake

$$
\begin{array}{rl}
{}^{1}\cancel{2}\text{ h} & {}^{12}\cancel{2}5 \text{ min} \\
-1\text{ h} & 40 \text{ min} \\
\hline
- & 85 \text{ min} \quad \times
\end{array}
\qquad
\begin{array}{rl}
{}^{1}\cancel{2}\text{ h} & {}^{85}\cancel{2}5 \text{ min} \\
-1\text{ h} & 40 \text{ min} \\
\hline
- & 45 \text{ min} \quad \checkmark
\end{array}
$$

Exercise 13.2

1. (a) 5 min 30 s + 5 min 30 s   (b) 1 min 20 s + 3 min 45 s
   (c) 2 h 25 min + 45 min   (d) 1 h 40 m + 1 h 40 min
   (e) 3 years 7 months + 4 years 5 months   (f) 10 years 7 months + 11 years 7 months

2. (a) 8 min 10 s – 7 min 2 s   (b) 13 min – 5 min 35 s
   (c) 9 h 20 min – 3 h 40 min   (d) 8 h 40 min – 3 h 50 min
   (e) 5 years 3 months – 2 years 3 months   (f) 8 years 6 months – 6 years 8 months

3. Application in real life.

   (a) Anisha practised for her school elocution competition for 35 minutes on one day and 45 minutes on the next day. How long did she practise in all?

   (b) Harish went to school for 11 years 6 months and college for 5 years 9 months. How many years of education is that?

   (c) A postman delivered parcels for 2 hours 15 minutes and letters for 3 hours 45 minutes. For how long was he on the beat?

   (d) Jayashree could swim a particular length in 3 minutes 22 seconds. After some practice, she could swim the same length in 2 minutes 40 seconds. By how much time had her speed improved?

   (e) A normal train from Chennai to Bangalore takes 6 hours 10 minutes. The Shatabdi Express takes 4 hours 45 minute. How much time do you save by travelling on the Shatabdi?

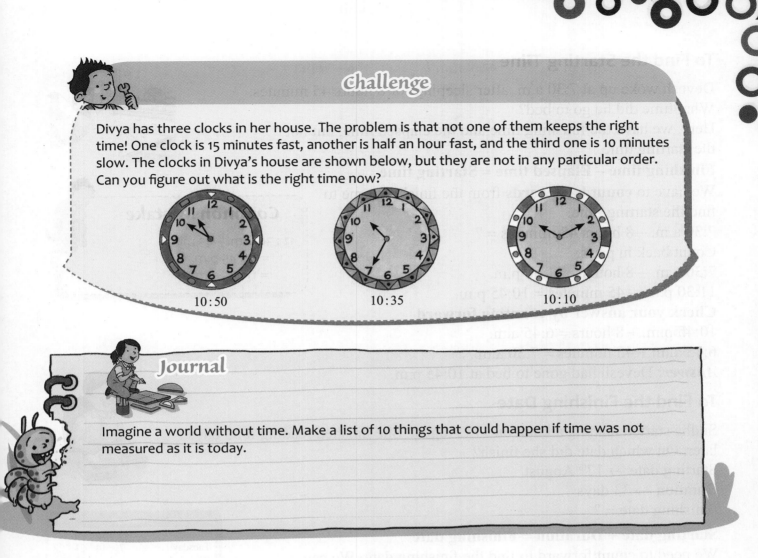

Journal

Imagine a world without time. Make a list of 10 things that could happen if time was not measured as it is today.

Finding the Starting Time or Finishing Time

To Find the Finishing Time

Ajay started the marathon race at 8:30 a.m. He finished 3 hours 32 minutes later. What time did he finish?

Starting time—8:30 a.m.
Finishing time—after 3 hours 32 minutes
To find out what time Ajay finished the marathon, we need to **add the elapsed time to the starting time**.
Starting time + Elapsed time = Finishing time
The time spent during an event or activity is the duration of the event or 'elapsed time'.
We have to **count forward** to find the finishing time.
8:30 + 3 hours 32 minutes = ?
Count in parts: 8:30 a.m. + 3 hours = 11:30 a.m.
             11:30 a.m. + 32 minutes = 12:02 p.m.
Answer: Ajay finished the marathon at 12:02 p.m.

Common Mistake

11 : 45 a.m. + 30 minutes
  = 12 : 15 a.m. ✗
  = 12 : 15 p.m. ✓

To Find the Starting Time

Devesh woke up at 7:30 a.m. after sleeping for 8 hours 45 minutes. What time did he go to bed?

Here, we have the finishing time and the elapsed time, but not the starting time.

Finishing time – Elapsed time = Starting time

We have to **count backwards** from the finishing time to find the starting time.

7:30 a.m. – 8 hours 45 minutes = ?

Count back in parts:

7:30 a.m. – 8 hours = 11:30 p.m.

11:30 p.m. – 45 minutes = 10:45 p.m.

Check your answer by counting forward

10:45 p.m. + 8 hours = 6:45 a.m.

6:45 a.m. + 45 minutes = 7:30 a.m.

Answer: Devesh had gone to bed at 10:45 p.m.

Common Mistake

12 : 30 p.m. – 45 min
    = 11 : 45 p.m. ✗
    = 11 : 45 a.m. ✓

To Find the Finishing Date

Sudha started reading a book on 17th August. She finished reading it 33 days later. On which date did she finish?

Starting date → 17th August

Duration → 33 days

Finishing date = ?

Starting date + Duration = Finishing date

We need to count forward to find the finishing date. We can do that in parts.

- 17th Aug to 31st Aug = 15 days (counting both days)
- 33 days – 15 days = 18 days
- 18 days after 31st August takes us to 18th September

Answer: Sudha finished reading the book on 18th September.

August					
Monday		6	13	20	27
Tuesday		7	14	21	28
Wednesday	1	8	15	22	29
Thursday	2	9	16	23	30
Friday	3	10	17	24	31
Saturday	4	11	18	25	
Sunday	5	12	19	26	

To Find the Starting Date

Rijul returned from his 21-day holiday on 10th July. When did his holiday begin? We need to count back in parts to find the starting date.

- 10th July to 1st July = 10 days
- 21 days – 10 days = 11 days
- 11 days before 1st July takes us to 20th June (30th → 20th June = 11 days)

Check your answer by counting forward

20th June to 30th June = 11 days

15 July to 10th June = <u>10 days</u>

    21 days

Answer: Rijul began his holiday on 20th June.

June					
Monday		4	11	18	25
Tuesday		5	12	19	26
Wednesday		6	13	20	27
Thursday		7	14	21	28
Friday	1	8	15	22	29
Saturday	2	9	16	23	30
Sunday	3	10	17	24	

Exercise 13.3

1. Fill in the missing information. Use a.m. or p.m.

	Starting time	Elapsed time	Finishing time
(a)	1:05 p.m.	4 hours 40 minutes	
(b)	11:15 a.m.	2 hours 45 minutes	
(c)		5 hours 15 minutes	6:00 p.m.
(d)		3 hours 20 minutes	3:20 a.m.

2.

	Starting date	Duration	Finishing date
(a)	21st May	16 days	
(b)	19th January	19 days	
(c)		13 days	2nd April
(d)		24 days	10th May

3. Application in real life.

(a) Apoorva's school Sports day is on March 20th. He wants to start practising 30 days earlier. When should he start? (Take February to have 28 days.)

(b) Nikhil's birthday party started at 11: 45 a.m. and finished 3 hours 40 minutes later. When did the party finish?

(c)  Meera started knitting a muffler on Independence Day. If she completed it in 25 days, on which day did she finish it?

(d) Prachi started practising the *veena* at 1:15 p.m. and finished 1 hour 20 minutes later. What time did she finish?

(e) Madhur joined a 2-week driving class that got over on September 3rd. When did it began?

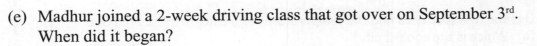

Measurement of Temperature

Temperature is the measure of how hot or how cold something is. We use thermometers to measure temperature.

Celsius Scale

The metric system uses a scale called the **Celsius scale** in the thermometer. On the Celsius scale, **water freezes at 0°C and boils at 100°C.**

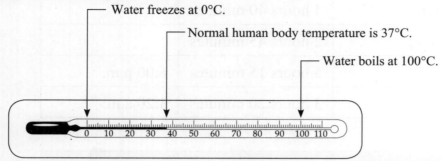

— Water freezes at 0°C.

— Normal human body temperature is 37°C.

— Water boils at 100°C.

Knowledge of outdoor temperature helps us in judging the weather conditions.

0°C – 10°C: Cold weather   20°C – 25°C: Mild weather   30°C – 35°C: Hot weather

10°C – 20°C: Cool weather   25°C – 30°C: Warm weather   35°C – 40°C and above:

                                             Very hot weather

Exercise 13.4

1. Circle the temperature that is close to the situation described. One has been done for you.

    (a) Warm day   (b) Hot bath   (c) Hot milk
        35°C/5°C   42°C/10°C   45°C/15°C

    (d) Cold drink   (e) Ice   (f) Feverish person
        5°C/30°C   0°C/100°C   38.5°C/35.8°C

2. Read these temperatures.

    (a)   (b)   (c)   (d)   (e)

         10°C   40°C   50°C   20°C   80°C
      5°C   35°C   45°C   15°C   75°C
         0°C   30°C   40°C   10°C   70°C

   About ____ °C   About ____ °C   About ____ °C   About ____ °C   About ____ °C

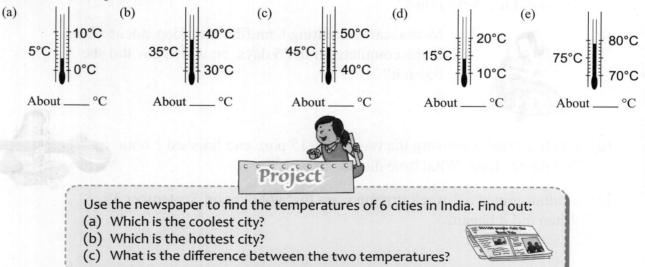

Project

Use the newspaper to find the temperatures of 6 cities in India. Find out:
(a) Which is the coolest city?
(b) Which is the hottest city?
(c) What is the difference between the two temperatures?

Chapter Check-Up

1. Fill in the blanks.

   (a) 3 h 20 min = _____ min

   (b) 560 min = _____ h _____ min

   (c) $11\frac{1}{2}$ min = _____ s

   (d) 980 s = _____ min _____ s

   (e) 15 min – 3 min 20 s = _____

   (f) 4 years 7 months + 2 years 8 months = _____

   (g) 2 h 40 min + 3 h 30 min = _____

   (h) 3 years 3 months – 1 year 4 months = _____

2. Find the time.

   (a) 3 h 20 min after 11:45 a.m.

   (b) 4 h 50 min before 7:20 p.m.

3. Find the date.

   (a) 13 days after 28th August

   (b) 25 days before 16th November

4. Read the temperature.

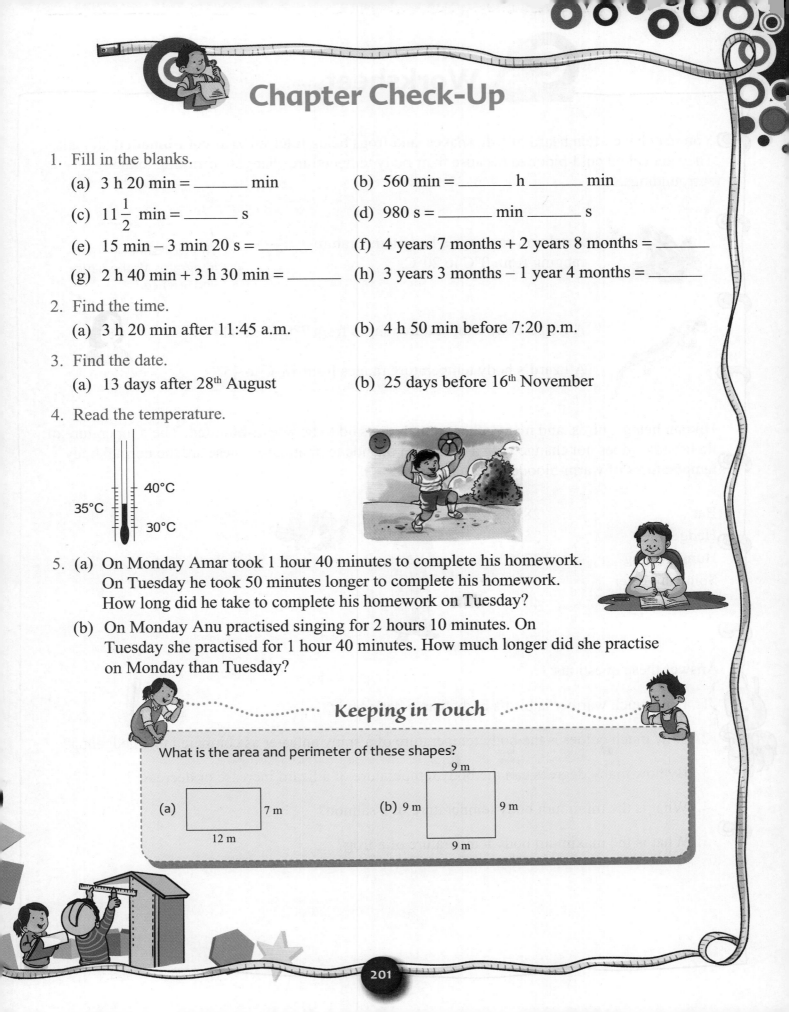

5. (a) On Monday Amar took 1 hour 40 minutes to complete his homework. On Tuesday he took 50 minutes longer to complete his homework. How long did he take to complete his homework on Tuesday?

   (b) On Monday Anu practised singing for 2 hours 10 minutes. On Tuesday she practised for 1 hour 40 minutes. How much longer did she practise on Monday than Tuesday?

·········· **Keeping in Touch** ··········

What is the area and perimeter of these shapes?

(a) 7 m 12 m

(b) 9 m 9 m 9 m 9 m

You may have often heard of fish, snakes, and frogs being referred to as **cold-blooded** animals. They are called cold-blooded because their body temperature changes according to their surroundings.

A salmon can have a body temperature ranging from 0°C to 20°C.

This worksheet integrates Mathematics and Science.

A frog's body temperature ranges from 7°C to 30°C.

A lizard's body temperature ranges from 18°C to 45°C.

Human beings, birds, and many other animals are said to be **warm-blooded**. The temperature of their bodies does not change with a change in outside temperature. These are the normal body temperatures of warm-blooded creatures:

Bat	–	28°C
Hedgehog	–	35°C
Human being	–	37°C
Spiny ant eater	–	30°C
Bird	–	40°C

Answer these questions:

1. How much warmer is bird's body than a bat's body?

2. How much colder is the body temperature of a spiny anteater as compared to a hedgehog?

3. By how many degrees can the body temperature of a lizard increase or decrease?

4. What is the minimum body temperature of a salmon?

5. What is the maximum body temperature of a frog?

Mapping Skills

Looking Back

Nandu was writing to his pen friend Jeanne, who lives in Paris, France, to explain to her where he lived. This is how he did it.

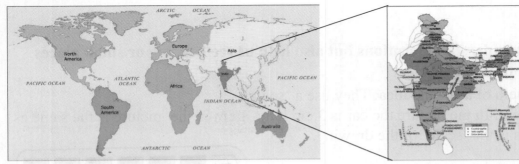

India enlarged from the world map.

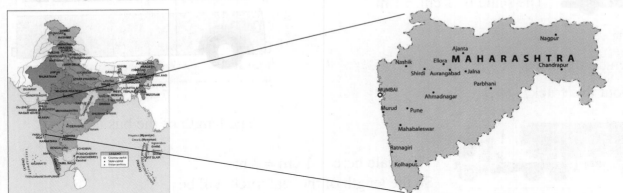

Maharashtra enlarged from the India map.

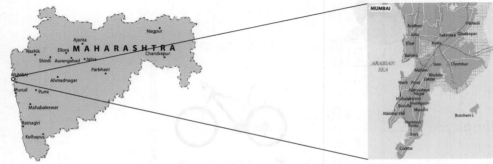

Mumbai enlarged from the Maharashtra map.

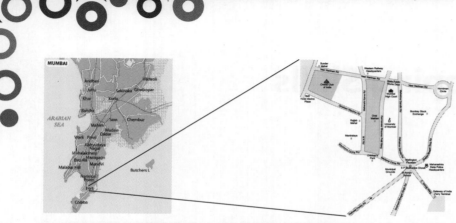

South Mumbai enlarged from Mumbai map.

From this Jeanne understood that Nandu lived in a country called _____, in the state of _____, in the city of _____, and in the _____ locality.

Scales in Maps

Maps not only help us understand locations but also help us see how big or small places are in comparison to other places.

Maps do this with the help of a special idea. They use a '**scale**'.

This is the picture of a car. In the picture the car is 3 cm long. 1 cm in the picture is the same as 1 m of the real car. This is the 'scale' of the drawing.

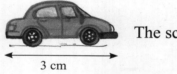

3 cm

The scale is 1 cm = 1 m

So the length of the car is 3 m.

What about this truck?

6 cm

The length of the bus is 7 m.

7 cm

The scale here is 1 cm = 2 m
So the length of the real truck will be
6 × 2 m = 12 m.

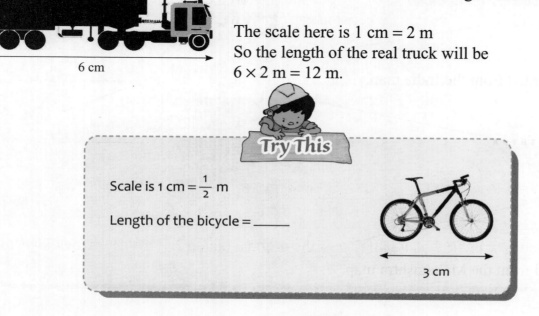

Try This

Scale is 1 cm = $\frac{1}{2}$ m

Length of the bicycle = _____

3 cm

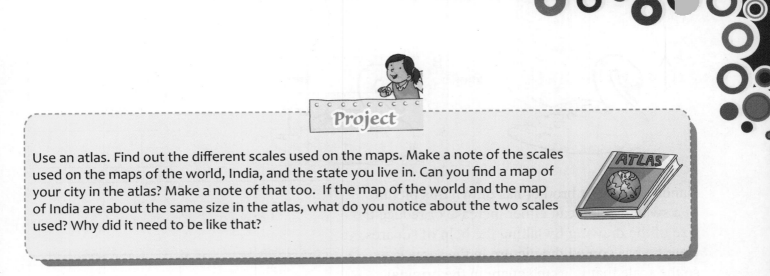

Project

Use an atlas. Find out the different scales used on the maps. Make a note of the scales used on the maps of the world, India, and the state you live in. Can you find a map of your city in the atlas? Make a note of that too. If the map of the world and the map of India are about the same size in the atlas, what do you notice about the two scales used? Why did it need to be like that?

This is a photograph of Nandu. He wants to send it to Jeanne, but since it is too small he takes it to a photography shop to get it blown up to double its size.

The larger picture has twice the length and width of the original picture. Measure the diagonals of the two pictures. What do you notice?

What is the area of the first picture?

Is the area of the second picture double that of the first picture? Calculate the areas before you answer. What is the relationship? Why has it happened?

Nandu also reduced the size of the original photo by half so that he could use it for the school identity card.

Diagonals

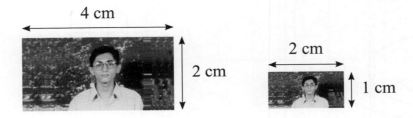

Find the area of the new picture. Is it half that of the original picture? What about the diagonal?

A

B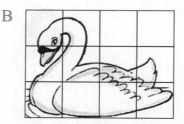

C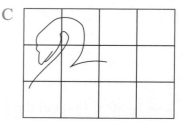

Nandu's younger brother has drawn this picture of a swan. Nandu can either increase or reduce the size of the drawing by taking the help of squares. Here he has copied the picture in the same size; so the scale that is 1 cm square in the original picture (A) is 1 cm square in the copy (B). Complete the picture by copying it square to square in C.

Use the squares on the right to enlarge the same picture using the scale 1 cm = 2 cm.

Try This

(a) Reduce the picture of Papa Bear to Mama Bear by copying the picture on the 1 cm squares.

(b) Then reduce the picture of Mama Bear to that of Baby Bear by copying it on to the $\frac{1}{2}$ cm squares.

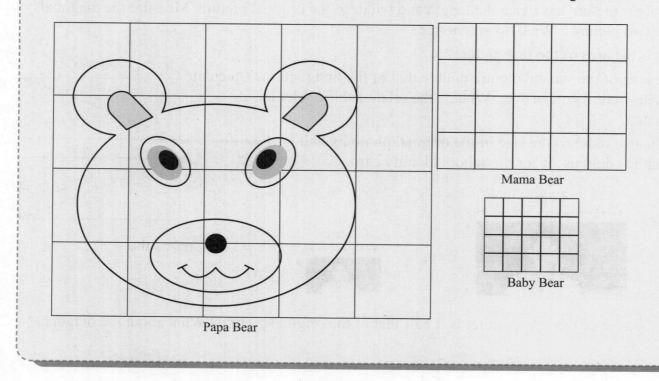

Papa Bear

Mama Bear

Baby Bear

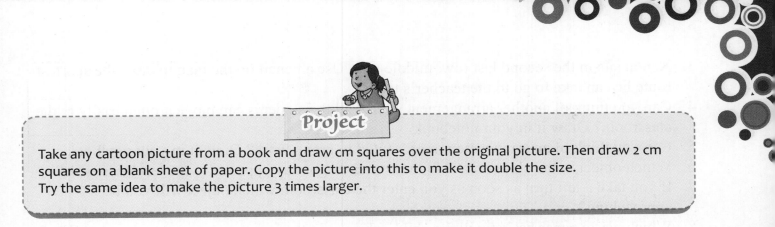

Take any cartoon picture from a book and draw cm squares over the original picture. Then draw 2 cm squares on a blank sheet of paper. Copy the picture into this to make it double the size. Try the same idea to make the picture 3 times larger.

Keys in Maps

This is a map of Nandu's classroom. The 'key' tells us the meaning of the different symbols used in the map.

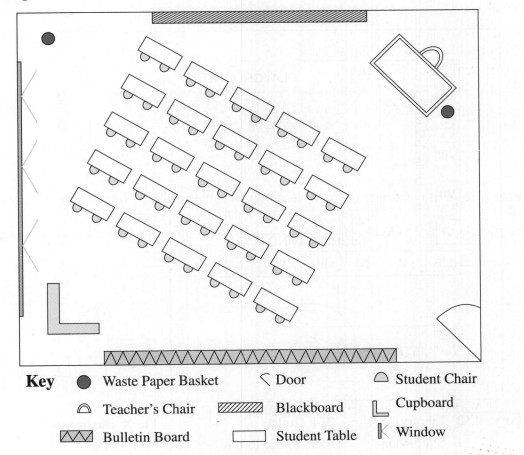

Key ● Waste Paper Basket ⌇ Door ⌂ Student Chair

⌂ Teacher's Chair ▨ Blackboard ∟ Cupboard

▨ Bulletin Board ▭ Student Table Ⅱ Window

Study the map with the help of the key and then answer these questions.

1. Why do you think the teacher's desk has been placed in the corner?

2. Is the seating arrangement for the students a good one? Say yes or no with reasons.

Did you know that while writing the light source should be on your left if you are right handed?

207

3. Nandu sits in the second last row, middle seat. Use a pencil on the map to draw the shortest route he can take to go to the teacher's table.
4. Can you think of another arrangement so that all the students can move around easily in the classroom? Draw it in your notebook.
5. Can you think of an arrangement more suited to group work? Draw it in your notebook.
6. Which object in the classroom is in the corner diagonally opposite to the teacher's table?
7. If you take a left turn as soon as you enter the classroom which object will you be approaching?
8. Which waste paper basket will the child, who sits in the last row, extreme right, use? Why?

This is a map of Nandu's school.
Study the map, the key, and the scale carefully before answering the questions.

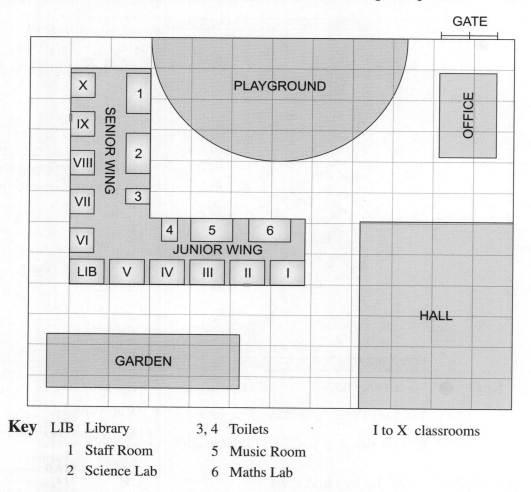

Key LIB Library   3, 4 Toilets   I to X classrooms
      1 Staff Room   5 Music Room
      2 Science Lab   6 Maths Lab

1. Has the school office been placed well in the school plan? Why?
2. When you enter the school from the junior wing side, why are the classrooms on the left of the school building and the activity rooms on the right?
3. If you stand in the garden facing the Junior wing, what do you have to your right?
4. A red line has been marked to show the windows in Classes II and IX. Draw a red line to show the window in all the classrooms.

5. Use the map of Nandu's classroom on page 207 to help you mark answers a, b, c on the map on the previous page.
    (a) A blue line to show the blackboard in Class IV.
    (b) A green dot to mark the teacher's table in Class X.
    (c) A yellow line to mark the door in Class VII.

Direction in Maps

Another important thing that maps show you is **direction**.
You must have often seen this on many maps.
You know that they stand for North, East, South, and West.

Red, Blue, Yellow, Black, and Green are marked on this grid.

Black is to the east of Red
Orange is to the west of Blue
Green is the southernmost colour.

I remember my directions starting from the North and going clockwise with this sentence —Nine Elephants Shift Wood.

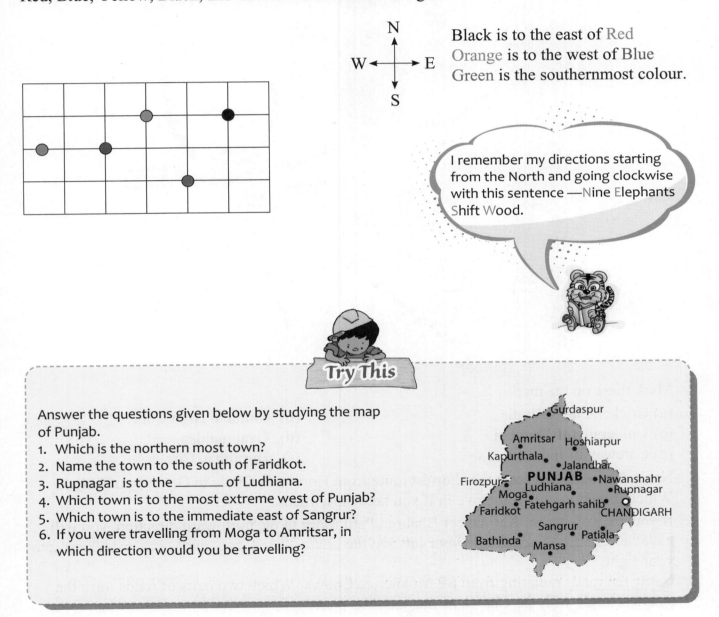

Answer the questions given below by studying the map of Punjab.
1. Which is the northern most town?
2. Name the town to the south of Faridkot.
3. Rupnagar is to the _____ of Ludhiana.
4. Which town is to the most extreme west of Punjab?
5. Which town is to the immediate east of Sangrur?
6. If you were travelling from Moga to Amritsar, in which direction would you be travelling?

This is the area Nandu lives in Mumbai.

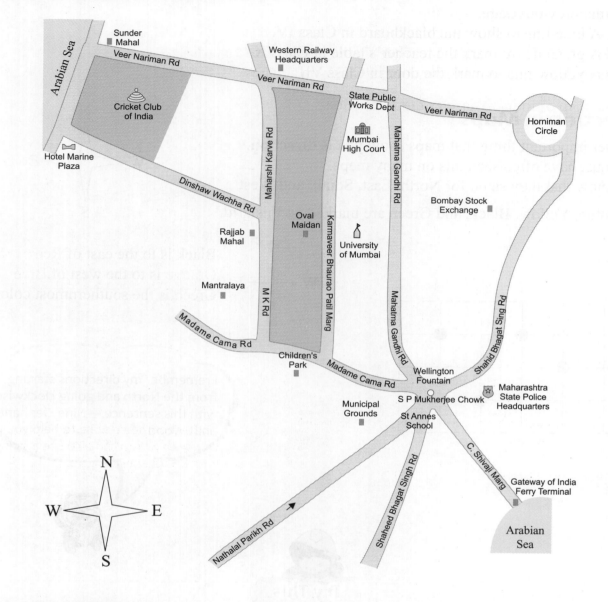

1. Mark these on the map.
   (a) Cricket Club of India
   (b) Mumbai High Court
   (c) University of Mumbai
   (d) Oval maidan
   (e) Gateway of India
   (f) Horniman Circle

2. Name the roads that form the shortest route from Horniman Circle to Gateway of India. Which direction will you move in if you take those roads?

3. If you are walking on Karmaveer Bhaurao Patil Marg in the northward direction, you will have the _____ to your left and the _____ and _____ to your right.

4. Name the roads radiating from SP Mukherjee Chowk. Which two pairs of roads form the smallest angle with the Chowk as the common point?

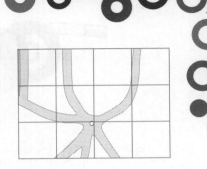

5. If you are walking on Veer Nariman Road towards the sea, in which direction will you be walking?

6. A small portion of the map has been further reduced to 1 cm squares. Can you identify the place on the larger map? Enlarge this to double its size by copying it on to 2 cm squares.

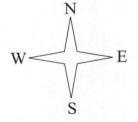

Use the map of India to answer these questions.

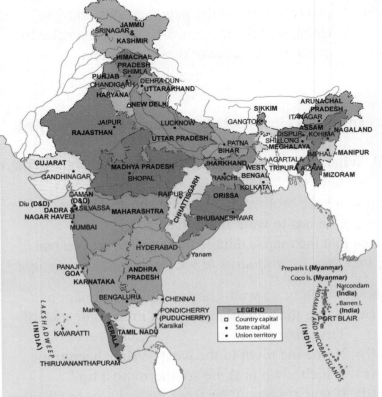

Scale 1 cm = 320 km

Use a centimetre scale to help you in Question 6. You can also use a string with knots at every 1 cm.

1. Name the state at the southernmost part of India.
2. Name the state at the eastern most part of India.
3. Name all the states on the west coast of India.
4. Which state is to the west of Orissa?
5. Which state is to the east of Karnataka?
6. Keep the scale in mind and use estimation to answer these questions.

   (a) The approximate distance between Goa and New Delhi.

   (b) The approximate distance between Puducherry and Daman.

   (c) Which state is approximately twice the size of Sikkim?

   (d) Name four small states that are neighbours and have approximately the same area.

   (e) Orissa is approximately half/double the size of Andhra Pradesh (cross out the incorrect one).

Chapter Check-Up

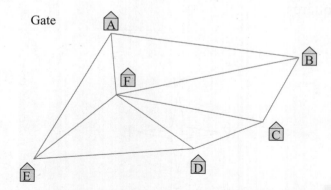

This is a map of the Khanna brothers' farm. Each brother has his own cottage in different parts of the farm. Raju, the postman, comes to deliver mail to them every day. He enters and exits the farm at the gate near A's cottage. Using a scale of $1\,\text{cm} = 100\,\text{m}$, use a ruler to measure and answer these questions.

1. (a) What is the shortest route that Raju can take to C? What is the distance on the map and what is the actual distance?

   (b) On one day only B and D have mail. What is the least distance that Raju can walk to them and back out of the gate?

   (c) The day that Raju has to deliver mail to all the brothers he uses the shortest route possible. Find that route and the distance he has to walk to do that.

   (d) Make a copy of the map given above so that the map is double the size. (**Hint:** *you can draw 1 cm squares on the map here, and then 2 cm squares in your notebook to copy into.*)

2. The map of Tamil Nadu given below shows some of its well-known tourist destinations.

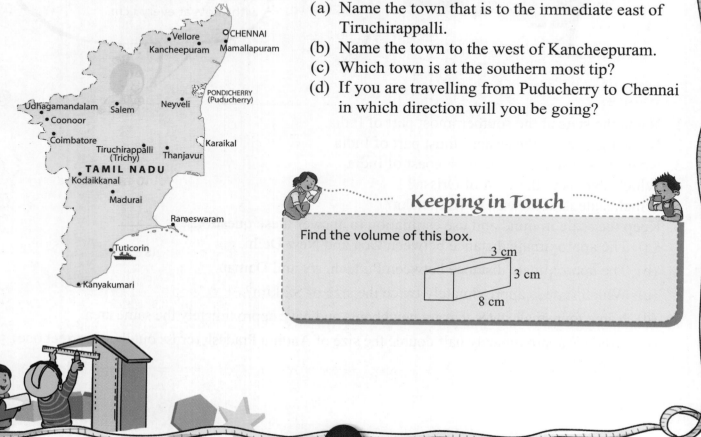

   (a) Name the town that is to the immediate east of Tiruchirappalli.

   (b) Name the town to the west of Kancheepuram.

   (c) Which town is at the southern most tip?

   (d) If you are travelling from Puducherry to Chennai in which direction will you be going?

Keeping in Touch

Find the volume of this box.

3 cm

3 cm

8 cm

The map below shows the route that Mahatma Gandhi took on his famous Dandi march to defy the British salt tax. The march began on March 12th 1930 from his ashram at Sabarmati in Gujarat and ended on 6th April at Dandi.

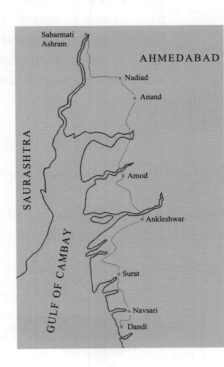

1. How many days was the march?
   Answer: _____

2. In which direction did Gandhiji walk on the salt march?
   Answer: _____

3. Some of his followers came from Goa. In which direction did they travel to meet Gandhiji at Sabarmati? (Use the map of India on page 211.)
   Answer: _____

4. Madhya Pradesh is to the _____ of Gujarat and Rajasthan is to its _____
   (Use the map of India on page 211.)
   Answer: _____

5. Which states does someone who is travelling from Kolkata to Sabarmati have to cross to get there? (Use the map of India on page 211.)
   Answer: _____

Looking Beyond

Enrichment Time

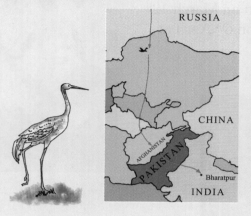

Birds from cold climates fly long distances in the same direction year after year to nest in a warm place. For several years the now-endangered Siberian cranes came from Russia to nest in the Bharatpur Bird Sanctuary in Rajasthan. The map shows that the birds first flew south towards Afghanistan and then turned towards the east to Bharatpur. We call this the **south-east** direction.

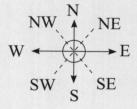

If the direction is between the north and east, it is called north-east direction.

If the direction is between the south and west it is the _____ direction.

If the direction is between the north and west it is the _____ direction.

Try this

In which direction is the minute hand pointing?

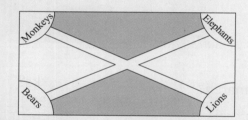

The elephant enclosure is in the _____ corner of the zoo.

The north-west corner of the zoo has the _____ cages.

Activity Bag

Draw a large square on the floor with chalk as shown. Four students may stand on the square with a card in hand showing each of the 4 directions. One student may stand in the centre. Slips may be prepared or the teacher may call out instructions for the student in the centre.

For example,

(a) Stand facing north. Take a quarter turn in the clockwise direction. Which direction are you facing?

(b) Face west. Take two half turns in the clockwise direction. Which direction are you facing?

(c) Face south. Take a quarter turn. Which direction are you facing?

Handling Data

Looking Back

1. The bar graph below shows the number of books read by students during the summer vacations.

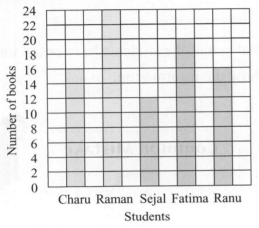

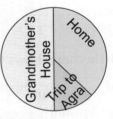

   (a) What does the vertical scale show? _____

   (b) Which student read the most number of books? _____

   (c) Which two students read the same number of books? _____

   (d) How many more books did Charu read than Sejal? _____

2.  This circle graph shows where Shariq spent his summer holidays. Read the graph to answer the questions.

   (a) Where did Shariq spend the maximum number of days of his vacation?

     _____

   (b) Where did he spend the least number of days?

     _____

   (c) Was he at home more or less than at his grandmother's house?

     _____

More about Circle Graphs

Circle graphs show all the parts of a whole. Here the whole consists of all the 24 students of class V-B.

The table shows the hobby classes that the students chose for the term. The circle graph shows the same information.

Music	12 students
Art	6 students
Gardening	3 students
Sewing	3 students

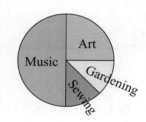

What is the total number of students shown in the graph? _____

12 out of 24 students have opted for music. That is half the students have opted for music. So $\frac{1}{2}$ the circle has been coloured to show the information.

6 out of 24 is $\frac{6}{24}$ or $\frac{1}{4}$ students have opted for art.

3 out of 24 is $\frac{3}{24}$ or $\frac{1}{8}$ students have opted for sewing.

3 out of 24 or $\frac{1}{8}$ students opted for gardening.

Common Mistake

$\frac{1}{4}$ ✗
$\frac{1}{8}$ ✓

Try This

This circle chart shows the weather for 4 weeks in Mumbai during the month of June.

(a) $\frac{5}{8}$ / $\frac{3}{4}$ of the days were rainy days. (Cross out the wrong one.)

(b) $\frac{1}{4}$ / $\frac{1}{2}$ of the days were sunny days. (Cross out the wrong one.)

(c) $\frac{1}{8}$ / $\frac{1}{4}$ of the days were cloudy.

If the circle chart shows 28 days.

_____ days were rainy.

_____ days were sunny.

_____ days were cloudy.

Exercise 15.1

1. This circle graph shows how Rishabh spent his day.

   A day has 24 hours. The circle has been divided into 8 equal parts with dotted lines. So each part represents 3 hours. You can fill in the details on the table with the help of the circle graph.

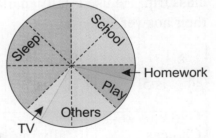

6 hours	
9 hours	
1 hour	Homework
2 hours	
5 hours	
1 hour	

2. 100 people were asked which kind of movies were their favourite. Look at the table that gives their replies, and colour and label the circle graph accordingly.

Adventure	24
Comedy	20
Mystery	20
Drama	36

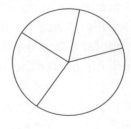

3. This circle graph shows the votes for the class election. If there are 40 students in the class, estimate the number of votes each person who stood for the election got.

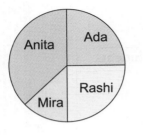

(a) (i) Ada   (*Hint:* $\frac{1}{4}$ *of 40*)

   (ii) Rashi

   (iii) Mira   (*Hint:* $\frac{1}{8}$ *of 40*)

   (iv) Anita

(b) Who won the election?

(c) Which two students got the same number of votes? How many more votes did Rashi get than Mira?

SCHOOL ELECTION!

Tally Marks

Bhupen was trying to find out from his classmates the most popular choice for a class trip. He used 'tally marks' to record their answer.

| is 1 || is 2 |||| is 4

卌 is 5   卌 || is 7   卌 卌 is 10

Choices	Tally marks	Number of students
Garden	卌 |||	8
Beach	卌 卌 卌	
Zoo	卌 卌 ||	
Planetarium	卌 ||||	
Museum	卌 ||	

1. Fill in the last column in the above table.
2. How many students are there in the class?
3. Which is the most popular place for the picnic?
4. Which is the least popular place for the picnic?
5. How many more students prefer the zoo to the planetarium?

Try This

Copy this table in your notebook. Collect the information with the help of tally marks as each student calls out the information.

Students in Class V who have brothers and sisters.

	Tally marks	Number of students
No brothers or sisters		
Only brothers		
Only sisters		
Both brothers and sisters		

Shefali has made these marks monthwise to count the number of days to her birthday. On which date did she start the tally marks? On which date is her birthday?

| ⦀ ⦀ | ⦀ ⦀ ⦀ ⦀ ⦀ ⦀⦀ | ⦀ ⦀ ⦀⦀ |

(**Hint:** First count the numbers in the middle to find which month it is.)

Exercise 15.2

1. Complete the tally chart.

Number of hours the students of Class V watch TV in a day.

Number of hours	Tally marks	Number of students
Less than $\frac{1}{2}$ hour	‖	
Between $\frac{1}{2}$ and 1 hour	⦀ ⦀ ‖‖	
Between 1 and 2 hours	⦀ ⦀ ⦀ ‖	
Between 2 and 3 hours	⦀ ⦀	
More than 3 hours	⦀	

2. Build a tally chart using these pictures.

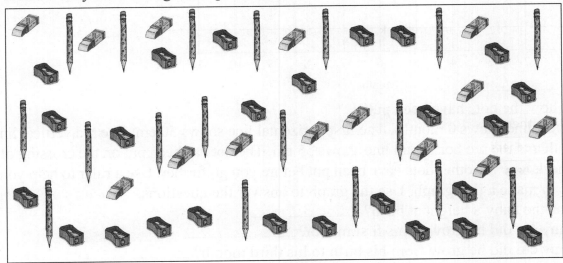

3. Use the pictograph given below to build a bar graph and tally chart:

Flowers in a Bouquet

Roses	🌹🌹🌹🌹🌹
Lilies	🌹🌹🌹🌹🌹🌹🌹
Asters	🌹🌹🌹
Tulips	🌹🌹🌹🌹
	🌹 Each symbol stands for 2 flowers

Line Graphs

Mrs. Menon kept a record of her baby's height from the time he was born till he was 12 months of age. She put a dot on the chart every time she took his height.

0 month (at birth)	–	50 cm
1 month	–	55 cm
3 months	–	65 cm
6 months	–	70 cm
9 months	–	75 cm
12 months	–	80 cm

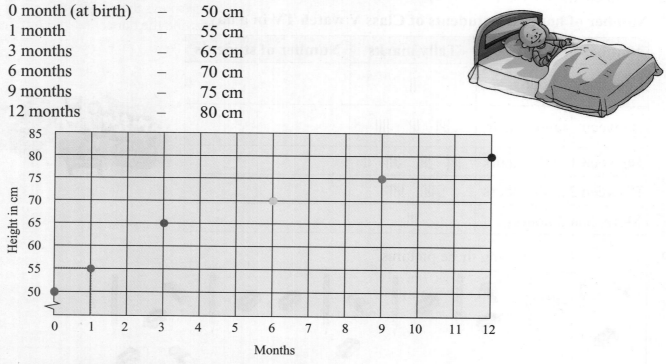

Can you see how the dots have been put?

The first vertical line shows 0 months. The first horizontal line shows 50 cm. The red vertical line shows 1 month and the red horizontal line shows 55 cm. The dot has been put on the crossing of the two lines. Check how the other dots have been put before you go further. Use a ruler to help you. Join the dots to make a line graph. Use the graph to answer the questions.

(a) What was the baby's height at birth? _____

(b) How many cm did he grow in his first month? _____

(c) How many cm did he grow from his birth to his third month? _____

(d) How many cm did he grow from 3 months to 6 months? _____

(e) What was his height at 12 months? _____

Exercise 15.3

1. This graph of the baby's weight shows you the baby's weight in kg for the first 12 months after birth. Answer the questions by looking only at the graph.

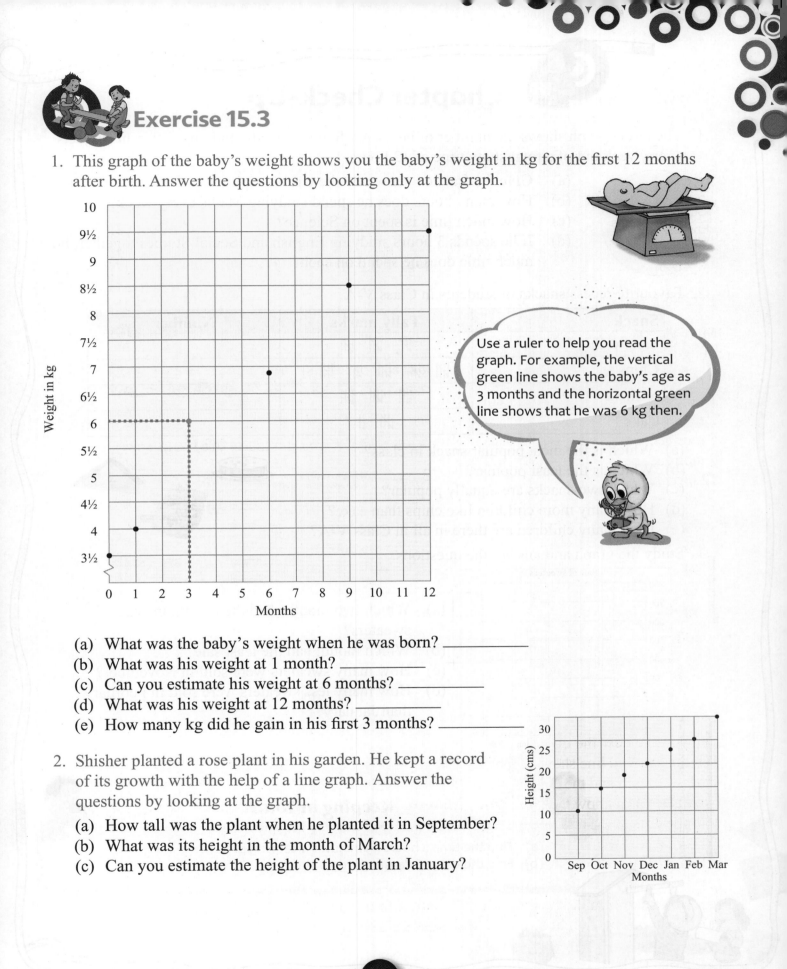

Use a ruler to help you read the graph. For example, the vertical green line shows the baby's age as 3 months and the horizontal green line shows that he was 6 kg then.

(a) What was the baby's weight when he was born? _____
(b) What was his weight at 1 month? _____
(c) Can you estimate his weight at 6 months? _____
(d) What was his weight at 12 months? _____
(e) How many kg did he gain in his first 3 months? _____

2. Shisher planted a rose plant in his garden. He kept a record of its growth with the help of a line graph. Answer the questions by looking at the graph.

(a) How tall was the plant when he planted it in September?
(b) What was its height in the month of March?
(c) Can you estimate the height of the plant in January?

Chapter Check-Up

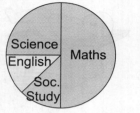

1. The circle graph shows the number of hours Anshuman spends studying different subjects every week out of a total study time of 12 hours.

   (a) Give the fraction shown by the circle graph for each subject.
   (b) How many hours does he spend studying Maths every week?
   (c) How much time is spent on Science?
   (d) If he spends 3 hours studying English and Social Studies together, how much time does he spend on each?

2. Favourite recess snacks of students in Class V-A.

Snack	Tally marks	Number
Sandwich	𝍷𝍷𝍷 𝍷𝍷𝍷 𝍷𝍷𝍷	
Chips	𝍷𝍷𝍷 𝍷𝍷𝍷 𝍷𝍷𝍷 𝍷𝍷𝍷 𝍷𝍷𝍷 𝍷	
Samosa	𝍷𝍷𝍷 𝍷𝍷𝍷 𝍷𝍷𝍷	
Cake	𝍷𝍷𝍷 𝍷𝍷	

   (a) Which is the most popular snack in class?
   (b) Which is the least popular?
   (c) Which two snacks are equally popular?
   (d) How many more children like chips than cake?
   (e) How many children are there in all in Class V-A?

3. Study the graph and answer the questions.

   Sale of sweaters

   (a) Which two months had the maximum sale of sweaters?
   (b) Which month had the least sale?
   (c) How many sweaters were sold in November?
   (d) How many less sweaters were sold in February than January?

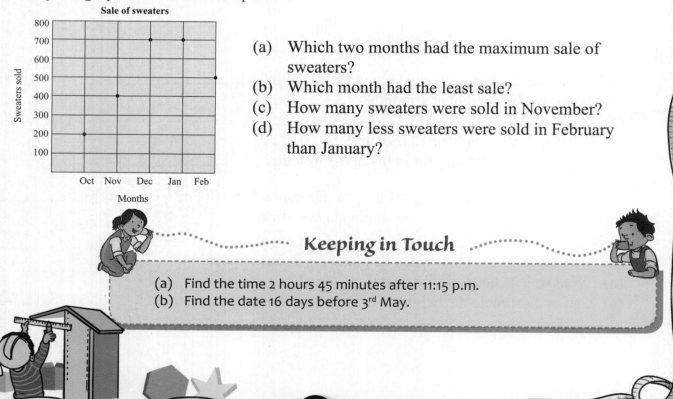

Keeping in Touch

(a) Find the time 2 hours 45 minutes after 11:15 p.m.
(b) Find the date 16 days before 3ʳᵈ May.

The following data shows the number of years the first five presidents of India served their term. Complete the table and graph given below and answer the questions that follow.

President	From–to	Number of years
Dr Rajendra Prasad (RP)	1950–1962	12
Dr S. Radhakrishnan (SR)	1962–1967	5
Dr Zakir Husain (ZH)	1967–1969	
Shri V.V. Giri (VVG)	1969–1974	
Dr Fakhruddin Ali Ahmed (FAA)	1974–1977	

This worksheet integrates Mathematics and Social Studies.

Answer the following questions.

1. Who was the longest-serving president?

Answer: _____

2. Who had the shortest term?

Answer: _____

3. Which two presidents served for the same number of years? For how many years did each serve as president?

Answer: _____

4. How many years did the first five presidents of India serve in all?

Answer: _____

Looking Beyond

Enrichment Time

Kunal wanted to make his family tree. He used this outline.
Read Kunal's family tree with the help of this outline and answer the questions given below.

Great Grandparents

Ragav-Saroja   Raja-Shymala   Padam-Ambika   Gopal-Uma

Grandparents

Ajay   m   Meera   Krishna   m   Lalitha

Parents

Ashok   m   Sudha

Kunal

Key:

Red – Kunal's mother's side of   Blue – Kunal's father's side   m – married
the family   of the family

(a) How many grandparents does Kunal have?

(b) How many great grandparents?

(c) If Kunal is called the first generation in his family tree, and his great grandparents are 4th generation, what will the generation above theirs be called?

(d) From the pattern can you tell how many people in that generation?

(e) Name Kunal's mother's parents.

(f) Name Kunal's father's grandparents.

Activity Bag

Use the idea shown above to make your own family tree. Get photographs wherever possible and stick it on the family tree.

Mental Maths

1. If today is 15th April, what will be the date after 20 days? _____

2. Are $\frac{3}{4}$ and $\frac{9}{16}$ equivalent?

3. Give XLIX in Hindu-Arabic numbers.

4. How many minutes in 5 hours?

5. Complete the pattern 10:30, 12:00, 1:30, 3:00 _____

6. Give the sum of the place values of 7 in 3794871: _____

7. A person who slept for 10 hours woke up at 8:00 a.m. When did he go to sleep? _____

8. How many hours in 600 minutes? _____

9. Build the smallest number using 6, 2, 8, 4, 0.

10. How many seconds in 6 minutes? _____

11. Give the reciprocal of $\frac{8}{11}$: _____

12. Complete the pattern: Monday, Thursday, Sunday, _____

13. S.P. = ₹ 320, C.P. = ₹ 500, Loss = _____.

14. One hour 20 minutes after 10:45 p.m. is _____.

15. Build the largest possible number using 5, 0, 3, 8, 7, 6: _____.

16. Two hours 15 minutes before 7:05 a.m. is _____.

17. Write 8381296 in the international system.

18. Complete the pattern Jan 1st, Feb 28th, Mar 1st, April 30, _____

19. How many days from 1st November to 31st January?

20. Give the prime factors of 71.

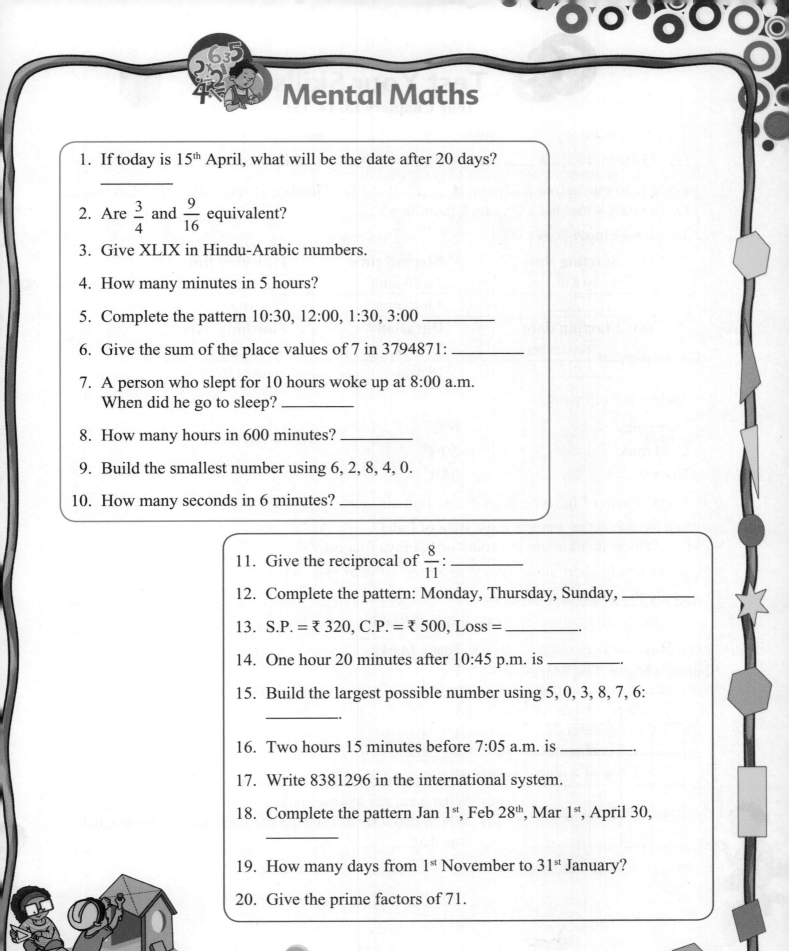

Test Your Skills

(For Chapters 13, 14, 15)

1. Fill in the blanks:

   (a) 330 min = ____ h ____ min

   (b) $7\frac{1}{2}$ min = ____ s

   (c) 3 h 20 min before 2:15 p.m. is ____

   (d) The date 15 days after 23rd March is ____.

   (e) 6 years 8 months + 2 years 8 months = ____

2. Fill in the empty boxes.

   (a)
Starting time	Elapsed time	Finishing time
9 : 10 a.m.	3 h 35 min	_____
_____	5 h 15 min	12:10 p.m.

   (b)
Starting date	Duration	Finishing date
27th November	35 days	_____
_____	18 days	January 10th

3. Match the following.

Warm day	6°C
Cold milk	50°C
Hot tea	35°C

4. Use the map of India on page 211 to find out:

   (a) Which is the western most state of India?

   (b) Which states are to the south of Madhya Pradesh?

5. Make a tally chart of the favourite writers of your classmates.

6. Study the graph to answer the following questions.

   (a) Fill in the table

   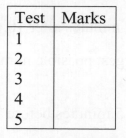

Test	Marks
1	
2	
3	
4	
5	

Shubha's Maths Test Marks

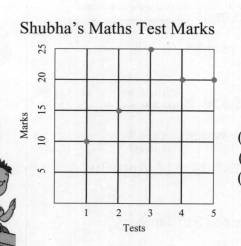

   (b) Which test did Shubha do best in?

   (c) What were her lowest marks?

   (d) Which two tests did she get the same marks? How much was that?

Answers to Selected Questions

Chapter 1: Place Value

Exercise 1.1

1. Across: 1. 10   6. 23,48,901   4. 99
   7. 976553200   8. 83,11,497

   Down: 1. 19,99,998   2. 63,45,121   3. 38,63,659
   4. 9,00,000   5. 91,20,412

3. (a) Sixty seven lakh nine thousand six hundred fifty four.
   6000000 + 700000 + 9000 + 600 + 50 + 4

   (b) Nine crore eighty three lakh ten thousand eight hundred nine.
   90000000 + 8000000 + 300000 + 10000 + 800 + 9

   (c) Two crore ten lakh twenty three thousand eight
   20000000 + 1000000 + 20000 + 3000 + 8

   (d) Forty five lakh ninety one
   4000000 + 500000 + 90 + 1

4. (a) 8,39,023 (b) 20,00,905 (c) 35,857 (d) 4,37,19000

5. (a) 9 lakhs (b) 30 lakhs (c) 3 thousands (d) 2 crores
   (e) 10 thousand

6. (a) > (b) > (c) < (d) <

7. (a) 11,12,589 (b) 10,00,479

8. (a) Smallest – 1,12,36,789 Greatest – 9,98,76,321
   (b) Smallest – 1,00,03,457 Greatest – 7,77,54,310

9. (a) 45,69,499 (b) 87,15,999 (c) 5,09,999 (d) 19,99,999

10. (a) 9,29,500 (b) 79,99,000 (c) 1,00,00,000 (d) 1,98,97,951

Exercise 1.2

2. (a) 1,000,000 (b) 356,400 (c) 1,013,913

3. (a) 712,801 Seven hundred twelve thousand eight hundred one.
   (b) 602,590 Six hundred two thousand five hundred ninety.
   (c) 1,016,800 One million sixteen thousand eight hundred.
   (d) 5,397,284 Five million three hundred ninety seven thousand two hundred eighty four.

4. (a) 30,000 (b) 6,000,000 (c) 100,000
   (d) 100,000

5. Indian
   (a) 8,50,009 Eight lakh fifty thousand nine.
   (b) 16,70,112 Sixteen lakh seventy thousand one hundred twelve.
   (c) 42,90,281 Forty two lakh ninety thousand two hundred eighty one.
   (d) 5,30,563 Five lakh thirty thousand five hundred sixty three.
   International
   (a) 850,009 Eight hundred fifty thousand nine.
   (b) 1,670,112 One million six hundred seventy thousand one hundred twelve.
   (c) 4,290,281 Four million two hundred ninety thousand two hundred eighty one.
   (d) 530,563 Five hundred thirty thousand five hundred sixty three.

Exercise 1.3

1. (a) 1350 (b) 2390 (c) 1010 (d) 92,410 (e) 11,000
2. (a) 600 (b) 5,300 (c) 6,900 (d) 14,900 (e) 58,000

3. (a) 2000 (b) 10,000 (c) 4000 (d) 36,000 (e) 98,000
4. (a) The municipal corporation spent ₹ 5,95,000 on repairing the roads.
   (b) 400 people attended the meeting of coin collectors in the city.
   (c) The Rajdhani Express was delayed by 5 hours.

Chapter Check-Up

1. (a) 10,00,000 + 1,00,000 + 900 + 40 + 8
   Eleven lakh nine hundred forty eight.
   (b) 70,00,000 + 8,00,000 + 90,000 + 8000 + 1
   Seventy eight lakh ninety eight thousand one.
   (c) 5,00,00,000 + 60,00,000 + 7,00,000 + 3,000 + 600 + 70
   Five crore sixty seven lakh three thousand six hundred seventy.

2. (a) 30,70,306 (b) 4,17,00,195 (c) 48,00,305
3. (a) 8 thousand (b) 60 thousand (c) 9 crore
4. Greatest: 7775321; Smallest: 1112357
5. (a) 79,99,000 (b) 15,10,000
6. (a) 5,09,999 (b) 13,80,969
7. (a) < (b) > (c) < (d) >
8. (a) A 15 year old boy would have lived for 131,400 hours
   A 15 year old boy would have lived for one hundred thirty one thousand four hundred hours.
   (b) 2,401,596 people travelled by planes this year. Two million four hundred one thousand five hundred ninety six people travelled by planes this year.
9. (a) 8:30 p.m. (b) 13,000
10. (a) XXIX (b) XII (c) LXXXI (d) XCV
11. (a) XXVIII (b) LXXXVI (c) XLIX

Worksheet

1. 3,28,05,000 1,70,75,200 96,29,091 95,96,960 85,11,965
   76,86,850 32,87,590 27,66,890 27,17,300 25,05,810
2. Canada 3. Sudan
4. Largest country – 32,805,000
   Thirty two million eight hundred five thousand.
   Smallest country – 2,505,810
   Two million five hundred five thousand eight hundred ten.
5. Thirty two lakh eighty seven thousand five hundred ninety.
6. crore

Chapter 2: Addition, Subtraction and its Applications

Exercise 2.1

1. (a) 31,629 (b) 1,41,717 (c) 1,14,781 (d) 1,41,779
   (e) 1,12,967 (f) 2,88,833 (g) 2,91,544 (h) 2,14,097
   (i) 1,86,500
2. (a) 5781 (b) 14,897 (c) 8,60,500 (d) 2,93,248
   (e) 11,397 (f) 13,220 (g) 10,155 (h) 4804
   (i) 59,113

3. (a)
   ```
     2 3 4 5 6
   + 5 8 5 5 7
   ─────────────
     8 2 0 1 3
   ```
   (b)
   ```
     7 7 7 2 6
   - 1 5 4 4 6
   ─────────────
     6 2 2 8 0
   ```

Exercise 2.2

1. (a)
   ```
    21  (−1) →   20
   +37  (+1) → +38
   ───            ───
    58             58
   ```
   (b)
   ```
    28  (+2) →   30
   +86  (−2) → +84
   ───            ───
   114            114
   ```

(c)
$$\begin{array}{rcl} 39 & (+1) & \to & 40 \\ +63 & (-1) & \to & +62 \\ \hline 102 & & & 102 \end{array}$$
(d)
$$\begin{array}{rcl} 72 & (-2) & \to & 70 \\ +46 & (+2) & \to & +48 \\ \hline 118 & & & 118 \end{array}$$
(e)
$$\begin{array}{rcl} 63 & (-3) & \to & 60 \\ +94 & (+3) & \to & +97 \\ \hline 157 & & & 157 \end{array}$$
(f)
$$\begin{array}{rcl} 47 & (+3) & \to & 50 \\ +86 & (-3) & \to & +83 \\ \hline 133 & & & 133 \end{array}$$
(g)
$$\begin{array}{rcl} 51 & (-1) & \to & 50 \\ +39 & (+1) & \to & +40 \\ \hline 90 & & & 90 \end{array}$$
(h)
$$\begin{array}{rcl} 93 & (-3) & \to & 90 \\ +47 & (+3) & \to & +50 \\ \hline 140 & & & 140 \end{array}$$

2. (a)
$$\begin{array}{rcl} 56 & (+2) & \to & 58 \\ -38 & (+2) & \to & -40 \\ \hline 18 & & & 18 \end{array}$$
(b)
$$\begin{array}{rcl} 80 & (+3) & \to & 83 \\ -27 & (+3) & \to & -30 \\ \hline 53 & & & 53 \end{array}$$
(c)
$$\begin{array}{rcl} 97 & (+3) & \to & 100 \\ -29 & (+3) & \to & -32 \\ \hline 68 & & & 68 \end{array}$$
(d)
$$\begin{array}{rcl} 63 & (-1) & \to & 62 \\ -31 & (-1) & \to & -30 \\ \hline 32 & & & 32 \end{array}$$
(e)
$$\begin{array}{rcl} 84 & (-4) & \to & 80 \\ -39 & (-4) & \to & -35 \\ \hline 45 & & & 45 \end{array}$$
(f)
$$\begin{array}{rcl} 96 & (+4) & \to & 100 \\ -63 & (+4) & \to & -67 \\ \hline 33 & & & 33 \end{array}$$
(g)
$$\begin{array}{rcl} 70 & (+2) & \to & 72 \\ -58 & (+2) & \to & -60 \\ \hline 12 & & & 12 \end{array}$$
(h)
$$\begin{array}{rcl} 64 & (-2) & \to & 62 \\ -42 & (-2) & \to & -40 \\ \hline 22 & & & 22 \end{array}$$

Exercise 2.3
1. (a) Profit ₹ 35   (b) Loss ₹ 10   (c) Loss ₹ 63   (d) Profit ₹ 114
2. (b) C.P. < S.P. = Profit ₹ 540   (c) C.P. < S.P = Profit ₹ 540
   (d) C.P > S.P. = Loss ₹ 180   (e) C.P. < S.P. = Profit ₹ 675
3. (b) C.P. + overheads = 1071   S.P. = 1235   Profit ₹ 164
   (c) C.P. + overheads = 2495   S.P. = 2300   Loss ₹ 195
   (d) C.P. + overheads = 7733   S.P. = 9818   Profit ₹ 2085
   (e) C.P. + overheads = 11188   S.P. = 10,050   Loss ₹ 1138
4. (a) Loss ₹ 750   (b) C.P. + overheads = ₹ 3750 Profit ₹ 250
   (c) ₹ 58   (d) ₹ 2110   (e) C.P. + overheads = 7220 Profit ₹ 780

Exercise 2.4
1. (a) ₹ 277   (b) ₹ 747   (c) ₹ 8970   (d) ₹ 8578
2. (a) ₹ 2190   (b) ₹ 2528   (c) ₹ 9650   (d) ₹ 72,050
3. (a) ₹ 1006   (b) ₹ 3955   (c) ₹ 9629   (d) ₹ 16776
4. (a) ₹ 1870   (b) ₹ 18490   (c) ₹ 1528

Exercise 2.5
1. (a) 5,135 copies   (b) 8,784 Kilometres   (c) 4,617 Kilometres
   (d) ₹ 4,38,465   (e) ₹ 3000   (f) 981 boxes   (g) 1,080 toys

Challenge (Page 38)
14 books

Exercise 2.6
1. (a) 336   (b) 5248   (c) 2085   (d) 10,973
   (e) 8270   (f) 26409
2. (a) 1279   (b) 59052   (c) 71774   (d) 10948
3. (a) ₹ 22   (b) 715 stamps   (c) 9601 Books   (d) 704 Pieces

Chapter Check-Up
1. (a) 49581   (b) 799908   (c) 8999   (d) 592683
   (e) 16743   (f) 55038
2. (a)
$$\begin{array}{rcl} 41 & (-1) & \to & 40 \\ +34 & (+1) & \to & +35 \\ \hline 75 & & & 75 \end{array}$$
(b)
$$\begin{array}{rcl} 73 & (+2) & \to & 75 \\ -58 & (+2) & \to & -60 \\ \hline 15 & & & 15 \end{array}$$
(c)
$$\begin{array}{rcl} 24 & (-2) & \to & 22 \\ +48 & (+2) & \to & +50 \\ \hline 72 & & & 72 \end{array}$$
(d)
$$\begin{array}{rcl} 92 & (-2) & \to & 90 \\ -39 & (-2) & \to & -37 \\ \hline 53 & & & 53 \end{array}$$
3. (a) Gain ₹ 3125   (b) ₹ 5527   (c) ₹ 855
4. (a) 9110   (b) 71880   (c) 591 people   (d) 1244 kilograms

Chapter 3: Multiplication, Division and its Applications
Exercise 3.1
1. (a) 251412   (b) 283156   (c) 328510   (d) 158219
   (e) 448592   (f) 3627744   (g) 2201384   (h) 3571875
   (i) 326027   (j) 3613732   (k) 2029060   (l) 54484540
2. (a) 1441, 14541, 145541, 1455541, 14555541
   (b) 11, 111, 1111, 11111, 111111
   (c) 3333, 33633, 336633, 3366633
   (d) 2222, 22422, 224422, 2244422

Exercise 3.2
1. (a) 248 Remainder 38   (b) 733 Remainder 28
   (c) 969 Remainder 2   (d) 397 Remainder 45
   (e) 693 Remainder 7   (f) 815 Remainder 6
   (g) 839 Remainder 10   (h) 696 Remainder 30
   (i) 809 Remainder 21   (j) 1316 Remainder 4
   (k) 1201 Remainder 20   (l) 562 Remainder 17

Exercise 3.3
1. (a) 20   (b) 11   (c) 125   (d) 15
2. 31
3. 224 Average - 56   312 Average - 78   212 Average - 53
   384 Average - 96   568 Average - 142
   (b) Class – 5   (c) Class – 3   (d) 340
4. 380   5. 48, 49, 51, 52 (one probable answer)   6. 60 km

Exercise 3.4
1. (a) How much money did Dhruv make?
   (b) How much more does the television cost than the washing machine?
   (c) How much did it cost each student?
   (d) How many packets were made?

Exercise 3.5
1. 189 pages   2. 391 kilometers   3. ₹ 1252   4. 24 houses   5. 225

Chapter Check-Up
1. (a) 312915   (b) 209430   (c) 1387826
2. (a) 238 R 2   (b) 409 R 5   (c) 2206 R 8
3. (a) 38 kg   (b) 23 days   4. (a) 405 km   (b) 23 marks
5. (a) 14 hour   (b) 63840   (c) 73   (d) ₹ 450

Chapter 4: Factors
Exercise 4.1
1. (a) 1, 2, 5, 10   (b) 1, 2, 4, 8, 16   (c) 1, 2, 3, 5, 6, 10, 15, 30
2. (a) 1, 2   (b) 1, 2, 5, 10   (c) 1, 2
3. (a)   (b)

Exercise 4.2
1. (a) 24, 38, 160   (b) 75, 190, 300   (c) 90, 200
2. (a) 72, 63, 60   (b) 36, 45
3. (a) 56, 92, 104, 700   (b) 42, 120

Exercise 4.3
(a) 3×17 (b) $2 \times 2 \times 3 \times 5$ (c) $2 \times 3 \times 3 \times 5$
(d) $2 \times 2 \times 2 \times 2 \times 2$ (e) $2 \times 2 \times 2 \times 3$ (f) $3 \times 3 \times 7$
(g) $3 \times 3 \times 3 \times 3$ (h) $2 \times 2 \times 2 \times 3 \times 3$ (i) $2 \times 2 \times 7$
(j) $2 \times 2 \times 2 \times 11$ (k) 2×31 (l) $3 \times 3 \times 5$

Exercise 4.4

1. (a) 3×3, 3×5 C.F. 3   H.C.F. 3
   (b) $2 \times 2 \times 2$, $2 \times 2 \times 2 \times 2$ C.F. 2, 2, 2   H.C.F. 8
   (c) 2×2, $2 \times 3 \times 3$ C.F. 2   H.C.F. 2
   (d) $2 \times 2 \times 7$, $2 \times 2 \times 2 \times 2 \times 2$ C.F. 2, 2   H.C.F. 4
   (e) $2 \times 2 \times 2 \times 5$, $2 \times 2 \times 2 \times 3$ C.F. 2, 2, 2   H.C.F. 8

3. (a) 20   (b) 4   (c) 1   (d) 2   (e) 2   (f) 4
4. (a) 2   (b) 8   (c) 5   (d) 16   (e) 4   (f) 9
   (g) 9   (h) 1

Chapter Check-Up

2. (a) 2, 3, 5, 7, 11, 13, 17, 19   (b) 22, 24, 25, 26, 27, 28
4. (a) 4   (b) 5   (c) 8   5. (a) 8   (b) 14   (c) 4

Chapter 5: Multiples

Exercise 5.1
2. 20, 40

Challenge (Page 69)
12 October

Exercise 5.2
1. (a) Common multiples – 18, 36, 54 ..... LCM 18
   (b) Common multiples – 10, 20, 30, 40 ..... LCM 10
   (c) Common multiples – 6, 12, 18, 24, 30 ..... LCM 6
   (d) Common multiples – 12, 24, 36 ..... LCM 12
3. (a) 16   (b) 50   (c) 40   (d) 200   (e) 80   (f) 400
4. (a) 48   (b) 180   (c) 90   (d) 105   (e) 150   (f) 288
   (g) 60   (h) 96

Challenge (Page 71)
$2 \times 24 = 48$ $4 \times 24 = 96$

Chapter Check-Up
1. Common multiples – 12, 24, 36 ..... lowest common multiple 12
4. (a) 60   (b) 70   (c) 54   (d) 45   (e) 120   (f) 240

Chapter 6: Fractions

Exercise 6.1

1. (a) $\frac{3}{12}$ (b) $\frac{9}{15}$ (c) $\frac{3}{18}$ (d) $\frac{3}{15}$ (e) $\frac{6}{15}$ (f) $\frac{12}{15}$

2. (b) $\frac{1}{4} = \frac{2}{8} = \frac{3}{12} = \frac{4}{16}$ (c) $\frac{2}{3} = \frac{4}{6} = \frac{6}{9} = \frac{8}{12}$
   (d) $\frac{2}{5} = \frac{4}{10} = \frac{6}{15} = \frac{8}{20}$ (e) $\frac{3}{4} = \frac{6}{8} = \frac{9}{12} = \frac{12}{16}$

3. (a) $\frac{1}{4}$ (b) $\frac{2}{7}$ (c) $\frac{7}{8}$ (d) $\frac{1}{3}$ (e) $\frac{1}{2}$ (f) $\frac{11}{15}$

4. (a) 6   (b) 14   (c) 4   (d) 7   (e) 75   (f) 49   (g) 3   (h) 4

5. (a) E   (b) NE   (c) NE   (d) NE   (e) E   (f) E

Challenge (Page 78)

Red: $\frac{1}{8}$, Blue: $\frac{1}{16}$, Green: $\frac{1}{16}$, Orange: $\frac{1}{8}$, Squares: $\frac{1}{16}$, Black: $\frac{1}{16}$

Exercise 6.2

1. (a) $\frac{2}{3}$ (b) $\frac{3}{4}$ (c) $\frac{2}{3}$ (d) $\frac{3}{4}$ (e) $\frac{2}{3}$ (f) $\frac{3}{5}$

2. (a) $\frac{1}{3}$ (b) $\frac{1}{2}$ (c) $\frac{3}{4}$ (d) $\frac{2}{3}$ (e) $\frac{1}{2}$ (f) $\frac{2}{3}$
   (g) $\frac{4}{5}$ (h) $\frac{2}{3}$ (i) $\frac{4}{5}$ (j) $\frac{1}{5}$

3. (c), (d), (f), (g), and (h)

Exercise 6.3

1. (a) >   (b) >   (c) <   (d) >   (e) <   (f) <   (g) >   (h) <
2. (a) >   (b) >   (c) >   (d) <   (e) <   (f) >   (g) <   (h) >

3. (a) $\frac{9}{21} < \frac{9}{19} < \frac{9}{16} < \frac{9}{15} < \frac{9}{10}$ (b) $\frac{1}{15} < \frac{3}{15} < \frac{6}{15} < \frac{12}{15} < \frac{14}{15}$
   (c) $\frac{1}{6} < \frac{2}{3} < \frac{3}{4} < \frac{7}{8}$ (d) $\frac{3}{12} < \frac{2}{6} < \frac{2}{4} < \frac{7}{8}$
   (e) $\frac{1}{3} < \frac{1}{2} < \frac{2}{3} < \frac{3}{4}$ (f) $\frac{1}{2} < \frac{6}{10} < \frac{2}{3} < \frac{4}{5} < \frac{5}{6}$

4. (a) $\frac{10}{14} > \frac{10}{15} > \frac{10}{20} > \frac{10}{22} > \frac{10}{35}$ (b) $\frac{15}{19} > \frac{11}{19} > \frac{10}{19} > \frac{9}{19} > \frac{8}{19}$
   (c) $\frac{5}{6} > \frac{2}{3} > \frac{1}{2} > \frac{1}{5}$ (d) $\frac{3}{4} > \frac{5}{12} > \frac{2}{6} > \frac{1}{8}$
   (e) $\frac{5}{6} > \frac{3}{4} > \frac{2}{3} > \frac{3}{5}$ (f) $\frac{11}{12} > \frac{7}{9} > \frac{3}{4} > \frac{2}{3} > \frac{5}{8}$

Exercise 6.4

1. (a) $\frac{3}{8}$ (b) $\frac{7}{9}$ (c) $\frac{7}{8}$ (d) $\frac{4}{6}$ (e) $\frac{7}{10}$ (f) $\frac{3}{4}$ (g) $\frac{5}{8}$ (h) $\frac{7}{10}$

2. (a) $\frac{1}{2}$ (b) $\frac{1}{2}$ (c) $1\frac{1}{8}$ (d) $1\frac{3}{10}$ (e) $1\frac{11}{36}$ (f) $1\frac{3}{8}$ (g) $1\frac{23}{30}$ (h) $\frac{11}{12}$

Exercise 6.5

1. (a) $8\frac{1}{2}$ (b) $5\frac{5}{7}$ (c) $3\frac{2}{4}$ (d) $3\frac{17}{12}$ (e) $1\frac{37}{56}$
   (f) $5\frac{8}{10}$ (g) $4\frac{17}{12}$ (h) $5\frac{9}{10}$ (i) $5\frac{58}{36}$ (j) $6\frac{5}{4}$

Exercise 6.6

(a) $\frac{7}{6}$ (b) $\frac{1}{4}$ (c) $\frac{1}{12}$ (d) $\frac{1}{12}$ (e) $\frac{9}{28}$
(f) $\frac{1}{24}$ (g) $\frac{3}{10}$ (h) $\frac{1}{6}$ (i) $\frac{1}{8}$ (j) $\frac{47}{110}$

Exercise 6.7

(a) $2\frac{1}{3}$ (b) $5\frac{1}{5}$ (c) $9\frac{1}{7}$ (d) $1\frac{9}{10}$ (e) $4\frac{1}{4}$
(f) $\frac{2}{3}$ (g) $\frac{22}{3}$ (h) $2\frac{2}{3}$ (i) $4\frac{1}{4}$ (j) $5\frac{1}{5}$
(k) $\frac{9}{10}$ (l) $2\frac{1}{2}$ (m) $4\frac{1}{12}$ (n) $2\frac{7}{12}$ (o) $8\frac{45}{56}$

Problem Solving (Page 88)

(a) Add; $\frac{3}{4}$ of pocket money   (b) Add; $\frac{5}{8}$ homework
(c) Subtract; $2\frac{3}{8}$ times   (d) Subtract; $1\frac{5}{6}$ ribbon
(e) Subtract; $\frac{1}{15}$ cup

Exercise 6.8

1. (a) $\frac{7}{2}$ (b) $\frac{32}{5}$ (c) 4   (d) $\frac{10}{3}$ (e) 1
   (f) 0   (g) 12   (h) 24   (i) $\frac{25}{12}$ (j) $\frac{8}{17}$
   (k) $\frac{15}{12}$ (l) $\frac{1}{2}$ (m) 0   (n) $\frac{3}{5}$ (o) 8

Exercise 6.9

1. (a) $\frac{3}{8}$ (b) $\frac{8}{15}$ (c) $\frac{3}{8}$ (d) $\frac{35}{12}$ (e) $\frac{16}{15}$
   (f) $\frac{4}{35}$ (g) $\frac{1}{4}$ (h) $\frac{2}{15}$
2. (a) $\frac{7}{24}$ (b) $\frac{3}{8}$ (c) $\frac{5}{66}$ (d) $\frac{1}{3}$ (e) $\frac{5}{7}$
   (f) $\frac{1}{3}$ (g) 1   (h) $\frac{3}{7}$

Exercise 6.10

(a) 15   (b) 21   (c) 48   (d) 12   (e) 12   (f) 8
(g) $\frac{25}{2}$ (h) 6   (i) 9   (j) 10

Exercise 6.11

1. (a) $\frac{3}{7}$ (b) $\frac{1}{15}$ (c) $\frac{6}{35}$ (d) $\frac{1}{14}$ (e) $\frac{1}{36}$
   (f) $\frac{3}{64}$ (g) $\frac{1}{5}$ (h) $\frac{1}{49}$ (i) $\frac{2}{25}$ (j) $\frac{1}{18}$

2. (a) $\frac{6}{7}$ (b) $\frac{5}{6}$ (c) $\frac{3}{5}$ (d) 0 (e) $\frac{5}{8}$

   (f) $1\frac{2}{7}$ (g) 1 (h) 3 (i) $2\frac{2}{3}$ (j) $1\frac{1}{5}$

3. (a) $4\frac{1}{5}$ cans (b) 3 sheets (c) $\frac{2}{9}$ (d) $\frac{1}{20}$

   (e) 12 bowls (f) 4 people

Chapter Check-Up

1. (a) $\frac{4}{5}=\frac{8}{10}=\frac{12}{15}$ (b) $\frac{7}{9}=\frac{14}{18}=\frac{21}{27}$ (c) $\frac{6}{11}=\frac{12}{22}=\frac{18}{33}$

2. (a) $\frac{2}{3}$ (b) $\frac{2}{3}$ (c) $\frac{9}{10}$

3. (a) < (b) < (c) > (d) >

4. (a) $\frac{10}{13}$ (b) $1\frac{1}{2}$ (c) $\frac{13}{9}$ or $1\frac{4}{9}$ (d) $\frac{31}{35}$ (e) $2\frac{16}{45}$

   (f) $\frac{3}{17}$ (g) $\frac{7}{36}$ (h) $1\frac{3}{10}$

5. (a) $\frac{10}{7}$ or $1\frac{3}{7}$ (b) $\frac{28}{33}$ (c) 0 (d) $\frac{1}{6}$ (e) $\frac{5}{33}$

   (f) $\frac{8}{21}$ (g) $\frac{4}{35}$ (h) $\frac{8}{5}$ or $1\frac{3}{5}$ (i) $\frac{64}{3}$ (j) $\frac{35}{33}$

6. (a) 50 candles (b) $\frac{17}{4}$ or $4\frac{1}{4}$ hours (c) $1\frac{7}{12}$ hours

Chapter 7: Decimals

Exercise 7.1

2. (a) 8 (b) 4 (c) 1 (d) 5 (e) 6

3. (a) 4.7 (b) 58.96 (c) 5.78

4. (a) 1.3 (b) 0.27 (c) 14.2 (d) 8.43 (e) .05

5. (a) $\frac{11}{100}$ (b) $\frac{8}{10}$ (c) $\frac{11}{10}$ (d) $\frac{307}{100}$ (e) $\frac{584}{100}$

6. (a) 1.5, 1.6, 1.7 (b) 5.95, 5.96, 5.97

   (c) 12.1, 12.2, 12.3 (d) 8.04, 8.05, 8.06

   (e) 6.05, 6.06, 6.07 (f) 4.26, 4.27, 4.28

Challenge (Page 103)

   23.45 kg 11.5 years old 131.5 cm

Exercise 7.2

2. (a) < (b) < (c) > (d) = (e) > (f) >

   (g) > (h) < (i) <

Exercise 7.3

1. (a) 8.3, 8.06, 8.059, 8.013 (b) 4.2, 4.02, 3.8, 3.48

   (c) 19.46, 19.4, 1.95, 1.945 (d) 8.66, 8.06, 6.8, 6.08

   (e) 80.2, 80.002, 8.63, 8.6 (f) 3.91, 3.9, 3.09, 3.019

2. (a) 0.04, 0.14, 1.04, 1.14 (b) 19.09, 19.9, 20, 20.01

   (c) 14.19, 14.9, 19.14, 19.4 (d) 6, 6.23, 6.32, 6.4

   (e) 0.99, 1.1, 6, 9.09 (f) 7.02, 7.162, 7.2, 7.23

Exercise 7.4

2. (a) 26.91 (b) 16.09 (c) 10.8 (d) 612.2 (e) 12.5

   (f) 178.31 (g) 10.46 (h) 41.94 (i) 35.11

3. (a) > (b) < (c) > (d) = (e) > (f) >

Exercise 7.5

1. (a) 5.16 (b) 9.17 (c) 2.68 (d) 6.27 (e) 0.9 (f) 5.71

   (g) 0.39 (h) 1.96 (i) 4.85 (j) 3.72 (k) 8.35 (l) 3.05

2. 7.9 **3.** 11.04

5. (a) Arpita - 99.52 points, Akeel - 99.25 points,

   Edmond - 80.5 points, Jagriti - 80.2 points

   (b) 19.32 (c) 18.75

6. (a) 78.5 km (b) 9.25 cm (c) 5.83 cm (d) Swapneel; 0.08 seconds faster

Chapter Check-Up

1. (a) 0.073 (b) 0.009 (c) 0.0462

2. (a) 0.003 (b) 1.14 (c) 0.238

3. (a) Ninety five thousandths (b) One hundred and one thousandths

   (c) One and forty three hundredths

4. (a) > (b) > (c) > (d) =

5. (a) 8.87 (b) 28.95 (c) 2.55 (d) 22.09

   (e) 1.9 (f) 11.85 (g) 26.75 (h) 9.29

6. (a) Shamim (b) 37.5 km (c) 69.25 points

Chapter 8: More About Decimals

Exercise 8.1

1. (a) 1016; 101.6; 10.16 (b) 1560, 156, 15.6

2. (a) 47.7 (b) 92.4 (c) 21.6 (d) 129.2

   (e) 6.9 (f) 58.73 (g) 0.2 (h) .06

3. (a) 282.5 (b) 8.1 (c) 12.3 (d) 110

   (e) 1,673 (f) 319 (g) 140 (h) 800

4. (a) 10 (b) 10 (c) 100 (d) 1000

   (e) 10 (f) 100 (g) 100 (h) 1000

Exercise 8.2

1. (a) 0.06 (b) 12.4 (c) 0.05 (d) 3.4

2. (a) 9.13 (b) 0.13 (c) 45.37 (d) 56.2

   (e) 5.91 (f) 0.36 (g) 3.06 (h) 0.4

3. (a) 15.05 (b) 2.15 (c) 0.775 (d) 4.575

   (e) 1.85 (f) 0.65 (g) 0.534 (h) 9.045

4. (a) 4.28 (b) 72.5 (c) 0.09 (d) 0.00256

   0.428 7.25 0.09 0.0256

5. (a) 10 (b) 100 (c) 10 (d) 10

   (e) 1000 (f) 100

6. (a) 17.5 litres (b) 34.5 km (c) 0.22 m (d) 4.5 g

Exercise 8.3

1. ₹ 27.50 ₹ 92 ₹ 8.50 ₹ 12 ₹ 122

2.

Item	Quantity	Price (₹)
Toothpaste	2	57.00
Rice	5 kg	126.25
Wheat flour	5 kg	92.50
Biscuits	3 packets	35.25
	Total	311.00

Item	Quantity	Price(₹)
Soap	2	30.00
Rice	10 kg	252.50
Washing Power	1 kg	43.00
Biscuits	5 packets	58.75
Buns	6 pieces	25.20
	Total	409.45

Chapter Check-Up

1. (a) 16.1 (b) 63.36 (c) 0.20 (d) 0.08

2. (a) 1.85 (b) 2.93 (c) 6.66 (d) 4.5

3. (a) 57.6 (b) 0.83 (c) 9 (d) 0.0036

   (e) 5310 (f) 0.62 (g) 280 (h) 0.114

4. (a) ₹ 75 (b) ₹ 552.50 (c) ₹ 25.50

   (d) 12 m (e) 1.8 cm

Chapter 9: Shapes, Patterns and Nets

Challenge (Page 133)

Cards 3, 5, 6 will look different on a half turn. Since the 2nd row shows that they are the same, none of them have been turned. Card 4 is the only card that looks the same on a half turn. Therefore, card 4 is the card that has been rotated $\frac{1}{2}$ turn.

Chapter Check-Up

1. (b); (c); (e)

2. (a) $\frac{1}{2}$ turn (b) $\frac{1}{2}$ turn (c) $\frac{1}{4}$ turn (d) $\frac{1}{2}$ turn
   (e) $\frac{1}{2}$ turn (f) $\frac{1}{4}$ turn

Chapter 10: Geometry Basics

Exercise 10.1

2. (a) acute (b) obtuse (c) acute (d) obtuse
   (e) right (f) straight (g) right (h) obtuse

Challenge (Page 147)

1. ∠AOE 2. ∠AOD 3. ∠AOC 4. ∠AOB 5. ∠BOE
6. ∠BOD 7. ∠BOC 8. ∠COE 9. ∠COD 10. ∠DOE

Chapter Check-Up

1. (a) one (b) line (c) line segment (d) right angle
   (e) rays (f) 90°; 180° (g) acute angle

Chapter 11: Measurement

Exercise 11.2

1. (a) 12 cm (b) 9.6 m (c) 100 m (d) 380 cm (e) 87 cm
   (f) 720 mm (g) 0.70 m (h) 8 mm (i) 92 mm (j) 4.2 cm
2. (a) 6200 m (b) 120 m (c) 9100 m (d) 6.3 km
   (e) 1.1 km (f) 2.8 km
3. (b) 98 m 98 cm (c) 16.24 m (d) 11.2 cm
   (e) 28 cm 7 mm (f) 498 mm

Problem Solving (Page 159)

(a) 95 cm (b) 500 hops (c) 22.4 km (d) 1.63 m
(e) 50 books (f) 11 cm (g) 21.4 cm

Fill in the blanks (Page 160)

(a) 1.5 mm (b) 5.8 mm (c) 9.8 mm (d) 0.62 mm
(e) 80 mm (f) 300 mm

Exercise 11.3

1. (a) 19 kg 386 g (b) 0 kg 832 g (c) 2614 g
   (d) 8610 g (e) 3 kg 246 g (f) 11.296 kg
2. (a) 420 g (b) 900 g (c) 1600 g (d) 5190 g
3. (a) 0.125 kg (b) 0.9 kg (c) 0.12 kg (d) 9.5 kg
4. (a) 0.715 kg (b) 60 g (c) 2.375 kg (d) 1040 g
   (e) 12100 g (f) 8.008 kg (g) 0.932 kg (h) 350 g
   (i) 6.125 kg
5. (a) 20 eggs (b) 33.75 kg (c) 2.50 kg

Exercise 11.4

2. 1300 mℓ; 15,500 mℓ; 350 mℓ; 900 mℓ
3. 0.335 ℓ; 0.95 ℓ; 2.5 ℓ; 5.25 ℓ
4. (a) 400 mℓ (b) 8030 mℓ (c) 140 mℓ (d) 0.75 ℓ
   (e) 15350 mℓ (f) 0.1 ℓ (g) 4 ℓ (h) 1.84 ℓ (i) 1250 mℓ
5. (a) Yes (b) 6 cups (c) 1.2 ℓ

Exercise 11.5

1. (a) 29 m 6 cm (b) 8 cm 4 mm (c) 12 kg
   (d) 3 kg 250 g (e) 3 ℓ 150 mℓ (f) 8 ℓ 100 mℓ
2. (a) 3 m 50 cm (b) 5 cm 9 mm (c) 1 kg 100 g
   (d) 3 kg 750 g (e) 1 ℓ 700 mℓ (f) 8 ℓ 500 mℓ
3. (a) 4 m 25 cm (b) 9 m 65 cm (c) 350 mℓ
   (d) 3 kg 850 g (e) 27 kg 750 g

Exercise 11.6

1. (a) 9 g (b) 100 g (c) 500 g (d) 120 g (e) 30 ℓ
   (f) 1 ℓ (g) 100 g (h) 300 mℓ (i) 8 cm (j) 50 cm
   (k) 70 m (l) 2 mm
2. (a) kg (b) m (c) litres (d) cm (e) mℓ

Chapter Check-Up

1. (a) 800 m (b) 1.5 km (c) 8400 m (d) 18 cm (e) 7.2 m
   (f) 350 cm (g) 12 mm (h) 22 cm (i) 3 mm
2. (a) 0.85 kg (b) 90 g (c) 1.38 kg (d) 900 g
   (e) 1150 g (f) 2.2 kg
3. (a) 500 mℓ (b) 170 mℓ (c) 1.88 ℓ (d) 7250 mℓ
   (e) 0.2 ℓ (f) 0.95 ℓ
6. (a) 3 m 20 cm cloth (b) 8 kg 350 g (c) 3 ℓ 800 mℓ

Chapter 12: Perimeter, Area and Volume

Exercise 12.1

1. (a) 240 cm (b) 550 cm (c) 344 cm (d) 160 cm
   (e) 320 cm (f) 240 cm
2. (b) 20 cm (c) 44 cm (d) 72 cm (e) 100 cm (f) 120 cm
   (g) 164 cm (h) 220 cm (i) 252 cm (j) 368 cm
3. (b) 12 cm (c) 14 cm (d) 18 cm (e) 14 cm (f) 18 cm
   (g) 20 cm (h) 22 cm (i) 28 cm (j) 32 cm
4. (b) 10 cm (c) 16 cm (d) 24 cm (e) 30 cm (f) 43 cm
   (g) 58 cm (h) 75 cm (i) 96 cm (j) 139 cm

Exercise 12.2

4. (a) 45 sq.cm (b) 120 sq.cm (c) 65 sq.cm
   (d) 22.5 sq.cm (e) 18.9 sq.cm (f) 52 sq.cm
5. (b) 12 cm (c) 8 cm (d) 4.cm (e) 6 cm (f) 28 cm
   (g) 10 cm (h) 17 cm (i) 11 cm (j) 17 cm

Exercise 12.5

4. (a) 54 m (b) 156 m; ₹ 15,288 (c) 1400 m or 1.4 km
   (d) 25 cm; 625 sq. cm.

Exercise 12.7

1. (a) 60 cu. cm. (b) 60 cu. cm. (c) 384 cu. mm.
2. (a) 120 cu. cm. (b) 10 cu. cm. (c) 90 cu. cm.
   (d) 100 cu. cm. (e) 192 cu. cm.
3. (a) 3120 cu. mm. (b) 1485 cu. cm. (c) 384 cu. m.
4. (a) 168 cu. m. (b) 5 cm (c) 4 cm (d) 11 mm
5. (a) 1344 cu. cm. (b) 13,500 cu. cm. (c) 5400 cu. cm.

Exercise 12.8

2. (a) 20 mℓ (b) 60 mℓ (c) 75 mℓ
3. (a) 9 cu. cm (b) 30 cu. cm (c) 96 cu. cm

Chapter Check-Up

1. (a) Perimeter - 28 cm; Area - 49 sq. cm
   (b) Perimeter - 32 m; Area - 55 sq. m
3. (a) sq. cm (b) sq. cm (c) sq. m (d) sq. km
   (e) sq. km (f) sq. cm
4. (a) 64 cu. cm (b) 80 cu. cm (c) 48 cu. cm (d) 480 cu. cm
5. (a) 18 cu. cm (b) 12 cu. cm (c) 14 cu. cm (d) 12 cu. cm
6. Two, 8 sq. cm, 5 sq. cm
7. (a) 1290 m or 95,450 sq. m. (b) 16 m
8. (a) 90 cu. cm. (b) 512 cu. cm.

Chapter 13: Time and Temperature

Exercise 13.1

1. (a) 480 min (b) 660 min (c) 420 min
   (d) 560 min (e) 192 min (f) 282 min
2. (a) 12 h (b) 2 h 12 min (c) 2 h 10 min
   (d) 6 h (e) 6 h 50 min (f) 8 h 20 min

3. (a) 780 seconds (b) 300 seconds (c) 1560 seconds
   (d) 630 seconds (e) 900 seconds (f) 2700 seconds
4. (a) 14 min (b) 8 min (c) 4 min 40 s
   (d) 10 min (e) 1 min 33 s (f) 15 min 50 s
5. (a) 660 s (b) 8 min 24 s (c) 5 min
   (d) She jogged for the same time both days

Exercise 13.2

1. (a) 11 minutes (b) 5 minutes 5 seconds (c) 3 hours 10 minutes
   (d) 3 hours 20 minutes (e) 8 years (f) 23 years 2 months
2. (a) 1 min 8 seconds (b) 7 min 25 seconds (c) 5 hours 40 minutes
   (d) 4 hours 50 minutes (e) 3 years (f) 1 year 10 months
3. (a) 1 hour 20 minutes (b) 17 years 3 months (c) 6 hours
   (d) 42 seconds (e) 1 hour 25 minutes

Challenge (Page 198)

10 : 20

Exercise 13.3

1. (a) 5:45 p.m. (b) 2:00 p.m. (c) 12:45 p.m. (d) 12 midnight
2. (a) 5th June (b) 6th Feb (c) 21st March (d) 17th April
3. (a) 19th Feb (b) 3:25 p.m. (c) 8th September (d) 2:35 p.m.

Exercise 13.4

1. (b) 42°C (c) 45°C (d) 5°C (e) 0°C (f) 38.5°C

Chapter Check-Up

1. (a) 200 min (b) 9 h 20 min (c) 690 seconds
   (d) 16 min 20 s (e) 11 min 40 s (f) 7 years 3 months
   (g) 6 h 10 min (h) 1 year 11 months

2. (a) 3:05 p.m. (b) 2:30 p.m.
3. (a) 10th Sept. (b) 22nd October
5. (a) 2 h 30 min (b) 30 min

Chapter 15: Handling Data

Exercise 15.1

1. 6 hours – School
   9 hours – Sleep
   1 hour – Homework
   2 hours – Play
   5 hours – Others
   1 hour – TV

3. (a) (i) Ada – 10 votes
       (ii) Rashi – 10 votes
       (iii) Mira – 5 votes
       (iv) Anita – 15 votes

Challenge (Page 221)

22nd January: 12th March

Chapter Check-Up

1. (a) Maths $-\frac{1}{2}$ (b) 6 hours
   Science $-\frac{1}{4}$ (c) 3 hours
   English $-\frac{1}{8}$ (d) $1\frac{1}{2}$ hour on each
   Soc. Study $-\frac{1}{8}$

2. (a) Chips (b) Cake (c) Sandwich and *Samosa*
   (d) 19 children (e) 63 children
3. (a) December and January (b) October
   (c) 400 sweaters (d) 200 sweaters